CHEAP SCARES!

CHEAP SCARES!
Low Budget Horror Filmmakers Share Their Secrets

Gregory Lamberson

McFarland & Company, Inc., Publishers
Jefferson, North Carolina, and London

LIBRARY OF CONGRESS CATALOGUING-IN-PUBLICATION DATA

Lamberson, Gregory, 1964–
 Cheap scares : low budget filmmakers share their secrets / Gregory Lamberson.
   p.   cm.
 Includes index.

 ISBN 978-0-7864-3706-1
 softcover : 50# alkaline paper ∞

 1. Horror films—Production and direction. 2. Low budget films.   I. Title.
 PN1995.9H6L25   2008
 791.43'6164 — dc22   2008037277

British Library cataloguing data are available

©2008 Gregory Lamberson. All rights reserved

No part of this book may be reproduced or transmitted in any form or by any means, electronic or mechanical, including photocopying or recording, or by any information storage and retrieval system, without permission in writing from the publisher.

Cover photograph: "Brain Zap" frame grab from Brett Piper's *Shock-O-Rama* (courtesy of POP Cinema).

Manufactured in the United States of America

McFarland & Company, Inc., Publishers
 Box 611, Jefferson, North Carolina 28640
   www.mcfarlandpub.com

For my uncle, Bill Thompson, who enabled my first
encounter with the Living Dead

Acknowledgments

First, I'd like to thank my interview subjects for generously contributing their time to this book, and for their invaluable assistance in assembling the necessary photographs: J.R. Bookwalter; Justin Wingenfeld; Robert Craig Sabin; Devi Snively; Jerry Gold; Roy Frumkes; Larry Fessenden; Scooter McCrae; James Lorinz; Brett Piper; Stephen Biro; Paige K. Davis; and Justin Channell. It was a pleasure speaking to all of you.

Thanks also to Mike Raso and Jeffrey Faoro at POP Cinema, not only for authorizing the use of so many images, but for distributing my films on VHS and DVD, and for working so hard to promote them.

Thanks to Nick Mamatas for encouraging me to write this book in the first place, and to filmmaker Joseph Fusco and author Jeff Strand for critiquing its manuscript. And to Gregory Dohler and Henrique Couto for supplying me with photos.

And an extra special thanks to my beautiful wife, Tamar, for holding down the fort while I tackled this project, which—as always—turned out to be so much bigger than I had anticipated.

Table of Contents

Acknowledgments	vii
Preface: Who the Hell Does This Guy Think He Is?	1
Introduction: So You Want to Make a Horror Film	5
1. J.R. Bookwalter: The Filmmaker Next Door	9
2. Strange Bedfellows	24
3. Justin Wingenfeld: The Inside Man	29
4. Screamwriting 101	38
5. Robert Craig Sabin: Going Hollyweird	48
6. This Gun for Hire	60
7. Devi Snively: Trippin' from Festivals to the AFI	65
8. Development Hell	76
9. Jerry Gold: Brief Legal Briefs	85
10. Making a Budget	96
11. Roy Frumkes: Producing Screams and Laughter	103
12. Pre-production	126
13. Larry Fessenden: The Art of Horror	137
14. Production	154
15. Scooter McCrae: Micro-Budget Maverick	163
16. Directing	181
17. James Lorinz: Acting Scared	186
18. Post Production	199
19. Brett Piper: Renaissance Man	206
20. Distribution	221
21. Stephen Biro: Unearthing Films	232

22. Promotion	242
23. Paige Kay Davis: Marketing Mayhem	250
24. Justin Channell: New Blood	261
25. The Martini: Last Words	270
Index	273

Preface

WHO THE HELL DOES THIS GUY THINK HE IS?

FADE IN:

When I was in high school, dreaming of becoming the next George Romero, there was no Internet. If I craved motion picture industry information, I perused old issues of *Variety* and *The Hollywood Reporter,* provided by my uncle, William Thompson, who has been in theatrical distribution and exhibition all his adult life. When I wished to learn about horror films, I read *Famous Monsters of Filmland* and *Fangoria.* And when I sought to learn the tricks of making low budget films, I read *Super 8 Filmmaker* and Don Dohler's wonderful *Cinemagic.* There were few other options.

My love of monsters began at the ripe old age of four, when my mother took me to see movies at our town's single screen theater and bought me comic books on the walk home. In the pages of those comics I discovered garish advertisements for products that set my imagination on fire: Aurora's line of glow in the dark model kits based on Universal's classic monsters. I cut out the images and moved them around the screen of our black and white TV, creating my own movies, minus the celluloid. It wasn't long before I started collecting the models and watching the features starring those creatures. I still remember the school night my mother woke me to watch *King Kong* for the first time: Kong was already battling that pterodactyl for Fay Wray on Skull Mountain. It was like an epiphany, and I've wanted to tell stories about monsters ever since.

I had a rocky relationship with my first grade teacher. As a peace offering, I drew a picture of my favorite monsters for her. She returned it to me covered in red ink: "Next time, draw a party picture." Apparently she failed to grasp that my illustration was a "party picture." I learned early on that "this thing of ours" is often the target of artistic discrimination, and that there is a lack of imagination in the public education system. But if my teacher thought she could dissuade my love of horror, her assault on my creativity had exactly the opposite effect. You need to be stubborn to be a filmmaker.

Five years later, Uncle Bill took me to a double feature of *Kong* and *Night of the Living Dead* at a revival theatre in Washington, D.C., and later to *Martin* and *Dawn of the Dead* during their original releases. Romero's work had a profound impact on me. Here was a guy who operated outside the Hollywood system, making revolutionary films on low budgets. Don Dohler was another Hollywood outsider who inspired me: his low budget features *The Alien Factor* and *Nightbeast* never played on the local TV stations where I grew up, but he offered tantalizing behind the scenes peeks at those 16m productions in *Cinemagic*. If Don could make his filmmaking dreams a reality, so could his readers—a sentiment he once expressed to me in a letter. Don had agreed to be interviewed for this book, but passed away before I could conduct it. I hope *Cheap Scares*! evokes his spirit in some manner.

Bill later sent me a flyer for *Document of the Dead*, a feature-length documentary on the making of *Dawn of the Dead*, directed by Roy Frumkes, a teacher at the School of Visual Arts in New York City. SVA was already a strong contender in my search for the right film school, but seeing that Roy had shot his documentary with a crew comprised of SVA students sealed the deal for me. I lived in the SVA dorm, at the time two floors in Sloan House, a YMCA (now a swank condominium) on 34th Street and 9th Avenue. My classmates Jimmy Muro, who later directed *Street Trash* and became Hollywood's top Steadicam operator, and Peter Clark, my future co-producer and director of photography, lived there too.

Peter and I left SVA after one year because we wanted to make features, not short films. We were inspired by Frank Henenlotter's *Basket Case*, which had been playing as a midnight movie at the Waverly Twin for a year, and Sam Raimi's *The Evil Dead* and Douglas McKeown's *The Deadly Spawn*, which played at the RKO National Twin on Broadway and 43rd street, where I worked as an assistant manager. All three films had been shot on 16m and were blown up to 35mm for theatrical exhibition, so we could do the same thing. Realizing we had to work on a similar production to gain necessary experience, we "made our bones" working for free on the 16m horror spoof *I Was a Teenage Zombie*. I learned as much during that four week shoot as I did during an entire year at film school.

Since then, I've written, directed and co-produced three micro-budget horror features—*Slime City*, *Undying Love*, and *Naked Fear*. All three played as midnight films in NYC, and all three were released on VHS, DVD, or both. I worked as an assistant director on the wretched *Plutonium Baby* and on Frank Henenlotter's excellent *Brain Damage*, and as both the assistant director and associate producer on the crime drama *West New York* and the sex comedy *Just the 4 of Us*. I've written two screenplays for hire, *The Soulless* and *The Curse of the Love Canal*, and I've turned two of my unproduced scripts into well received horror novels, *Personal Demons* and *Johnny Gruesome*. I've also worked as the publicist for low budget horror film producers, independent DVD labels, and film festivals. And I co-created, launched, and edited a popular horror entertainment website, *Fear Zone*. I've only made my living sporadically as a filmmaker, but I've always kept my hand in it.

I believe there's a genuine need for *Cheap Scares! Low Budget Horror Filmmakers Share Their Secrets*. John Russo's *Scare Tactics*, once considered the bible for low budget horror filmmakers, became obsolete the minute J.R. Bookwalter shot his Super VHS feature *Ozone*. Successive books have contained erroneous, or downright misleading, information: advertising copy for one claimed, "Horror movies get better distribution deals — so they're great for independent filmmakers." When I read that pearl of wisdom I wanted to scream like Janet Leigh in Alfred Hitchcock's shower. If you're going to invest your time, money, and life making a low budget horror film, you need someone to tell you the truth about its chances in the marketplace. Get ready for some tough love.

One topic I won't dwell on in this book is the viability of digital video versus film formats. Any feature shot on film stands a better chance in the marketplace, but a good film shot on Mini-DV or HiDef will not suffer solely because of its format. Digital filmmaking is here to stay, and low budget auteurs are not the only filmmakers using this technology. As far as I'm concerned, that debate is over.

For nearly 25 years, I've spent countless hours behind a typewriter or computer keyboard, on location, and in the filmmaking trenches. I've learned a thing or two, and I'm eager to share my experiences with you. Consider this book my class: 13 lessons and 13 in-depth conversations with other filmmakers and industry professionals. My subjects gave me enough anecdotes for three volumes, so I've edited my questions and their responses to squeeze in as much information as possible. Learn from what the filmmakers in this book have done right — and from what we've done wrong. We'll tell you how to develop, produce, and complete a feature film — and get it seen.

In the end, it's all up you, and it won't be easy.

But let's try to get there together.

Class is in session.

Introduction

SO YOU WANT TO MAKE A HORROR FILM

So you want to make a horror movie...

The first question you need to ask yourself is, "Why?"

Is it because you love horror and think you're the next Wes Craven or George Romero? Or because you think a horror film is an easy sell? Or because horror is hot at the multiplex right now? Or you've just graduated from film school and have nothing better to do with your time? Or you have money to burn? Or you think it would be a cool hobby? Or you believe that with today's digital video technology, anyone can make a movie that will sell?

Consider this: independent films are difficult to sell. With the so-called "democratization of film" resulting from the ready availability of professional quality digital video technology, more feature length films are being produced than ever before, and only so many of them can be distributed by professional companies. Each year, the Sundance Film Festival receives thousands of submissions. Only a handful are accepted for competition, few will actually find an interested distributor, and only one or two of those may receive more than a token release.

Pretty bleak, eh? It gets worse, because most film distributors share a similar disdain toward horror films — except when they love them, which is to say, when the cyclical nature of movie trends favors fright flicks. Theatrical horror films have become hot again: mediocre genre movies routinely gross $15–$20 million on their opening weekends — then disappear after two weeks. Even when horror is viewed as profitable, it's still dismissed as exploitation aimed at teenagers. People don't consider most horror filmmakers artists, or even craftsmen. For many people, horror is one step above pornography.

When a micro-budget horror film occasionally beats the odds and breaks through with mainstream audiences — like *The Blair Witch Project* or *Open*

Water—the marketplace explodes with similar product. But even a company like Lion's Gate can release only so many films over the course of a year, and smaller companies like POP Cinema and Unearthed Films are having a harder time getting their independent DVD product distributed. Retailers like Best Buy have mostly stopped carrying independent, alternative horror films in favor of mainstream studio films. The result is that too many low or "no budget" horror films are competing for a limited number of outlets—and most of the distributors acquiring low budget genre films aren't paying advances.

It's a tough business that is even tougher on independent filmmakers and distributors. The conditions of the marketplace can change drastically from the conception of your project to its completion. If you want to make a horror film because you think you'll make a fast buck, I strongly suggest you reconsider this course of action—unless you have enough money in the bank to complete your film, or you already have a distributor lined up. The latter can happen, but it is extremely rare.

The Hobbyist

There is nothing wrong with being a hobbyist filmmaker. By definition, if your principal means of income is not derived from filmmaking endeavors you are a hobbyist, or an amateur. Don't be offended; there is a big difference between being a non–professional and being unprofessional. I consider myself a semi-pro: I receive occasional royalty checks for my films and advances for my novels, and I sell copies of my work at conventions and through my website.

Hopefully, you want to make a horror film because you're passionate about films that inspire dread and revulsion, or allow you to communicate an idea or theme in a way that a more conventional film might not. Science fiction allows storytellers to examine society and humanity in ways that a standard drama does not, and horror—when executed properly—can deal with primal emotions such as fear of death and anguish over loss—as powerfully, if not more so, than more mainstream fare.

One day on location for *I Was a Teenage Zombie*, the director, John Michaels, declared, "I hate horror films." I found this extremely disheartening. A few years later, John became an Orthodox monk, and I heard he was producing recruiting videos for his order. I don't know how funny they are, but I'm glad he found his true calling. Presumably, his films are MOS ("Mit out sound," as the filmmakers who fled to the United States from Nazi Germany called silent films).

On *Plutonium Baby*, it was painfully evident that none of the key people behind it cared about making a good horror film; they just wanted to make some easy money. In that respect, they succeeded. Too bad it was so depressingly uninspired and poorly made.

Don Dohler, light meter, and friend. Photograph courtesy Gregory Dohler.

Do You Have What It Takes?

This question is just as important as "Why do you want to make a horror film?"

First of all, do you have talent? If you're uncertain, make several short films before attempting a feature and gauge your success. There are countless film festivals specializing in horror material; they want you to submit films to them because entry fees are what make them possible, and they want to show your film to encourage you to submit to them again in the future. Horror film festivals offer an excellent opportunity for you to show your work to strangers, and reactions from an unbiased audience are the best you can get. Even with all the contacts he's made in the horror field, Rodrigo Gudino, the publisher of *Rue Morgue* magazine, started out making short films which he took on the festival circuit. He was more concerned with developing his abilities from an artistic standpoint than leaping into production on a feature.

Perhaps you are talented, but you're channeling your energy in the wrong direction. You might think of yourself as a director, but you're better suited to be a screenwriter or a producer. If you don't recognize your own strengths and weaknesses, no one else will — until it's too late, and you're viewing your first assembly and wondering, "How the hell are we going to cut a salable feature out of this?"

Lamberson lines up a shot on *Undying Love* (1992). Note the sound blanket wrapped around the 16m camera.

More than anything, when I ask if you have what it takes to be a filmmaker, I'm asking you to look deep inside yourself to see if you have the guts and stamina to spend a year developing a project; to work 20 hours a day during production; to spend up to a year on principal photography, pickup shots, and re-shoots; another year on post production, when it looks like you'll never see the light at the end of the tunnel; another year seeking distribution for your finished film; and still another marketing it.

It takes commitment to be an independent filmmaker working with limited resources. When others see what we go through — and what sacrifices we must sometimes make — to realize our dreams, they often think we should be committed. Making a feature is an incredible test of who you are and whether or not you belong in this business.

Passion, talent, commitment, perseverance — these are all important qualities for any filmmaker, but they are especially important for low budget filmmakers who sometimes have nothing to run on but the fumes of their own belief.

Are you prepared to put your film project above everything else in your life, sometimes at great personal sacrifice, to realize your vision?

If so, let's make a movie.

1

J.R. Bookwalter
THE FILMMAKER NEXT DOOR

In many ways, J.R. Bookwalter is the quintessential micro-budget filmmaker: he was among the first to make and distribute feature length films shot on Super-8 film, Super VHS, and Mini-DV. Of course, he was fortunate to have a successful horror filmmaker bankroll his first epic — a filmmaker who specified in their contract that he could never be identified by name (and so J.R. refers to him as "The Master Cylinder"). But this horror icon's generous involvement resulted from J.R.'s chutzpa in approaching him in the first place. J.R. parlayed his experiences as a guerrilla filmmaker into a professional gig as a post-production supervisor and in-house filmmaker at Full Moon Pictures. When he discovered Hollywood wasn't everything it was cracked up to be, he returned to his indie roots in Ohio, where he runs Tempe DVD. He's racked up an amazing 32 credits as a film producer; 27 as an editor; 18 as an actor; 13 as a director; and 12 as a screenwriter.

You're easily the most prolific filmmaker featured in this book.
   I started at a young age and had the energy to have that kind of output. By the same token, I look back at the entire body of work and there's really only maybe a handful of things that I can say "Well, I'm kind of proud of that stuff." But they're all redheaded stepchildren: if I trash them, it's okay; if somebody else trashes them, I'm like, "Hey, wait a minute!"

You've written a number of the screenplays for your films, but you've only taken story credit on some of them, and other people have completely written some others.
   If I can criticize my own body of work, it's that I had some good ideas in some of the early stuff I wrote, but writing was not my strong suit. I always felt as a filmmaker that I could direct a certain way and edit a certain way, and somehow make it work. I know a lot of people struggle to try to get the perfect script and they want to put it all down on paper, but with me it was always

sort of the opposite. I wanted to just get to the editing phase, and the post-production phase, and put it all together there.

You directed The Dead Next Door ***when you were only 18.***
I was 18 going on 19 when it started, and then I was 22 or something when it finished, because it was over the course of, like, four years. It never occurred to me that I couldn't do it. I think that's what got me through four grueling years of making it — "Why can't I do it?" I think that sort of blind ignorance is how it actually came to be in the first place.

What inspired you to make the leap?
That wasn't my idea; that was the so-called "Master Cylinder," who kicked in the bulk of the money. I had gone up to Detroit after dropping out of college. They were in the early stages of starting *Evil Dead 2*. I'd read about it in *Fangoria* and thought, "That's only four hours away. Maybe I'll drive up there and just get a job as a production assistant or whatever." So I carted some of my short films up there and showed them, and The Master Cylinder turned to me and said, "Well, what are you going to do now?" I said, "Well, I'm thinking about doing industrial films or just PA work or whatever." And he's like, "No, you should be making a feature. Why don't you go out and make one?" Honestly, it hadn't occurred to me. He said, "Well, you should come up with something. If you do, send it up to me and I'll take a look at it. Maybe I'll help you out." I'm thinking, "Well, you don't have to tell me twice!" (laughs) The whole drive home I was coming up with ideas, and I banged out the script in a few days, and it was certainly within 30 days that I had stuff up to him.

What was the film's final projected and final budget?
When I sent him the script and a little prospectus, I was going to do it on VHS for $4,000, which is sort of ironic, because not so many years later I would be doing stuff on video for less than that (laughs). At the time that was absurd; we're talking about 1985, and it was just not done. Even movies like *Blood Cult*, which had gone straight to video, had been shot on Betacam or something, and they had spent like $100,000, so to even attempt something like that was absurd. But The Master Cylinder said, "Oh, let's make it $8,000 and then we'll try to shoot it on 3/4." The whole thing evolved over time, especially when we made the jump to Super-8 film. I found out later he'd had this fascination with wanting to shoot a feature on Super-8, but had never done it. I had certainly never shot anything that long so I didn't know what I was doing. The final budget, I think, when all was said and done, was $125,000, which sounds absurd by today's standards, but again, in the late 80s that was a pretty common budget for these kinds of movies. Certainly if we'd known going in, and planned for it, we could have shot that movie in 16m, if not 35mm. But there was a lot of waste and mistakes and learning experiences.

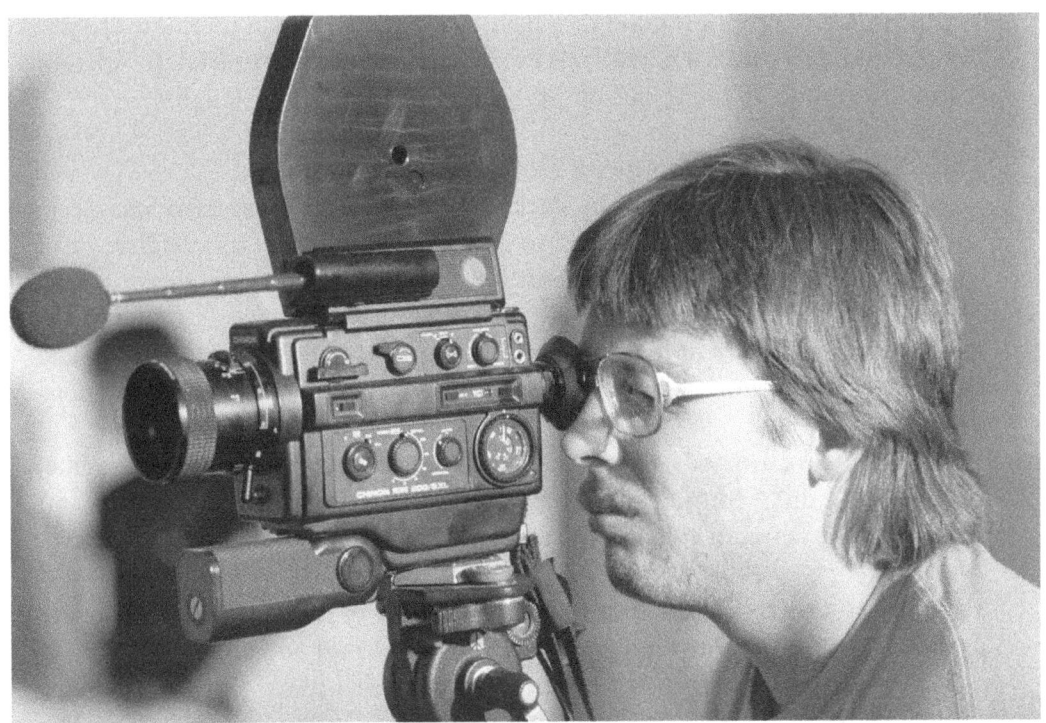

J.R. Bookwalter directing his Super-8 epic, *The Dead Next Door* (1988). Photograph courtesy J.R. Bookwalter.

It was a better time for raising money because home video was new.

Even if you went direct to video, the distributors were selling VHS tapes for $80 or $100, and there were so many places to sell those tapes that it was actually a lucrative business. You're lucky to get $10 for a DVD now.

I laughed while watching the extras on the DVD for The Dead Next Door. **I wrote** Slime City **on a manual typewriter. And that cardboard production strip board!**

Oh, yeah, what a nightmare. They were really different times. It seemed like there were a lot of us doing it, but somehow it was easier to be discovered. I wouldn't want to be starting to make movies now. If you don't become a YouTube star or whatever overnight, who knows how anybody's going to find you?

Were you a Cinemagic **subscriber?**

Oh, yeah, of course. I was obsessed with that magazine. On Cleveland television they used to play *The Alien Factor* all the time, my friends and I would always watch that movie. There was press on (Don Dohler) everywhere.

We relied on print magazines for three-month old film news. Now there are hundreds of websites that post current information daily.

Kids don't know how good they have it now, that's for sure. I know I sound like an old fart, but it's really true. Everything is so geared to instant gratification now. If you're not on MySpace, you're not hip. (laughs)

They didn't grow up with Super 8 Filmmaker *like we did.*
The thing about Super-8 film back when we were kids was there was a certain discipline there. You really had to go, "Okay, I'll make this edit here but I have to make sure this is the *right* edit." You really had to think about it.

It's amazing you were able to pull off the Washington, D.C., footage in The Dead Next Door, with the zombies outside the White House and those monuments.
Yeah, I dare anybody to try that now! Even at the time people were like, "You can't do this." But that's the kind of thing you do when you're young and stupid. "Well, why can't we do it? Let's just drive down there and *do* it."

You weren't able to use the first two weeks' worth of footage due to exposure problems. I can imagine the effect that must have had on you.
Two things went through my head, because it's like, "Oh, my God, the footage is underexposed, what are we going to do?" And the worst thing is, "Oh, my God, now I have to call The Master Cylinder and tell him I projected the film and we have to re-shoot all this stuff!" And then the third thing, I guess, was breaking the news to the cast and crew. We sat everyone down and we said, "Look, there's some problems with the camera, this, that and the other thing, and we're going to have to re-do a bunch of this stuff." And then we got the projector out and we showed them and said, "Here's what happened. We're just going to have to tough it out." And everybody kept going. One of my friends who worked on the film said, "It's like being in Jonestown, only without the Kool-Aid." (laughs)

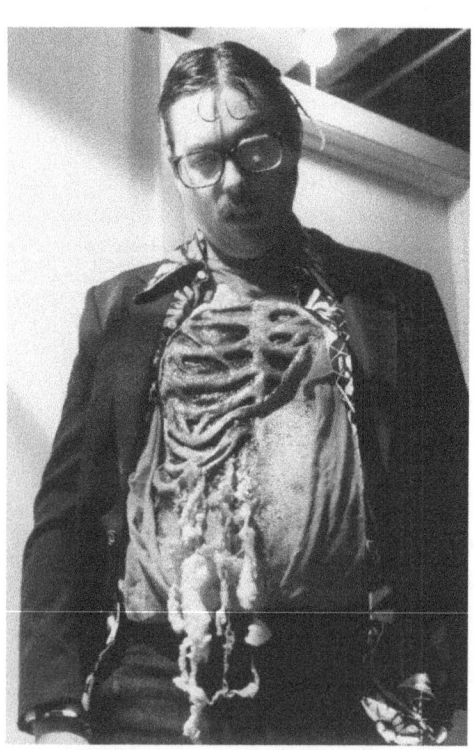

Bookwalter lets it all hang out in his *Skinned Alive* (1989) cameo. Photograph courtesy J.R. Bookwalter.

Guerrilla productions tend to almost dictate how and when things happen instead of the other way around. I always laugh when a first-time filmmaker tells

Robot Ninja Michael Todd (left) and Bookwalter (1994). Photograph courtesy J.R. Bookwalter.

me that they've storyboarded their entire film. I tell them, "Put those away right now."

Absolutely. You can prepare all you want, but until you're actually out there doing it... (laughs) And that's one of the reasons why I've always been a little bit down on film schools. They can teach you the nuts and bolts—"Here's how you shoot, you can be a cinematographer, you can be an editor."—but they can't really prepare you for what happens if you show up on your first day of shooting and it rains or snows, or there's some other mishap or act of God. You just have to go out there and get kicked in the nuts a few times, and you've got to think on your feet and figure it out.

What did The Master Cylinder say when you told him you couldn't use two weeks of footage?

He wasn't happy. But he was more pissed that we watched the film instead of the fact that we had to re-shoot the stuff, which was odd to me! I was like, "Well, we just saved you who knows how many thousands of dollars by not continuing..." Because we shut everything down for a couple of weeks to get our shit together. He was just pissed that I disobeyed his order and watched the stuff.

You could have shot the whole film without knowing.

If we had done that I think that would have been it for the movie. He probably would have just pulled the plug. What do you do? That actually hap-

Ozone (1993), Bookwalter's seminal Super-VHS feature, re-released on DVD by his Tempe DVD label. Photograph courtesy J.R. Bookwalter.

pened to a friend of mine, Tom O'Rawe, a filmmaker in New Jersey who made *Ghoul School*, which I was peripherally involved with. He shot a movie, he was originally going to do it for Camp Video with a $10,000 budget, called *Basement*, it was an anthology. He shot the whole thing on Super-8, and Mike Raso of POP Cinema was the cinematographer, ironically; it's a small world. My DP, Mike Tolochko, and I both told him, "You've got to overexpose the hell out of it, don't go by what the light meter says." We'd had our Super-8 film experience at this point. And they didn't listen, and 80 percent of the movie was pitch black and they didn't realize it until it was completely done.

Sometimes you can learn more from your mistakes than from what you do right. You never forget that pain you feel when you see something that you did really wrong. You never make that same mistake again.

Absolutely, and I beat that into people's heads when they ask me how to get into the business. You have to fall on your face because rarely does anyone have this great career where everything just works out for them. You have to fall on your face at some point, be it you make a movie that nobody likes or you screw up a bunch of the technical aspects and have to re-do them. Failure is an option, and it's a good thing, actually.

Did you form Tempe Video specifically to self-distribute The Dead Next Door?

No, that was a leap I took later because originally The Master Cylinder had hooked it up with this company in North Carolina called Electro Video, run by a guy named Tony Elwood. He was one of the guys who had worked on *Evil Dead 2* effects or something, and he had his own Super-8mm film called *Killer*, and he was selling it on his own. So The Master Cylinder had given it to him and he put it out. I think I got my hands on it maybe two years after that. It must have been '91 when I started Tempe Video.

Were you unhappy with how Electro handled the film?

It was really like The Master Cylinder gave them the movie just so he could say, "Here, I saw it through to the end, the movie is getting a release." I'm not going to sit here and say that he buried it, but that's essentially what happened. He just kind of took the first deal that someone said yes to, just to get it out of his hair and maybe get me out of his hair too, I don't know. (laughs) I was happy. I remember *Fangoria* always had those Marshall Video ads on the letters page and one day there was *The Dead Next Door*, and I was like, "Wow, it's finally coming out!"

You don't seem to be very fond of two of your follow-up features, Robot Ninja and Galaxy of the Dinosaurs.

I went out to L.A. in '89 with a friend because a mutual friend was doing makeup effects for this movie *Beverly Hills Corpse*, starring Linnea Quigley. It

Bookwalter directs *Polymorph* (1996), his first Mini-DV feature, a "cabin in the woods" alien invasion movie. Photograph courtesy J.R. Bookwalter.

turned out to be something that David DeCoteau was making, which wound up being called *Murder Weapon* by the time it was released. And *Murder Weapon* was the start of his Cinema Home Video label. He had done this movie called *Deadly Embrace* with Jan Michael Vincent and had gotten some astronomical check that he wasn't expecting, like $250,000, and he decided to start a home video distribution company. Of course, when he did this, in '89, the market was just starting to tip in the other direction, so it maybe wasn't the best time to get into it. He sunk all his money into starting this company and I came in at the right moment, because the sound house where we were mixing *The Dead Next Door* is where he had mixed his stuff, so we kept running into each other. Long story short, we made *Robot Ninja* and then *Skinned Alive*, and then *Ghoul School* was the third one, and these were 16mm films, which I thought was a step up even though the budgets were a big step down, because these were really shot for $15,000 plus some lab costs. *Robot Ninja* is probably my least favorite film. It's that sophomore slump, I guess, because I felt like I was in such a good place after *The Dead Next Door*, even though I was kind of a little bitter about how long it had taken. I felt like, "Ah, I wasted all these years and I gotta get on and do something else right away." And so I think a lot of that bitterness and anger sort of came out on film in *Robot Ninja*.

There were sort of two eras of Cinema Home Video. The first was making these three 16mm movies. And then that kind of dried up, and DeCoteau went off and produced a bunch of stuff for Charlie Band and Full Moon. And at some point I moved out to L.A., and I moved back to Ohio after about a year and a half, and made what I call "The Six Pack," which was six Super-VHS movies that he was doing for this outfit called Rentrak, which at the time was a pretty lucrative home video thing, where independent retailers would get their product on a revenue-sharing plan. And that's where *Zombie Cop*, *Kingdom of the Vampire*, *Chickboxer*, *Maximum Impact*, *Galaxy of the Dinosaurs*, and *Humanoids from Atlantis* came from. It was six movies in seven months.

What was the average shooting schedule on those?

About a week. They were done in twos. It was two movies for five grand, total. The first two were *Zombie Cop* and *Kingdom of the Vampire*. The second two movies were for five grand. And then when we got to the third set, the economic situation was starting to be less, so the challenge was making two movies for $2500. It's one of those things, I've done it since, where I get involved with a company, and it's too much of a good thing, and I burn myself out, and then I wind up hating life. (laughs)

You know something's wrong when the budgets get smaller instead of bigger.

Oh, absolutely. But you're consumed by it. And when we started that deal, he wanted to do twelve of those movies. Literally twelve movies in the space of a year. I think it was one week for writing, one week for prep, one week for shooting, one week for post, and then repeat—for a year. I can't even imagine. (laughs) I mean, we did six in seven months. I never would have made it! By the time we got to the last of those six, that was the first time that I thought, "Okay, I have to just hang this up, this isn't working, I don't know if I want to do this anymore." That lasted for a few months until the script for *Ozone* happened to fall into my lap, and that re-inspired me to get back out there. But making those six movies in seven months was a pretty soul crushing experience.

Was *Ozone* **the first film on which you used the Film Look process?**

Yes, because that was one of the faults of the six Cinema Home Video movies. I thought, "Man, if he had just paid to have these Filmlooked, people might have accepted them more." As it was, people were just merciless, like, "Ah, it's just shot on video crap." At the time the Filmlook technology was $5,000 or some ridiculous amount. But there was a producer out in California, Dave Sterling, who was offering low budget filmlook for $500 or something, and that's what we used on *Ozone*. For the DVD version it's a completely different story; that was done more recently, on the computer.

After *Ozone* **you produced a couple of things for John Russo, and then you did** *The Sandman*. **Setting a horror film in a trailer park was a cool idea.**

Witchouse 3: Demon Fire (2001), starring Debbie Rochon and Brinke Stevens. Photograph courtesy J.R. Bookwalter.

It seemed like such a depressing environment, especially the trailer park we picked to shoot in. You couldn't have found a worse location! There were just the absolute dregs of society at that place. In the original script, the girlfriend didn't live in the trailer park, she lived in a house near it, so it took some of the action out of there. But when I rewrote it, because we were making it for a lot less than what I originally intended, I thought, "Well, it's kind of better that she lives in the trailer park with everybody else and that kind of keeps all the action central to that location." That was another thing where I tried something that didn't really work. I can't say I got cocky after *Ozone*, but I was like, "Now I've got my footing back, and I want to try something that depends a little less on the gimmickry and more on the storytelling and acting." But I don't think it was quite successful. It was on the path to the right idea, I guess.

Polymorph *is probably my favorite of your films. On the DVD extras, the cast members say that you didn't want to make the film, but no one says why.*

By the time I did *The Sandman* I was just so exhausted, and at that time I was publishing *Alternative Cinema* magazine, so I had another distraction. Ariauna Albright and James Edwards were sort of cheerleading for me to do this, because they were actors and they were bored, and their egos were like, "We've got to be on screen or we're not alive." (laughs) I could have gone for another year without making a movie. I told Ariauna, just to get her off my back, "Okay, here's a big file folder full of old ideas and stories and stuff, go through it and see what you like."— thinking, "Maybe she won't do it and I'll be off the hook." Well, she came back with this old *Polymorph* idea of mine, which really was very different from what we wound up doing because it was just the four kids in a cabin in the woods. None of the gang and drug runner stuff was in there. I grudgingly said, "Okay, what the hell, let's do it, we can make the thing for eight or ten grand and have some fun." By the time it was done, and I was cutting it together, I was going, "Wow, I'm actually kind of glad I did this." The stuff that I was attempting on *The Sandman* with the characters and working with actors started to click on *Polymorph*, more so than the effects, and I had more fun with that stuff.

Was this your first time shooting on Mini-DV?

Yeah, the Sony VX-1000 camera had literally just come out. Somebody said *Polymorph* was the first feature shot on Mini-DV. I don't know if that's true, but it's certainly the first feature I know about. We were going to shoot it on Super-VHS-C, the same way we had done *The Sandman*, and then Dave Wagner, who had written *Ozone*, read about this camera and wanted to buy it. He said, "I'll help you with this movie and we'll make it on Mini-DV." Dave was the sound guy and I was the camera guy, and that was pretty much it. That was actually a fun film to make. The first day wasn't so fun, because I scheduled that big confrontation with all those people in that little cabin. I was like, "What in the hell was I thinking?" Halfway through that scene I went outside and I was so frustrated. It was not off to a good start. But we got through that day. My solution was just to shoot as much footage as I could and figure it out later. Then that night, a bunch of us were actually staying at that cabin because it was maybe 45 minutes away from where I lived. We had this fun campfire and cookout and I have very fond memories of that whole weekend, of the whole shoot, really. That sense of fun kind of crept into the movie.

Judging by some of your DVD extras, you have a laid back demeanor on set.
I know most filmmakers live for "Action!" and "Cut!" They want to be in that moment, they want to be on set with the actors, and I'm the exact opposite. I can't stand being on the set. I just want to get it over with as quickly as possible. Especially in a remote location. I'm like, "I don't have a good bathroom to go to, I have to eat crappy food." It's a big inconvenience for me. I know it sounds horrendously spoiled but I'm being honest here. I don't let that show to the people that I'm working with. To me it's like, "We're not heart surgeons, we're not curing AIDS, we're just making a movie. So let's just keep it all in perspective and keep it on an even keel." Everybody that I've ever worked with has pretty much said I'm very laid back and very easy to work with. Whether they know it or not, I always know what I want and communicate it to them easily and nobody's ever confused.

Did you sell* Alternative Cinema *to E.I. Cinema when you moved out to L.A.?
I probably would have kept doing *Alternative Cinema*, but during *Polymorph* I had to stop shooting because I had a very strict schedule for the magazine. That was kind of the turning point for me where I said, "I have to get rid of this thing. Do I want to make movies or do I want to publish a magazine?" One was conflicting with the other. We made *Bloodletting* after *Polymorph*, and the next year, '97, I felt like, "The grass is just growing under my feet." I wanted to get rid of some stuff, clean my slate and kind of, not start over, but I wanted to take the experience I had, and I felt pretty positive about everything and figured, "No time like the present. Let's go to L.A. and try it." The first six months I was in L.A. I didn't have a job. I'd set myself up so I had some money coming in: I sold the magazine, I sold some equipment I had, I was doing some freelance graphic design work for Cinema Home Video. Then David DeCoteau came to me and started picking my brain about editing and mixing a movie he was going to make for Full Moon called *Shrieker*. I thought that was going to be a one-time thing, but it ended up being the next five years of my life.

Shrieker was only a $150,000 movie, but they had shot it 35mm anamorphic. DeCoteau had not been a big supporter of the shot-on-video stuff after we had done those first six years ago. He wouldn't even watch the stuff that I made after that, even though it was much better. I was using the exact same equipment because I had a Macintosh with Adobe Premiere. I was doing it down and dirty, kind of using the technology for something you really weren't supposed to be doing, because the technology wasn't quite there yet. This was before Final Cut Pro, before Hollywood's acceptance of this kind of stuff. But we were doing it for this 35 anamorphic show and I was like, "Wow, this is kind of cool." And then I cut *Curse of the Puppet Master,* then within six or eight months they got rid of their post production supervisor and brought me in to do all of it. In the year that followed, the burnout process came, because I felt like, "All I'm doing is fixing other people's screw-ups here." We were the last line of defense to try to make those movies better. They would half-ass the shoot and then we'd have to throw CGI or cool title sequences or whatever to make the movies better.

You can't fix everything in post.
You wouldn't know that working for Full Moon! We really did become a band aid.
But it quickly got out of hand because it's like what you said, some of these directors, had only 10 day shoots, or 15 day shoots or whatever. You have to allow a certain amount of time for the post to try and clean up a lot of the messes. The first *Witchouse* was a big one. That was the one and only time I saw Charlie Band come downstairs and literally sit with one of my editors and re-cut the entire movie because it was so bad. And it's still not very good, but it's a lot better than it was. I remember sitting down with Ariauna Albright, it was the first thing she was in for them, and she was in tears. She was like, "Oh, my God, this movie is so horrible. It's the first thing I'm doing for them. They're never going to hire me again." To salvage a movie like that is not my idea of fun. It is a creative challenge.

It must have been an amazing experience to go from making your guerrilla movies in Ohio to shooting a 35mm in that giant house in Romania, whatever the budget was.
I think it was like $80,000, and then some more for the post. It was the one movie I made where I really felt like a filmmaker. I had my own driver! (laughs) The cast went in a van from the hotel, and I had my own driver, and it was a 45-minute drive to the location, and it just gave me time to think. "Hey, I'm getting paid! I don't have to use my own money; I don't have to grovel. I've got a budget, and I'm getting paid, and I have a per diem, and I'm in a foreign country for the first time of my life." That was one of the best months of my life, making that movie.

How long was the shoot?
It was nine days, and only eight in Romania.

You commented that you'd made your sole contribution to that franchise. But then you directed the third one, another nine day shoot, for $26,000. I think Witchouse 3: Demon Fire ***may be your best film. It was deceptive the way the first act makes you think the whole film is going to take place in that house, that it's going to be another one of those movies, but then you're in a car, you're on a beach, you're in a parking lot...***

That was my biggest thing with the Full Moon movies, you never really see establishing shots beyond the one house you're shooting in, and it's so claustrophobic. I was like, "There's this dialogue with the girls in *Witchouse 3* where they're coming back from shooting footage at the street fare." It was shot in the parking lot of Full Moon on a Sunday morning, when they had a farmer's market going on in the background, so you just see some tents and people tearing stuff down, and it looks like there's maybe something going on back there, and that's it. That's all I needed to sell it. You see that and you see a closed off street. The whole movie was a model of simplicity. I wasn't going to put my name on it, it was a dare to even make it for the money we made it for. I was just going to put a pseudonym on it and crank it out, but I was cutting it together and it was like *Polymorph* again. "Huh, what happened here? Somewhere along the way this actually worked out."

It says something about what's wrong with this business: you shot an $80,000 film in 35mm, and the reward was working with a quarter as much money on the sequel.

The first *Witchouse* did big business because it came out on video right as *The Blair Witch Project* was in theaters, so there was this big witch mania. *Witchouse* had a pretty good box cover, but not much else. I thought the movie sucked, and a lot of other people thought it sucked, too, but that didn't matter because they didn't know that until after they'd rented it. Blockbuster bought a lot of copies, Hollywood Video bought a lot of copies. And those numbers got back to Charlie, and Charlie thought, "Oh, we've got to do another one."

Witchouse 2 did a lot less than the first one because we came out on DVD around the time that *Blair Witch 2* was in theatres, which I thought was a much better movie than *Blair Witch* #1, but it didn't matter because people felt like they got burned on the first one. *Witchouse* #1 wasn't a very good movie. People saw it, but they didn't like it, so they kind of avoided the second one despite the good reviews. And then the third one got even better reviews than the second one, but it was the law of diminishing returns at that point. The movies were getting better, but nobody cared.

It was probably a miscalculation to link the films together with those titles.

I begged Charlie to just call the third one *Demon Fire* and not make it a *Witchouse* movie, but he insisted on pushing it that way. What are you going to do? It's one of the titles that I got the DVD rights to from him as part of another deal. It's one that keeps selling; I'm almost out of the third pressing and then that will be it. That one's definitely had some legs on it, people still discover it.

Watching Deadly Stingers, **the biggest surprise for me was in the opening credits. You didn't edit this one, so to me, it didn't feel like a Bookwalter film.**
It's so depressing that you say that, because it's how I feel about it, too. I just couldn't stand talking to or even being around Charlie Band and I just wanted out of that whole situation. It was the only movie I ever made where I knew going in, and I told him, "My magic hat is fresh out of rabbits."

When you quit, did you go straight back to Ohio?
No, I just moved back to Ohio in March, 2006. I turned my attention full time pretty much to my own DVD stuff.

You mean re-releasing your films?
Yeah, trying to get all my old stuff out and picking stuff up by other filmmakers. It's kind of a boutique business, a one-man band. But that was what I wanted. I really burned myself out making all these movies. I think it was over 13 movies for Full Moon in two and a half years. They had a nickname for me: I was "Big Daddy." I remember after delivering *Stingers* it was like, "Big Daddy has left the building." (laughs) That's it, I don't want to be Big Daddy anymore. I just want to go back and do something quiet and have a simpler life. This was too much of a grind, especially when the passion was kind of squeezed out of it.

When someone submits a film to you for consideration, what are your hopes when you put that disc in?
Boy, I am so picky, I'm lucky I put anything out! (laughs) There are times when I have to compromise and put stuff out that I'm maybe not so fond of, but I think other people might like it. I'm lucky if I like two films a year that I put out, that I would recommend to people. It's tough, because if you don't put out a steady stream of product, you don't get paid for the previous releases and then you don't have a business. I don't like that aspect of it. I almost feel like Charlie Band sometimes, only not as soulless. (laughs) If I was in another situation I wouldn't put this film out or that film out. And then I'm really surprised because I'll send stuff out and read the reviews, and people really like it, so what the hell do I know? It's such a weird industry.

2

Strange Bedfellows

Filmmaking is a collaborative medium. It's also a medium filled with egos that are easily bruised in high pressure situations. The three driving creative forces on most films are the director, the producer, and the writer, usually in that order. Sometimes one person fills two of those roles, which almost guarantees him final say on most matters. Many people subscribe to "the auteur theory," which proposes that a film's director is its author. In general, I disagree with this philosophy, although it's clearly the case if the director in question is a real artist, like James Whale, Alfred Hitchcock, Orson Welles, or Stanley Kubrick. Sometimes a filmmaker assumes all three roles to exert as much control over a project as possible, then delegates much of the producer's responsibilities to a co-producer, line producer, or production manager

The screenwriter writes the script, which might start with his original idea, or one by the director or the producer. He might base his screenplay on an existing screen treatment, or be hired to re-write an existing screenplay written by a previous writer, or may adapt material from another medium, such as a novel, a comic book, or a magazine article. A screenwriter's contribution to a film is often just as important as that of the director, which makes the disparity in their pay scales (when there is pay) a possible source of contention.

For the purposes of this book, a micro-budget movie is one that costs under $100,000 to complete, and a low budget film is one that costs under $1.5 million. *Brain Damage* and *Street Trash* were shot on 35mm for $900,000 — two decades ago. To a micro-budget filmmaker like me, these are dream budgets, but by Hollywood standards, they were very low. I completed *Slime City* on 16m for $50,000; *Undying Love* on 16m for $35,000; and *Naked Fear* on Hi 8 for $7,000. Mind you, these were all produced in the 20th century. For a better comparison, *Just the 4 of Us*, an unreleased indie sex comedy written and produced by Robert Craig Sabin, shot on Mini–DV over 20 days, cost $25,000. For micro-budget filmmakers making $4,000 features, these budgets may seem luxurious. A friend of mine, Greg Sterlace, has shot three character driven films for under $1,000 each.

If a director comes onto a project after a screenplay has been written, he may request certain modifications. If he develops the script with the writer, his ideas may be incorporated from the beginning. Some directors rewrite existing scripts or bring on another writer to rewrite it for him. And then there are directors who actually recognize a good screenplay when they see it, fall in love with the material, and see their job as preserving the original content as well as interpreting it.

The director is the primary mover on a project once financing has been raised. Hopefully, he will communicate his vision in ways that inspire all of his collaborators, including cast and crew. A director sets the tone for a project by providing leadership and clear thinking. Show me a director who yells at his teammates and stomps his feet when things don't go his way, and I'll show you an egomaniac who really has to beat the odds to make a good film. Film history is full of directors who achieved greatness despite belligerent personalities, but on those films, the cast and crew were well paid. That is not likely to be the case on a low or micro-budget film. Treat your people with respect and courtesy if you expect them to commit themselves to your vision.

Leslie Culton in Brett Piper's *Drainiac* (2004). Photograph courtesy Brett Piper.

The producer is responsible for raising money for a project, whether out of his own pocket, or through private investors, or through a company. A producer may be involved on a creative basis. Regardless, he has an obligation to protect investor capital, and may have approval over casting and other matters. A creative producer may assemble the entire team. A good producer will also protect the screenplay and the director from negative distractions or outside influences. And when the film has been completed, he will most likely be the individual responsible for negotiating a distribution deal and dealing with the production company's attorney and accountant. Of the three principle players named so far, the producer is who will be responsible for ongoing business matters long after the screenwriter and director have moved on to other endeavors.

Teamwork

Even when I've written, directed, co-produced, and edited a feature film, I've shunned the credit, "A Greg Lamberson Film." I think such credits are fueled by ego. If you are the creative force behind a project and make all of the key decisions, you still rely on a small army of dedicated individuals to realize your vision. Some of the filmmakers profiled in this book have largely made some films with only one other crew person. But doesn't that increase the amount of credit that person should get as well? The only time I want to see such a credit is if it prevents a filmmaker from listing his own name ten times at the end of a film, which is completely ridiculous and egocentric.

You need a team of creative people to make your movie, but before that you need to assemble your principal partners—writer, director, producer—and draw up written agreements defining each person's role, responsibilities, and equity in the film you've chosen to make together. If you take nothing else away from this book, I want it to be this: you must have a written agreement with every person with whom you make a film, even if they're your best friend; *especially* if they're your best friend. Otherwise, you run the risk of seeing a lot of hard work go down the drain, and the rights to the project may become

"Slime Guys" on the courtyard set they built for Frank Henenlotter's *Brain Damage* (1988). Left to right: Brit Petrucelly, Lamberson, Ed Walloga, Joe Warda, Peter Clark. Photograph courtesy Karen Ogle.

entangled in such a way that you are unable to salvage your film in any fashion. Written agreements are designed to protect everyone involved in as many scenarios as possible. Filmmaking can be highly stressful, and your best buddy today may be your bitter rival tomorrow. Signing agreements with your partners is not a sign of paranoia; it's an indication of common sense — and *professionalism*. If you choose not to sign written agreements, or put off signing them until after production wraps, you're not only risking your own efforts, but those of every single person who is investing their time, creativity, devotion, and resources to your project.

Seal the Deal

Once you and your partners decide you're serious about making a movie, the first thing you should do is find a qualified attorney. I don't mean your cousin Louie, the ambulance chaser; get an attorney who represents other clients in the entertainment industry, who grasps the nuances that agreements and negotiations entail. You don't go to an ear and throat doctor when you have chest pains, do you? At this stage, you simply want a partnership agreement that assigns credit, responsibilities and profit participation. Who has final say on creative decisions? Who has final say on business decisions? If the project never gets off the ground, or stalls in mid-production, or collapses during post production, do the screenplay rights revert to the writer, the director, or the producer? If the film isn't made, when may the partners dissolve their partnership? A decent entertainment attorney will address all these concerns in a written agreement, even if it's only two or three pages long. Once you've signed that document, the next step is to set up the terms of your partnership as it pertains to investors, whether that means a Limited Partnership, a Joint Venture Agreement, or a Limited Liability Corporation. If you absolutely cannot afford to bring in an attorney, then draw up a simple letter of agreement between the partners, cover as many bases as you can, and include a clause that you will have a more comprehensive agreement drawn up by an attorney when you have seed money to properly develop your project.

I co-produced *Slime City* with Peter Clark and Marc Makowski, initially on a $35,000 budget. Frank Henenlotter, the director of *Basket Case*, was a customer at the Times Square video store where Peter and I worked, and when he saw we were serious about making our movie, he referred us to his producer, Edgar Ievans, who in turn referred us to their attorney, Gerald J. Gold. Because we were investing our own money in the project — almost one half of the total budget — we already had seed money with which to pay Jerry. At that time, he advised us to form a Limited Partnership Agreement, which limited us to 25 investors. He also drew up an agreement between the three of us, as well as contracts for our cast and crew. Because we weren't paying people, the contracts specified the manner in which they would be entitled to receive Net Profits in the film (after unpaid production expenses were covered, the three of us received deferred salaries, and then investors would recoup their investment.) Jerry also negotiated our deal when a foreign sales rep provided us with completion funds, and our first video distribution deal in the U.S.

Marc and I co-produced *Undying Love* with Ed Walloga, Jr., my assistant director on all three of my micro-budget films, for a total budget of $35,000. This time, I was the primary investor and Marc and Ed provided the balance of the budget. Since it was just the three of us, Jerry advised us to use a simple Joint Venture Agreement, and I modified the contracts he had already created for the cast and crew. We completed the film on time and on budget, with no partnership issues, and Marc and I used the exact same formula on *Naked Fear*, which cost $7,500. For more advice from Jerry, read Chapter 9.

Get to know potential partners before they become actual partners. If someone says they can raise money for you, find out how before you get into bed with them. Define your responsibilities to each other and the production. Never assume that what seems like commons sense — or ethical behavior — to you means the same thing to your partners.

3

Justin Wingenfeld

THE INSIDE MAN

Justin Wingenfeld grew up in Pittsburgh, the land of George Romero's living dead, but a beat up VHS tape of Lucio Fulci's *The Gates of Hell* made just as big an impact on him as Romeros' films did. He attended Pittsburg Filmmakers, affiliated with Point Park College, before surviving a miserable experience as a production assistant on Troma Entertainment's *Citizen Toxie*. At POP Cinema, an indie DVD distribution and production company known primarily for goofy sexploitation horror films, he runs Alternative Cinema, the catalogue and warehouse department for the company's multiple labels: Seduction Cinema, Retro Seduction Cinema, Shock-O-Rama Cinema, and Retro Shock-O-Rama Cinema. He worked on several of their in-house productions in various capacities before directing Debbie Rochon and Julian Wells in *Skin Crawl*.

How did you end up at E.I. Independent Cinema, which is now POP Cinema?
I was living in Ohio briefly because my wife Trinity was in grad school at Miami University, outside Cincinnati. She went on to graduate, and we were both looking for jobs in our fields. Trinity's a biochemist, and I wanted to try to get into filmmaking, so it was basically New York or Los Angeles, and we decided we preferred to live in New York and started looking there. A friend of mine named Mike Watt bumped into Mike Raso at one of the conventions and Mike Raso asked him if he was interested in working for him. Mike Watt said, "I don't really want to move to New York, but I do have a friend who is looking for work in the film business in New York," and he gave me Mike Raso's number and I called him. I started work just a few weeks later, and now I run the catalogue department, filling customer and company orders. I've had one feature film produced and I'm hoping to do another one soon; I'm working on screenplays right now.

What did you do on some of POP's other movies?

I worked as a line producer on a few of the erotic movies. My pseudonym was Christian Right on those, because everyone used fake names, mostly as a joke. Then the catalogue department got busier, so I had to concentrate on that. They wanted to produce a horror movie, they had wanted to for a long time but the opportunity had never arisen, but then I gave a script I'd written called *Death is a Bitch* to Zach Snygg, who worked for them for a long time. He read it and liked it and talked them into letting me make it.

What script notes did Mike Raso give you?

Mike didn't actually read the script, he had way too much on his plate. He basically trusted Zach and gave us a small amount of money to go out and shoot it over the course of about three weeks. It was the last time that EI, now POP Cinema, shot on Betacam. It was going to be shot on film, and then it was cut back to 24p, and then right before we started shooting it was cut back to Betacam. But I think that the cinematographer, John Fedele, who's also in the movie, did a fantastic job and made it look as good as it possibly could.

Did you have to rewrite the script so it would be more like a POP Cinema production?

To tell you the truth, as far as the actual story and degree of nudity went, they had absolutely nothing to do with it. That was all me. I wanted there to be a lot of nudity, I wanted there to be a lot of sex in it, it had nothing to do with what I thought would sell or anything. I think there's an extreme lack of nudity and sex in — not just American horror movies, but in American movies in general. I think there's a real weird and kind of unsettling fear of sex and sexuality in American culture which I don't get and I've never understood. I've never been able to figure out exactly what it is that people find so objectionable about sex in movies.

Why did you decide to make Skin Crawl *through POP Cinema instead of on your own?*

It was not too dissimilar to things they had done so it made sense to go to them with it. It took a little bit of effort to talk Mike into it. He didn't want me to direct it at first, only because I'd never directed a feature before, which I certainly understood. Once John Fedele came on as director of photography and Zach came on as producer, I think he relaxed a little bit. I was willing to let someone else direct it if that was the only way to get it made, but I really wanted to direct it myself.

What formulas do you follow when you construct a screenplay?

I have tried writing treatments, using index cards, writing outlines, and I have always found precisely the same problem that I have found when I've just sat down and written a screenplay from the beginning to the end, which is, I can't figure out which direction I want the story to go. I don't find that doing anything other than just writing the actual screenplay has helped me at all. It just adds a whole new level of frustration. I get more accomplished just running things over and over in my head, and just retaining that information than I do writing treatments or synopses for myself. If it works for you that's great, but there are no rules. When it comes to movies, when it comes to rock 'n' roll, when it comes to any kind of art, there are no rules. I've found that what helps me is to stand up, walk around the room, and actually recite the story out loud to myself. I'll have conversations with myself playing two characters. Often the dialogue is actually what's driving the movie. The dialogue is what can create entire scenes and an entire plot point can come out of a conversation two characters have, and you say, "That's interesting. What if *this* happens?"

What did pre-production on Skin Crawl *entail?*

It was a pretty fair amount of work and most of it did fall on me as far as securing locations and casting the movie. Zach and I cast the movie together for the most part. Debbie Rochon and Kevin Shinnick, who played three of the main characters between the two of them, each brought on a couple of actors. I contacted and interviewed their candidates over the phone. We were under such a time crunch that I couldn't really audition much. The whole casting process took a couple of weeks. And securing locations was a major pain because you have to deal with insurance, and how long you're going to be at each place, whether or not they want credit in the movie, that kind of stuff. The rest of it, as far as crew and equipment and stock and all that stuff went, was all in house, so it was more about getting the go ahead from Mike.

How did you budget for post production when you know all the editing is going to be done in house?

To tell you the truth, as far as the budgeting of the whole movie goes, I don't know too much about it. The only hints I got about budget were whether or not I was allowed to do something. A lot of times I was told, "You can't do this, you can't do that. Whatever you've already done, that's just going to have to be good enough." When it came to editing the movie, Brett Piper was a paid staff member, basically developing projects and tweaking things that he had in the can and working on other things. For the few weeks that he and I edited together I came in after hours on my own time.

What was your actual shooting schedule?

We shot a total of 15 days. We didn't shoot on the weekends. We had to stop shooting for a little while because there was a scheduling conflict that

Justin Wingenfeld mans the POP Cinema table at Rock and Shock in Worcester, Massachusetts. Photograph courtesy Henrique Couto.

ended up throwing a monkey wrench in the whole thing. It was just a very minor problem that ended up being a big problem. A couple of actors' schedules and a couple of location schedules didn't mesh, so we ended up having to postpone part of the shoot for about a month before we finally picked up those scenes, and that only took about two days.

Were you able to rehearse?

Yes, luckily. And again, I did that on my own time. I believe two Saturdays in a row I had most of the principal cast over to my apartment and we did a read through. I think that was a really big help, because it really got everybody in tune with their character, and then we weren't on the set when we were actually supposed to be shooting a scene, and they weren't suddenly saying, "Well why am I saying this?" or "Why am I doing this?" because that had already been discussed. The things we talked about on the set were things like blocking. That's why I think rehearsal is so important. People say, "Oh, it's not necessary, and it's a waste of time," and I don't agree with that. I think it's essential.

I like that the film is a serious attempt at horror and not the typical POP fare.

Well, it's a far cry from *Play-Mate of the Apes* and *Kinky Kong*. I sincerely think that they were not expecting much. I think that they were definitely throwing me a bone. "Okay, let's get this pipe dream that Justin has of being a filmmaker out of his system. We'll let him make a movie. We can afford to blow this little bit of money on this movie and then maybe we can make that back and he can forget about it." When Mike started seeing footage from the movie, and he started seeing a rough cut being put together, he told me a number of times that he was surprised at how good it was. I wanted to do something that was unlike anything else E.I. had done, just in atmosphere. There's humor in it, but it's kind of a sarcastic, mean spirited humor as opposed to the goofy, sophomoric kind that's in a lot of the Seduction stuff.

E.I. was always more about juvenile comedy and sexploitation than straight horror.

Yeah, when Alternative Cinema first started, it was purely a catalogue company. They acquired movies from other companies and sold them as a mail order thing. A lot of them were horror movies, but pretty much whenever they started producing their own movies, the most obvious thing to produce for next to nothing was adult stuff. But they filled in a niche that just wasn't being filled, which was very softcore erotica that couples could sit and watch together or people could put on at a frat party. It was very light, it was very silly, and there wasn't anything particularly offensive about it. Even if it wasn't your cup of tea, you could possibly still sit and watch this, if only for the offbeat humor. And that worked for a while, but unfortunately it just became kind of stale, because there was a pattern there, a formula, and they never strayed from it. Technically, *Skin Crawl* was their first in-house horror movie.

Why did it take three years to complete?

Frankly, we finished principal photography and there was an editor on staff who was going to edit the movie. He was busy with other projects, so it

Key art for *Skin Crawl* (2007), written and directed by Justin Wingenfeld for Shock-O-Rama Cinema. © Pop Cinema, L.L.C.

Erin Brown ("Misty Mundae"), Brett Piper, and Justin at the Fangoria Weekend of Horrors in Chicago. © Pop Cinema, L.L.C.

kept getting postponed. First it ended up being a couple of months, then it went to about six months, and then that guy left the company. Once he left there was basically no one on staff to do it and Mike didn't trust me to do it myself. During that time I actually sat at home with a VCR and edited the movie on paper. By that time we had an editor on staff. I gave my notes to him as a guideline, he ended up not paying much attention to it and edited the movie the way he wanted to, leaving out entire plot points and lines of dialogue which explained what was going on, so the movie didn't make any sense. I remember watching it and thinking that for half the movie I couldn't understand how he thought it made sense to edit it the way he did. The other half was fine. And time just passed. It went from six months to a year, to two years, to three years. And you know, probably once a month for that entire time I would go into Mike's office and ask him about *Skin Crawl*, and once every few months he would come into my office and say, "I bet you're wondering what's going on with *Skin Crawl*. Well, we're doing some other things, blah, blah, blah." I don't necessarily think he was just stringing me along. I got the feeling he really did not know when we were going to get a chance to finally finish this movie. Now mine was far from the only movie that took that long to come out. *The Seduction of Misty Mundae*, which Mike directed, was shot around the same time as *Skin Crawl*, and that didn't come out until a few months before *Skin Crawl*. So I know it wasn't just my movie. To be brutally frank, I have never gotten a straight answer as to why it took so long, and I don't think I ever will get one.

Tell me about the first cut off the film.

It was okay for a first cut but it didn't make a lot of sense. Characters did things and said things and things happened that seemed completely unmotivated. You couldn't figure out what the hell was going on! I'm watching it and going, "Well, this shot's missing, this line's missing, and this entire scene is missing." All the stuff was missing because he cut it out, I guess because he thought it was boring or whatever. For all I know, Mike could have told him to cut it out. That cut of the movie got shelved and it sat for another year or so—

So that wasn't your cut at all?

That's the cut that was done after I had edited it "on paper," when I had written down all of the time codes for the beginning and ending of each shot that I wanted, with the corresponding take number and everything, it was a huge pain in the ass. But as I said, he didn't pay attention to it, so really it wasn't my cut of the movie. After about a year of it just sitting there Mike said, "Brett is going to finish editing your movie." I was both happy and apprehensive about that. I was happy because I knew Brett would do a good job, and I liked him and had worked with him on his moves and enjoyed working with him, but I was apprehensive because I didn't know how it would look to have my feature debut as a director edited by an established director. I thought that might look like, "Well, obviously Justin needed a lot of help in making this movie."

The biggest difference came in Brett's idea of going back in time and looking at things multiple times, which at first I honestly didn't like. When I first saw it I thought it was like a gag, I thought it was a gimmick. I didn't think it was necessary at all. But then I tried to be objective about it. I said, "Okay, don't look at it like this is something you worked on, that this is your movie, be objective." And when I really stopped and looked back I thought that it did make it a lot more interesting, and that it added a different twist to it. So I finally said, "Okay, I have to admit that works pretty well." He had edited up to the point where we see Howard's point of view of the day's events, and then he and I edited the rest of the movie together. A handful of scenes stayed the way they had been, but he and I went through and re-edited most of it. And then we sat and tweaked it. The other cool part was I got to sit there and work with him on all the digital effects. He physically did them, but I told him exactly what I wanted: "I want this effect, I want this to look like this..." We had some sequences with these weird colors, and these weird flashes, and the image gets skewed.

POP premieres a lot of their films at the Pioneer Cinema in lower Manhattan...

I don't think *Skin Crawl* was a big enough project to warrant it. I think that had I not been involved, and it was just something they happened to have picked up, even with those actors in it, it would have gotten even less of a push than it did. It was kind of released as a companion piece to *Chainsaw Sally*; those were both released around the same time, one right after the other.

I was pleasantly surprised not to see the actresses' faces and chests all over the box.

Yeah, it was a nice change of pace.

The good thing about film being such a collaborative medium is that if you surround yourself with people who know what they're doing, they make you look better.

Yes, that's true. People do forget sometimes that it is collaborative, and what makes it interesting is that it's not just one person's vision, it's a group's vision. The performance is the creation of the director and the actor, and the way the movie is shot is a collaboration between the director and the cinematographer, and the director and the editor, and the director and the special effects people. That's why I feel it's important for directors to collaborate with each member of the crew.

4

Screamwriting 101

"If it ain't on the page, it ain't on the stage."

How many times have you heard this expression?

A screenplay is a blueprint for a movie. You might think that's an oversimplification that doesn't give enough credit to the screenwriter, but can you imagine constructing a building without a blueprint? The screenplay is the single most important component in a motion picture's development. It tells the story, identifies the characters, and sets the entire project in a direction. You need a script to attract talent to your project and you have no business seeking financing or starting pre-production without a completed script, unless you've obtained the rights to a work from another medium, like a novel or comic book.

I was the 1st AD (assistant director) on *Plutonium Baby*—the *second* 1st AD. The first crew for the production resigned en mass four days into a projected 10-day shoot. Scott Coulter, who had just supervised the special effects on *Slime City*, enlisted the Slime Guys to save the day. Four of us obtained the necessary camera equipment and traveled to Connecticut, where we discovered utter chaos. Chief among the problems was that there wasn't completed screenplay; the writer sat holed up in the hotel turning out pages as we shot. The actors didn't have time to prepare and the director was overwhelmed. It was a disaster. When shooting wrapped, the producer only had half a movie, and after viewing a 37-minute rough cut, he had to pony up funds for another week of shooting. I'm not saying all of these production missteps would have been avoided if the filmmakers had started with a complete script—just most of them.

Screenwriting has become an extremely attractive and profitable way to earn a living. Screenwriting courses are popular at film schools and numerous magazines on the craft pepper bookstore racks. And yet, as well paid as he may be, the Hollywood screenwriter is still just a cog in the machine. Often, the first thing that happens when a writer sells his first screenplay is the production company hires another screenwriter to "punch up" the material. The original screenwriter has now been removed from the process. But he has his first credit, and hopefully, he'll get an invitation to the premiere…

This all too common scenario is why many independent filmmakers choose to remain in a smaller pond, with greater creative control, rather than work their way up the ladder in the big, shark infested waters known as Hollywood. Micro-budget filmmakers are the most independent of the indies, and we often feed at the bottom of the smallest pond because we have no choice. Whether you're shooting a Hollywood blockbuster, a $1 million independent feature, or a $4,000 micro-budget horror film, I believe this axiom is true: If it ain't on the page, it ain't on the *screen*.

A poor director can make a good film from a very good screenplay, but even a talented director has trouble fashioning a decent movie from a bad screenplay. It's important to put as much work as possible into your script, to make it as fresh, entertaining, and suspenseful as you possibly can, *before you go into production.*

Learning the Craft

How does one go about learning the craft of screenwriting? There are several ways: watch movies in the theater; listen to commentary tracks on DVDs; read screenplays and interviews with screenwriters; enroll in film school. But take all the information you obtain with a grain of salt — even from me. If we all follow the same rules, patterns and paradigms, tomorrow's movies will resemble one another even more than today's do. To create something worthwhile, avoid the cookie cutter mentality advocated by individuals, organizations, and corporations that profit by your subscription to their manifestos. Most important, *write*: force yourself to sit down, start a draft, and complete it.

Breaking the Rules

With the abundance of instructional screenwriting services and products available to burgeoning wordsmiths, it's no surprise there are dozens of different methods and paradigms available to screenwriters. The individuals behind these theories need to convince you of the validity of their methods so you'll attend their seminars and purchase their books, DVDs, and CD ROMS. You know they've successfully marketed their products when they write a follow-up book on the exact same subject. At SVA, Roy recommended *Screenplay* by Syd Field. In this book, Field breaks down the three-act screenwriting structure into easy to understand terms. The book sold well, so, like a Hollywood blockbuster, a sequel followed. The first half of *The Screenwriter's Handbook* recaps material from *Screenplay;* the second elaborates on the concept of the "midpoint," a point halfway in a script when the course of action subtly changes direction. In other words, in his second book, Field unveils a four-act structure. I recommend the former book, but not the later. And Field has written at least *seven* screenwriting books.

TITLE SEQUENCE

Old woodcuts, accompanied by modern turns on MADRIGAL MUSIC ... the flavor of witchhunting days. The TITLES are superimposed over these.

SHOCK CUT TO

INT — HOSPITAL — DAY

A three-thousand-pound female patient is falling on NANCY FUCHS, crushing her to the floor.

NANCY

Oh, shit!

All this is slightly, then heavily, SLOWED DOWN.
Her long brown hair pirouettes in the air.
Her intense eyes search desperately for escape.
Her aquiline features convulse with pain.
And as the woman is laboriously dragged off, we hear:

NANCY's VOICE OVER

The patient was a case of senile psychosis. Her family had faked reports of heart failure to get her committed. Two other nurses were helping her out of a wheelchair when she threw herself on me.

During this, we.........................DISSOLVE INTO....

INT — DOCTOR'S OFFICE

.... an X-ray of the damage inflicted by the fall, as the Doctor's Voice picks up the thread:

DOCTOR OS

Why did she do it?

NANCY OS

Cause she was crazy! She thought I was a chair, or she was angry at me for removing the chair, who knows? I never found out.

DOCTOR OS

Ok. Well, these are the X-rays they forwarded to me. These first are the Lumbary Myelograms. They show nothing,

Page 1 from Roy Frumkes's unproduced screenplay *The Psychic*. Frumkes's style here is highly visual, with creative techniques to suggest editing rhythms.

In what parallel universe could slavishly following a road map possibly be construed as an act of creation? Learn the basic rules offered by these "experts" so you're aware of them, then decide which ones best help you construct the story *you* want to tell — and toss the rest into your cyber shredder. Some rules really are made to be broken, and in this day and age, when so many mainstream films exist purely to satisfy corporate needs, it's up to independent filmmakers to create fresh and exciting material. *Dare to be different.*

Screenwriting Programs

Many screenwriting programs are available which make writing, organizing, and editing easier. Most people I know use Final Draft; I use Movie Magic Screenwriter. I chose that program because it includes a novel writing function, which I needed when I adapted an un-produced screenplay, *The Forever Man*, into my first novel, *Personal Demons*. The first time I wrote a screenplay using this program was like a dream come true: all I had to do was turn it on and I was off and writing. The margins were pre-set and I mastered — or at least comprehended — the various basic functions within minutes. I turned out a feature length script in only two weeks, thanks to all the time I saved, and I was able to convert the material to Final Draft when necessary. It really is a brave new world.

But as any science fiction fan knows, with the advancement of technology comes an undercurrent of danger, and screenwriting software is no exception. I'm astounded by the number of programs out there that take you by the hand and guide you through the writing process, offering prompts when you need to see a character again, or if you've passed the pre-designated page where an act point should occur, at least according to the paradigms. Allowing a machine to dictate the beats of your story is even worse than obeying a paradigm. Technology is a tool, *not* a creative partner.

Proper Format

If you write a screenplay you intend to show to an agent, producer, director, star — or any professional in the film business — you must present your material in proper screenplay format. I can't count how many times people have asked me to critique scripts which they've composed using a basic Word program: no headers, ragged dialogue columns, quotation marks around dialogue, character names in CAPS every time they appear in the narrative...

If you can't take the time to learn proper formatting you must not be serious about your craft. Yes, in this instance I'm preaching conformity: there's a time and a place for everything, and you want your screenplay to look professional whether you're trying to sell it to a big studio or convince an investor that this will make a great micro-budget film. If you can't afford a screenwriting program, there are numerous templates available for free on-line.

Hollywood folks are inundated with so many screenplays that they look for any excuse to weed down their T.B.R. (to be read) piles. You're not being an independent visionary by stubbornly retaining your self invented, sloppy screenwriting format — you're just being lazy. It's easier to find pros and semi-pros willing to work on your project if they believe it's worth doing, and they'll form their initial opinions on your professionalism based on your presentation.

A screenplay has a header on every page. It has one-inch margins on all but the left hand side, which has a one and a half inch margin to accommodate holes and brackets when screenplay copies are assembled for distribution. Lines of narrative description run between 55 and 65 characters. Dialogue columns used to be three inches wide; now they're four inches. I'm no longer surprised when I see scripts formatted with one inch margins on both sides, five-inch dialogue columns, and 10-point fonts rather than 12; the perpetrators of these scripts are deliberately attempting to make overwritten screenplays appear to be a desirable length, but they aren't fooling anyone.

There's a practical reason for using standard screenplay format as well: one page of a script should approximate one minute of screen time. There are exceptions, but this is accepted as the norm. When an assistant director makes up his shooting schedule, or a script supervisor times your script, it's a lot easier for them to do so with the content presented in the industry standard. I've included various screenplay samples throughout this chapter which employ the basic format I'm describing. If your script doesn't look anything like them, you have homework to do. I'm talking about presentation, *not content*.

Camera Angles

As an independent filmmaker, you have more control over your script, budgetary considerations aside, than a writer working for a studio. If you know you're going to direct your script yourself, feel free to employ camera angles if it better enables you to tell your story. But if you're directing your own script, why do you need to specify these angles? Just communicate your ideas to your Director of Photography or storyboard artist. I sometimes specify camera angles for my opening scene, just to set the tone, or for an important sequence in which specific camera angles are necessary to understand my intent.

Write What You Don't Know

Here's an axiom I *disagree* with: "Write what you know." I see it all the time in guidebooks. What a boring approach to storytelling! Should a film student only write about film school? Should a bartender only write about bar-

MAIN TITLE SEQUENCE

Bright RED TITLES over a black background are INTERCUT with the following SHOTS:

INT. SCOTT'S BATHROOM — NIGHT

We are in the darkened bathroom of SCOTT KELLY, an intense looking 25-year-old with sharp features and medium length, dark brown hair. Scott enters, flicks on the light and closes the door behind him, a look of grim determination on his face.

Bending over, he RUNS WATER in the bathtub.

He peels off his T-shirt, drops it on the floor, and UNZIPS his fly. There is no music, just RUSHING WATER.

The tub is full now. Water DRIPS steadily from the faucet.

Scott dips a naked leg into the hot water.

He is sitting in the bath tub now, his back against the wall. Taking a deep breath, he raises his right arm on the porcelain rim and makes fist.

And picks up a GLEAMING RAZOR BLADE with his left hand. He presses the razor blade against his right and steels his nerves. Then he cuts his wrist with the blade, but we do not see the wound.

Now he cuts his left wrist, and this time we see the action in gruesome CLOSE UP: the razor slices into his flesh, and a second later a line of blood appears.

He drops the razor blade into the water.

Leaning against the tiled wall, he closes his eyes. We hear his HEARTBEAT, which grows steadily slower.

The razor blade rests on the bottom of the tub. Scott's blood spreads INTO FRAME, obscuring our VIEW until we see only deep red.

END TITLE SEQUENCE

                                           HARD CUT TO

Page 1 from Greg Lamberson's *Undying Love*, which played as a midnight movie in New York City in 1992 and was released on video as *New York Vampire* in 1998.

tending? How many times have you been at a party and someone has said, "You should make a movie about my life"? Do you take these people seriously? Do you ask them to tell their life story right then and there? Not likely.

Unless you've been to the moon (without a rocket) or you've rescued POWs or saved the life of the President, your life just isn't interesting enough to justify 100 minutes of screen time. Don't write what you know—*use your imagination*. You can certainly imbue your characters with aspects of your life, using your experiences to add layers of realism to your creations. But when telling a cinematic story, forget about that magic moment when you decided to become a filmmaker. Save it for your memoir — or your instructional filmmaking book!

Does Size Matter?

Someone once told me the ideal length for a Hollywood screenplay is 100 — 110 pages. I suggest that 90 pages is the ideal length for a script for a low budget or micro-budget movie.

But shouldn't a screenplay operate on its own terms regardless of the film's budget? In a perfect world, yes. But if the world was perfect, you wouldn't be struggling under the constraints of a small budget, would you? Check out the running time of some of the direct-to-DVD features in your collection or at your local video store. You'll see that most of them run between 75 minutes—acceptable for a micro-budget film, but not for a Hollywood feature — and an hour and a half.

The length of your script affects your shooting schedule and therefore your budget. Even if you're not paying your cast and crew, you have to feed them. Insurance may cost more. With a greater running time, editing will take longer. When you enter the finished product in festivals, you may pay larger entry fees. Finally, you show the finished product to your best friend, who tells you, "It was kind of long..."

Basic Structure

A story has a beginning, a middle, and an ending. Most screenplays have a First Act, a Second Act, and a Third Act, and begin with the words "FADE IN" and end with "FADE OUT"—the Hollywood equivalent of "Once upon a time" and "...happily ever after." If you have a 90 page script, each act will run approximately 30 pages. Feel free to adjust this however you wish; Act One can be 25 pages, Act Two 40 pages, and Act Three 25 pages, or any variation you choose. Remember, these are guidelines, not absolutes. I doubt anyone ever told William Shakespeare, "Sorry, but your play has five acts, not three. We can't produce it."

Each act has its own climax, and that climax generally jerks the story in a (hopefully) surprising direction. In my films, the First Act Point has occurred

```
FADE IN

INT. GARAGE — NIGHT — 1975

Grease, junk and old broken cars, left in the dark to rust. A pair
of dim headlights stare dully out of the shadows.

Three GUNSHOTS ring out. A shadow falls across the headlights,
clinging to them for a moment, then sliding off. A soft THUD.
The shadows claim a new corpse.

                    MICKEY V.O.
          On June 13th, 1975, Elizabeth Bendini was
          shot three times; once in the stomach, twice in
          the head. Her body was driven to a nearby
          swamp and dumped. It was subsequently
          infested by insects and devoured by wildlife
          and rot.

We linger on the car in the shadows. Is it a trick of the light, or
do the headlights grow brighter?

                    MICKEY V.O. (CONT'D)
          Her body got off easy. What happened to the
          rest of her wasn't so pretty.

CUT TO

BLACK AND WHITE AD

The same headlights, the same car, is pictured in the personal page
of some local rag. It looks ... less than impressive.

INT. BEDROOM — DAY

MIKEY reads out loud from the paper.

                    MIKEY
          "... If you find Muffin, please call 555-6247."
          Isn't that a heartbreaker?

Mikey is a twenty-seven year old chain smoker. His boyish good
looks are off-set by a cynical twinkle in his big brown eyes.
```

Page 1 from Robert Craig Sabin's award winning screenplay for *Carma*, never produced. This scene establishes the premise of a haunted car in record time.

at the 20-page mark, with a dramatic murder. In *Slime City*, Alex (Robert Sabin), transformed into a slime monster, savagely beats a homeless man to death. In *Undying Love*, a model named Camilla (Julie Lynch) reveals herself to be a vampire femme fatale when she slays her possessive photographer (Robert Sabin again). And in *Naked Fear*, Randy Carver (Tommy Sweeney) saves the life of his new roommate (Robert Sabin!) by stabbing to death a home invader. In each instance, the murder advances the storyline, creates new conflicts, and builds suspense.

A Visual Opening

Movies are motion *pictures*, not motion words. Make your story visual and cinematic. Most script readers expect a dramatic story "hook" by the 10-page mark, and will discard your screenplay if they don't see it. Alexander Beck, *Slime City's* foreign sales agent, criticized me for not beginning the story with some horrific act. I wanted the film to start on a normal note, with Alex moving into his new apartment building, a la *Rosemary's Baby*. Beck was right; I forgot I was making an exploitation film (or didn't even realize it). In *Undying Love*, a suicidal young man named Scott Kelly is cursed with eternal life when he hooks up with a vampire. I opened the script and the movie with Scott's attempted suicide, then followed that with the introduction of my vampire villain, and followed that with a scene in which Scott meets the woman who will indoctrinate him into vampire society. All of the main characters, conflicts and themes were introduced in the first 10 pages.

Avoid Clichés

The horror genre is unfortunately typified by hoary clichés: as the heroine searches the dark barn, a cat/bird/stegosaurus bolts from its hiding space; startling her; the masked killer isn't really dead, and our heroine just dropped her meat cleaver; our heroine — God, she's brave! — goes out in the woods alone, with only the light of the full moon to guide her way; our heroes and heroines — two of each, and don't they look old for high school students? — make a wrong turn on the wrong road at the wrong time in a storm that is *so* wrong. We've seen it all before. When you've finished your first draft, read through it and search for moments like these. With a proper twist, you may be able to resuscitate one or two of them for a good jolt. If not, cut them now — because it may be impossible to cut them in the editing room.

What clichés drive you crazy when you watch a horror film? Make a list. A *long* list. How about when characters are all named after famous horror film writers, directors, and stars? It's been done several hundred times. Or when a famous director makes a self conscious cameo in a film and all but winks at the camera? It's a distraction from the atmosphere you should be working hard to establish. How about when a character takes an elevator to the 13th floor? Do you know that many buildings don't even have thirteenth floors? Or when a character goes to room — shudder — #666? That one's been done a thousand times, and recently Biblical scholars revealed that the 6-6-6 number is biblically inaccurate anyway. Don't recycle someone else's gags just because you've seen them before; your audience has seen the exact same films.

Finish Your First Draft

Do you have trouble finishing what you start? Take my advice: plow through your first draft and do some major fine tuning when you do your second draft. Most people procrastinate, and look for reasons to procrastinate. "I was at my halfway point, but I decided to go back and fix the beginning." Fix the beginning when you fix the whole script. Work your way through your opening, then your first 10 pages, and so on until you've written your final "FADE OUT." You'll have a complete draft that you can polish and re-work to your heart's content, and the toughest part will be over.

Rewriting Your Script

In publishing, ninety percent of writing is rewriting. This has been true for me when I've written novels, but less so when I've written screenplays. As a screenwriter, I now write on a pretty instinctive level and pacing comes naturally to me. But rewriting is still an important part of the process. You think your script is in the best shape it can be? Read it out loud. I guarantee you'll give your dialogue another polish. Think it's fully cooked now? Ask a few actor friends to read it out loud in front of you. Here comes Draft #3. Remember: the smoother your dialogue reads, the easier it will be to interest good actors in your project.

Robert Sabin once told me, "Filmmaking is about building relationships."
Screenwriting is about building movies.
Start writing.

5

Robert Craig Sabin
Going Hollyweird

Robert Craig Sabin was the first friend I made when I moved to New York City to study filmmaking at The School of Visual Arts. I cast him for my first narrative short film, *Cult Figure*, and wrote *Slime City* for him to star in. When Peter Clark and I worked on *I Was a Teenage Zombie* to gain production experience, we roped Robert into taking one of the supporting acting roles so he could undergo the same baptism of fire. We've worked on five features together, including one he wrote and produced. He's the best screenwriter I know, and has co-created an innovative Internet horror anthology series, *5 Minute Horror*. He's experienced first hand the horror of Hollywood development, having written everything from direct-to-DVD Walt Disney sequels to historical dramas to adapting two novels based on the world's most popular 500-pound serial killer.

Living in Florida, you knew you wanted to be a filmmaker, yet you attended NYU as an acting major.
They didn't have a film program at my high school, just a theatre program. The closest you could get to filmmaking at Boca Ciega was acting and directing. So it was sort of a natural progression to go to NYU's drama department. While I was at NYU I tried to transfer out of the acting program and into the writing program, but for whatever bureaucratic reason they said I couldn't do that. As it turns out, I think it was for the best because studying writing at college probably would have led me into the most fatuous existence. The acting program was interesting because it sent you to various acting studios across the city, so it wasn't NYU administering the program, it was Stella Adler and Lee Strassberg and the Experimental Theatre program in Soho, so you were getting a kind of real acting training, and it took you out of the university realm and into the theatre realm.

For years I had no idea that acting wasn't your primary goal. Did you just use your acting experience as a way to observe what was going on?

Yeah, I don't know if you remember, on *I Was a Teenage Zombie* there was one point where they wanted me for a shot and I wasn't on set at that particular moment, I was out getting lunch or something like that, and John Michaels said, "He's never here and he's always writing in that book!"(laughs) I had no knowledge of filmmaking at all until I started working on this stuff. But even then it wasn't the actual making of the movie that interested me, for me the real joy is the writing of it. That's really always been my ambition, to write a brilliant script and then find a good director who thinks it's a brilliant script and wants to actually make that script.

What did you learn about acting on I Was a Teenage Zombie?

Well the good thing about *Teenage Zombie* was that it was unabashedly a comedy. The people on the set who had the most input were comedy people, like George Seminara, and there seemed to be a real attempt to joke it up as much as possible. Consequently, I never really felt like I had to worry about character or motivation or anything like that. It wasn't really about emoting, it was about finding the moment and playing the joke of the moment. I feel I was more successful in that. I think my real weakness is when I have to do that "acting stuff" of really exploring character and motivation and sort of resonating emotionally. I have to say, I really enjoyed working with those people, it was a very fun set. It also demystified the process of getting a laugh on camera. I remember when we watched the dailies and the various screenings and my scenes did as well as anyone else's, and I was surprised and pleased by that.

How was Slime City *the next step for you?*

I knew you when you wrote the first draft of *Slime City*, so the impressive thing was seeing it progress from an idea to a script, and then you actually went out and found money and got it made, and that was very impressive to me, that you could start with an idea, really follow through with it. I thought that was amazing. What was also pretty cool was, as opposed to the kind of slapdash aspects of *Teenage Zombie*, where someone would say, "Hey, let's try this joke!" and throw it in there, we were very devoted to the script on *Slime City*. There was a lot of integrity and commitment to the vision of that script. It was more focused, and we were all very excited to be on that set. It was amazing to see that these things could actually occur.

Even though Mary Huner played two roles, and we were paying so much attention to the special effects, did you feel the weight of being the leading man at all?

I went into it thinking I was going to do the best I could do and I never took responsibility for more than that. I think more than the weight of being the leading man was the weight of living on the set, you know, having your home be the set. The special effects were probably more challenging than the role itself, and I say that not because there wasn't a lot to explore in the role, but because as an actor I probably wasn't able to invest emotionally as much as I should have. You know, it's funny; I've always felt bad about the performance I gave you in *Slime City*. It's just a little stiff, a little wooden, and it just feels like I'm watching the entire film and I'm not quite in synch with it. If there was a responsibility as a leading man, I don't think I quite lived up to it. But I think more than that was the special effects and the homelessness that resulted from the shoot.

I've always thought you had real presence in it. I've also always felt I failed Mary because I never filmed the necessary reaction shots of her for the ending, which is one of the reasons why it's so funny instead of scary.
Well you know, as a first film it was such an ambitious project and there was so much to do, especially on that last week. There was so much to accomplish and I think you were pulled in so many different directions. We were all finding our feet, and I think that Mary learned a lot from the whole process and was a better and more fearless actress at the end of it all.

What do you remember about the special make-up effects process?
I remember that Scott Coulter and Tom Lauten were Tom Waits fans, and as they were making the appliances for my face I kept falling asleep in the make-up chair. I remember that they got very, very good at removing the applications. As the shoot progressed, they removed them quicker and quicker, and by the end of the shoot they didn't even bother taking it off, they just left before we got the last shot, so I was sort of left to my own devices pulling off strips of latex from my face. I don't think anyone was conscious enough to be aware of just how funny it was.

And would you wake up with stuff still glued on your face?
Oh, yeah, for weeks. Bits had gotten into my pores, and a week later I was still discovering little dabs of black glue all over my face.

They poured all that methylcellulose in your hair...
Yeah, I blame that shoot for my baldness.

For Undying Love **I cast you in a supporting role because I didn't want to ask you to make that kind of commitment again for no money.**
I just enjoyed being on the set, I enjoy working. And I have to say it was a real hoot. I was dating this girl at the time who only knew me as a waiter, and then suddenly there I was on the set, and she came onto the set too, and she was an actress, and I don't think she'd ever been in a movie. She'd never

gotten close to that, so even though I didn't have a big part I felt like the big man for that day.

We teamed up you and Tommy Sweeney up for Naked Fear, **and I'd argue that film was more about acting than anything else.**

Yeah, I' would agree with that. And Tommy was great to act with. He has such a seething presence onscreen, and off screen he's still a little intimidating. He just looks mean, like a badass. The fun thing about Naked Fear was there were some comic opportunities, and because it was about character, because it was about people talking and getting to know each other, I actually felt a lot more comfortable overall in terms of what I was doing. I was of course a lot older by then. That one was a lot of fun; of the three films it felt more like my kind of movie.

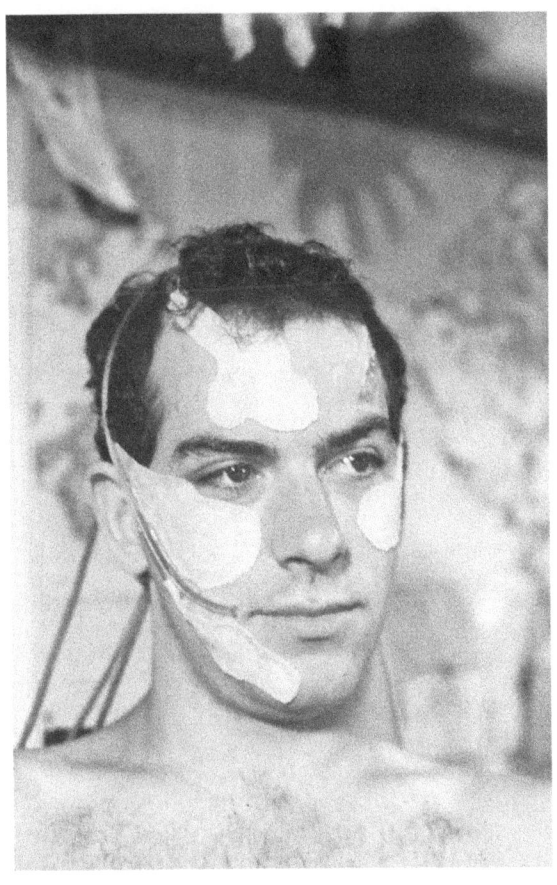

Robert C. Sabin, with condoms attached to his face, for *Slime City* (1988). The tubes enabled Scott Coulter to inflate the condoms for an "air bladder" effect. Photograph courtesy J. Scott Coulter.

While you were still on the East coast you wrote and produced Just the 4 of Us.

I had written something called *Hunting Season*. My friends were all very impressed with *Hunting Season*, we'd done a full read, everyone really wanted to get involved with it, they thought it would make a cool movie. It had also just done well at the Austin Heart of Film screenplay competition. We decided to put on a play to raise money to shoot the movie. The play that we put on was called *Forum*, about two couples who try to fool around with each other and the interesting things that occur afterward. The play went very well, it really scored with the audiences. I remember feeling amazed at the laughter and the applause that would break out. But I had friends who said, "You can't do *Hunting Season*. That's going to be miserable for your first feature. It's exteriors, in the snow, at night. You couldn't ask for a worst case scenario." So we reworked *Forum* as a movie, and I think we made about $5,000 from the show and we put out feelers and ended up raising about $25,000.

And after that shoot you made the move out west.

Yeah, when I went to Austin people lined up to tell me that I had to go to California. Abby and I were living in Pennsylvania and in July we made the abrupt decision to move out there at the end of August. We found an apartment on-line and got a U-haul and loaded everything up and drove across the country. It could have been a nightmare, and I think Abby still regards it that way. We had a cat in the cab and our four-and-a-half year old daughter, who was as good as gold. We pulled up to our apartment and immediately felt at home. And then I tried to call all these Hollywood contacts I'd made in Austin now that I was in town but they really didn't want to hear from me anymore. So from there I basically rebuilt some sort of contact base.

Did you have an agent when you moved out there?

I did not. Lawrence Mattis and I had parted ways. It's very frustrating: you go to an agent and say, "This is the next script I want to work on." And they say, "No, no, you can't work on that script. That will never sell." So you give them a list of 10 ideas and they go, "No ... no ... no..." And it sucks that you have all these script ideas and they keep saying no to all of them. Lawrence and I couldn't agree on what my next script was going to be. I wanted to write a comedy about JFK and the Cuban missile crisis and he didn't think that would be a good sell. He was probably right, but you know, what the hell? Let me write it. I was reading a book about the civil rights era, and came across one story that I'd never heard before that I thought was

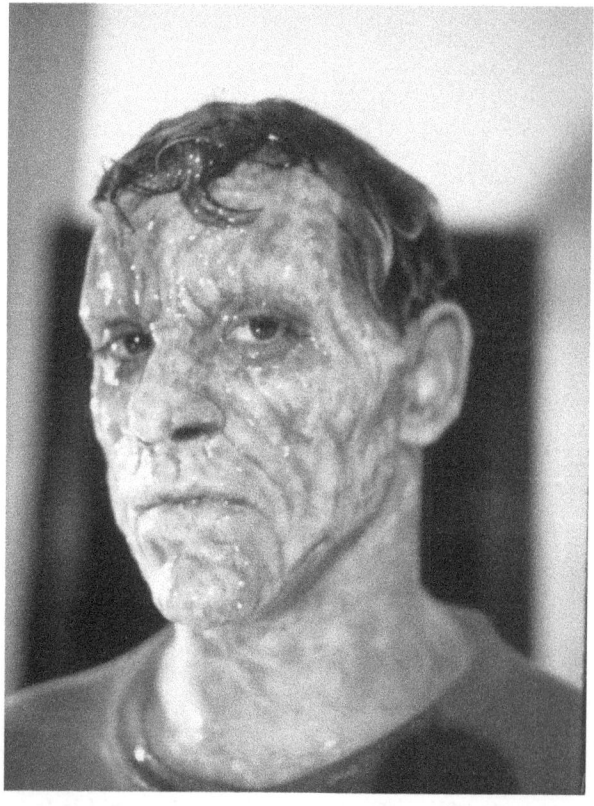

Robert C. Sabin in Scott Coulter's Zachary makeup for *Slime City* (1988). Photograph courtesy J. Scott Coulter.

Vampiress Camilla (Julie Lynch) bites off Renny Field's (Robert C. Sabin) tongue in *Undying Love* (1992), released on VHS as *New York Vampire* (1998). Photograph courtesy Karen Ogle.

amazing and I wrote it up as a screenplay and I went to this pitch meeting at this writers' group that I'd joined. There was a producer at the pitch meeting and she took the pitch and said, "That's an amazing pitch, I want to read that script." So I gave her the script and she said it was one of the best scripts she'd ever read and she took me around to agents and producers and created an audience for me out here.

And you went through some development with this?
 Showtime read it and made an option offer on it, but before I could accept the offer they withdrew it and then got out of the movie business altogether. That's one of the frustrating things about what's going on out here right now, the market for cable TV movies has dried up, nobody wants to make them anymore, they all want series.

But that script did get you another agent.
 I got an agent through this *Blue Bomb* script, called *One Thin Wire* now, and this agency had a lot of connections in the animation field. They sent me to Disney. It was kind of funny, Disney read *Hunting Season*, which is a very foul mouthed script, every other word is "fuck." People are dying left and right,

the body count is very high, and the execs at Disney were like, "Oh, this is great!" They liked it probably because they couldn't make it. So they scheduled a meeting for me and I went out there to meet with them, but they never showed up at the meeting. Before I even got home from that aborted meeting they made me a job offer to come in for a punch-up session because they felt guilty. So they sent me the script for *Lion King 1.5* and I had to read it and write jokes. And you go in, and you read them the jokes that you've written, and they give you $1,500 and you go home. It's a really wonderful thing. I haven't done it in a couple of years, but I really did enjoy it.

Let's talk about your biggest credit so far.

That was *1952* at HBO. I wrote the script, once again based on a true story, and my agent sent it to Jeffrey Levine at Baltimore Spring Creek, Barry Levinson and Paula Weinstein's company. And they liked it and took it to HBO. First they said no, but it got to Sidney Lumet, who's one of my idols, and Sidney Lumet read it and loved it and was attached as director for a brief, beautiful period.

It was all going to happen, then.

Yeah, it was all going to happen. But then HBO asked me to rewrite it. I rewrote it along the lines of having one character star in it, and then they gave it to somebody else to rewrite. Ultimately they just decided that after all the rewriting it had gotten too far away from the truth and they didn't want to get sued, so they decided not to make it.

So they asked you for changes and then the changes turned them off?

Exactly, exactly. At that point Greg Kinnear was on board to act in it and Mick Jackson was going to direct, Sidney Lumet had left after the first rewrite. They had a production office set up and everything and then it just kind of fell through. That was very disappointing. I thought for sure it was going to get made.

There are supernatural aspects to Carma, **but you could kind of categorize it as being in a genre similar to** Ghost; **it's very "audience friendly."**

Most of my screenplays seem to revolve around death, which is a hard sell for a comedy. *Carma*'s about death. *Hero's Funeral* has death in the title. My next movie called *Whacked*, was about a guy cursed to die one thousand times. And what occurred to me maybe two years ago while trying to work on some horror ideas because my friend Bari is such a huge horror fan. We would discuss ideas and I would say, "Hey, wouldn't it be funny if instead of killing you, a serial killer made you give him the names of five people, and he'd kill those people. How would you feel about that?" It was a funny idea to me, and then I started thinking, it's actually a horrible idea if you invest in it emotionally and get rid of the irony. That was sort of a revelation to me. If you come up with a high concept horror comedy idea and take it very seriously and have real characters and sort of go with how insane the situation is, what you wind up with is horror. Horror and comedy are very conducive to each other as genres, they're very similar. I think that a lot of the stuff that I'm writing for 5 Minute Horror is stuff that in different hands could be comedy. But by taking it seriously, by going ahead and saying, "This is real, we're going to posit that this situation is a real situation," and you start to explore the details and the honest reactions you get to a very horrible place.

Let's get into 5 Minute Horror's creation.
 Me and my friend Bari Willerford were sitting around Starbucks—

Things really happen there?
 They really do. Bari calls it "the office." He's there all the time. Anytime he needs to get writing done, he's there. He's actually a successful actor, he played Joe Louis in *American Gangster*. The HBO job had just fallen through, and there wasn't much happening at Disney, and we were basically whining to each other about how frustrating it was that we had to depend on other people for our livelihood. So we came up with this idea. Originally it was going to be a DVD that we'd send to a subscriber base, but it evolved into a website where you could stream short horror videos that would be no more than five minutes long. They would all be short and sweet and straight to the point, and there's no FCC regulations with the internet — yet — and hopefully there won't be, so we can explore sexual things, have nudity, and go further with the gore, and have language that you couldn't have in a lot of Hollywood films, because they don't want to chase away that particular audience. And finally, something that I've always thought is pathological about the movie industry is that they work very, very hard to gather an audience for this movie, for this product that they've put out, they spend a lot of money, they herd them in — and then they let them go. They say, "All right, you've seen our movie, now you can go." Then the audience spreads out goes out to the four winds. And what we're going to do instead is engage that audience. When we get a subscriber we're going to make sure we know who that subscriber is, why that person's subscribing, what that person likes, and give him more of it, continually contacting and interfacing with that person so that we're actually building an audience instead of letting it go after a presentation of the product. But a key part of that is continual roll-out of videos. We have to be able to let them know every week, "Okay, there's something new on the website, check it out." And I think that if we do that, we stand a chance, especially with how popular streaming video is these days.

At this point, you've produced three pilots. Tell me what your involvement was on each segment.

My involvement in the first one, "Tasty," was just as a producer. I was there on the set to help out and provide money from my credit card. My daughter is in the movie, she gets her throat slit, and that was pretty much it. We cast friends in the other roles.

So you've already broken a taboo that I haven't: you're killing off your own family members.

Yes (laughs). You'll get there. Susanna is a very cool kid, and she wanted to do this from the get-go. It was very fun to see her work with that prosthetic —

Just like you did in Slime City.

Yes, yes! Like I did. The second was "The Accomplice," and I wrote that. That's the one about the serial killer who gives his victim an out, she can give up a list of five names rather than be killed herself. I also wrote "Super Sex," in which we explore a more sexual realm. If superheroes really existed, what would happen on a date with Superman? It's been talked about for years, but no one's ever done it, so we went ahead and did it. The amazing thing to me is how surprising people find the ending. We had actors come in and say, "So why am I resisting her? She's beautiful." And then we explain, "Well, you know that when you have sex with her it's going to kill her." And they're like, "Oh, God!" And that was a lot of fun.

What are the production values on these?

We're budgeted for $7,000 per five-minute picture. We shoot them in a day, two in a weekend is how it works. We have some very creative and talented people aboard. We've got this director named Dale Fabrigar. He's very good at taking this measly budget and making it look like a solid piece of film.

You were hired to write the Chaingang *screenplay based on two of Rex Miller's novels about that character,* Slob *and* Slice.

Chaingang is a very interesting power fantasy. I think Rex Miller's serial killer books are generally about a level of control and hatred towards the rank and file and superiority over the rank and file. This sense of superiority seems to be the through line in his work. I think it comes out the most in *Slob*. Here's this guy who's been spurned by people all of his life, and yet he believes himself to be superior to them. When he kills, he's kind of like a tourist in a land of monkeys. At the same time, you respond as if his murderous impulses are controlled by them. It's in the book that he loses control, and I came to the conclusion that the reason he loses control is because he's back in the big city, where there's just so much to do in terms of killing people.

What always struck me about the character is that he's this big killer, ala Leatherface, but he's also got this Hannibal Lecter–like brilliance, although Miller makes it clear his intellect functions on the level of an idiot savant.

The interesting thing is you never see him use his intellect in any way except covering up his crimes. Every once in a while they talk about his intellect, but he really just snatches people off the street and kills them. It's not like Hannibal Lecter, who insinuates himself into his victims' lives and comes up with some sort of ironic death for them that's sort of wonderfully brilliant to watch take place. Bukowski is more like, "Hey, girl, you want to be an actor?" and grabs them off the street. That's one of the things, I have to say, that was disappointing for me. He had that precognitive aspect that sort of gave him the jump on everyone.

You see the wheels turning when he lures people to their deaths, but that's where the idiot savant thing comes in, it's all on automatic.

He seems to be an excellent con man. That's what's interesting to me about making the movie. In a book, you kind of take it for granted, but in a movie, you have to wonder, how do you pull that off? You have this huge, six-foot-seven, five hundred pound person. He's got to be scary to look at, and he spends most of his time in a sewer, so he's got to stink. And there he is, driving around in a car, and you've got to wonder, how does he pull that off, how's it going to happen?

And this was before My Space.

Yeah, exactly. He needs a good My Space page. What's also interesting to me is, Rex Miller, as I understand, was also morbidly obese, and I think that *Slob* was his perfect self, if you will.

What directions were you given in terms of tackling the books, and what's your working relationship with the other writer involved?

They wanted to use *Slob*, the first book, and they wanted to use *Slice*, one of the sequels, but they weren't sure how to use them. So Jeremy Anderson (the co-writer) and I decided that *Slob* would serve as the first act, and would have to be whittled down appropriately, and *Slice* would be the second act. Of course, you have a baby in *Slice*, and he has this cool relationship with this whack job woman. So that was the way we outlined it. They sort of liked the outline at first, but as we started turning in the pages they weren't as crazy about it, primarily because Joel Bender had really, seriously fallen in love with the first book and kept saying, "Don't make anything up, don't change anything, whatever's in the book I want in the script." Honoring that request was our biggest challenge, not fixing the structural problems that are adherent in adapting these things, just leaving them in for a little while and then going back and fixing them later.

What was the logic behind doing a big Chaingang *movie, with, I'm assuming, the definitive offing of the main character from the second book, rather than just doing the first book and allowing room for a potential franchise?*

I think what really interested the director about combining the two books is that in the first one, Chaingang is basically just a killing machine, but in the second one he has that weird relationship with the girl and he procreates. That was very interesting to him, and to us as well.

So the character's evolution appealed to you?

And a very sick arc it is. You know, he basically has this baby and guts the mother to get the baby out. It's very interesting to see in this particular context, how he keeps his murderous urges towards her in check because he needs her to have the baby. It's also this sort of stab at humanity. We all said, "Well, we've never seen that before. We've never really seen a serial killer sit around and have a kid." In the first one, he's just killing people. It's random until he focuses on Eichord, the cop, and he doesn't do that until toward the end of the book. That's when things pick up speed, and very abruptly. We needed more meat to the movie.

Have you ever gotten into a situation where you've done work for someone on a promise of money that's never come through?

Oh, yeah. The first couple of years I was out here I would write whatever I could. If someone asked me to write something I'd say, "Sure," thinking maybe it would go somewhere. That sort of became, "Well, I don't want to write unless I believe that this person has a shot at getting it made, or at least getting it seen." And that kind of turned into, "I have better things to do than write for other people who don't pay me at all." Because it really is very, very difficult to get something made out here. It's difficult to get the eyes of the people that you need to green light something. The conclusion I've come to is I've got as good a shot as most people I know, in fact better than a lot of people I know, so why write for them when I could work on my own script and get it to the appropriate executive?

A lot of these wannabe producers just want to have a finished script so they have a property to show around. They're knocking on the same doors you might just as well be knocking on yourself.

Exactly. I can sit down and pound out a script that I think has a good chance of going at this studio or that studio and I don't have to fight with anyone to get it written. It's just me doing the job to the best of my ability. If I team up with somebody or if I write for somebody it becomes a different thing.

What steps do you think people living outside LA or New York need to take if they want to take this seriously?

That's really problematic because different things work for different people. I was actually more attractive to people in LA when I wasn't living here. So I would say, play that as long as you possibly can. If you have people interested in you, chances are they're interested because you're an unknown, out of town commodity, which means that they have discovery rights. The minute you get into LA, that disappears. You become just another LA writer, another schmuck with a screenplay. So really play the "Aw, shucks" thing as long as you can. Just because people say, "You should be out here, you should be out here," doesn't mean you should and doesn't mean that when you do move out here they're going to return your calls.

6

This Gun for Hire

As an indie filmmaker, I enjoy writing and directing my projects. I tried directing someone else's screenplay once, but the screenwriter was also the producer, and our relationship deteriorated during pre-production to the point where I bailed on the project. But what about screenwriting for hire?

I dabble in freelance writing. I'm a fast writer and I'm able to construct workable screenplays with a minimum of development, so writing screenplays for other people always seems like a good idea when such opportunities present themselves. But my experiences with this kind of work have yielded mixed results. For one thing, writing a screenplay for someone else requires you to serve that person's vision, even when your brain screams that the person approving your work lacks imagination or common sense. If you accept the check, you must be willing to subvert your own instincts, even if this means creating work you consider inferior. Or you walk. For another, I often find that prospective producers lowball me on the screenwriting fee, and then when I accept their meager compensation they delay payment, and continue to delay it, to the point of madness. On one occasion, I concluded the producer was lying about having funds and I walked.

This can be a sleazy business, and there are producers out there who won't think twice about leading you on if it means they wind up with a screenplay they can then show around to potential money people. If they strike out with these financiers before they've paid you a dime for your hard work, they're not out any money and they move on to the next sucker — er, screenwriter.

If you partner with a director and a producer, and the three of you agree that you will write a screenplay for no money down, but shall receive compensation as soon as financing is raised, go for it if you believe in the project. If you agree that none of you shall make a dime until your film is completed and sold, and then you shall each receive equal participation, use your best judgment. Just remember, if the film is never sold, or even made, you're the only member of this triumvirate who has fulfilled all of his contractual obligations; the producer is out nothing but photocopying expenses, and the director is out nothing but time wasted on a project that went nowhere. You'll be out much more time and effort than either of them. In an arrangement such as this, it's wise to sign an agreement which provides a "reversion of rights" clause: if, after a suitable period of time—say, one year—the producer and director are unable to raise money for the production, all rights to the screenplay should revert to the screenwriter with no strings attached.

My Number One rule for screenwriters writing screenplays for hire is this: *if you're writing for money, do not commit a single word to paper until you've received an advance for your work.* Never give credence to a producer who keeps delaying payments.

The Soulless

Nicanor Loreti is a horror journalist and filmmaker based in Argentina. He has written for *Fangoria* and is a contributor to *Lo Cosa*, a slick South American entertainment magazine for which he reviewed *Slime City* and my novel *Personal Demons*. Thus began a long distance, on-line friendship between us. Nicanor wrote, directed, and shot *El Kuervo*, a micro-budget ghost story short, and has worked in different capacities on several feature length productions. In 2006, he contacted me with a proposal: POP Cinema, which, as E.I. Cinema, released *Undying Love* on VHS under the title *New York Vampire*, and as Shock-O-Rama Cinema released *Slime City* on VHS and DVD, offered to fund Nicanor's project *The Soulless* for $3,000 to $5,000 (the U.S. dollar stretches far in Argentina) and he asked me to co-write the screenplay with him.

Our arrangement called for Nicanor to provide me with a story treatment. I would write the first draft of the screenplay, and he would rewrite my draft so it would more accurately reflect his point of view. I read his treatment and agreed it would be fun material to tackle. I liked its ambiguity: Nicanor suggested some characters and scenes, which made it easy for me to satisfy his requirements, yet left me a lot of room to create and develop my own concepts. There

Alex (Robert C. Sabin), fully possessed by the evil Zachary in *Slime City*'s climax (1988). Photograph courtesy J. Scott Coulter.

was no structure, so I knew the spine would be mine no matter how many changes he made in his draft, and the fact that he intended to rewrite my draft relieved me of the burden of realizing every one of his ideas.

From the beginning, Nicanor was upfront that I would be paid very little for my efforts, almost nothing. But as a stay-at-home father, I needed money, and screenwriting is something I can do in my free time, on my own schedule, at home. Whenever I agree to write a screenplay for hire, I request the following payment schedule: ⅓ upon signing, ⅓ upon reaching the halfway mark of the script; and ⅓ upon completion. I generally include a rewrite in my fee, but I insist on getting everything I'm owed by the completion of the first draft; that way, there's less chance of me getting screwed, and if the producer doesn't want me to do the rewrite, so be it. He's already gotten more than his money's worth.

I knew *The Soulless* would be a simple assignment and no rewrite would be required. I decided the low fee would be satisfactory if I was able to write the script during the equivalent of one work week, but spread out over as many as three. Because we were talking about such a low figure, I told Nicanor I wanted him to pay me ½ of my fee upfront and ½ upon completion. After receiving the first payment, I wrote the script in a week and a half; I knew that if I took any longer he would want to see pages as I churned them out, and would comment on my work while I was still writing. No writer needs that kind of pressure, and I hate when producers demand to see my work before I'm ready to show it.

In the end, I was pleased with how the script turned out. I made it very visual, with interesting characters and a strong sense of foreboding. It was a tight little piece that made Nicanor happy. His friend, filmmaker Albert Pyun (*Cyborg*, *Dollman*), called it "brilliant." Despite a plethora of nudity and violence, Mike Raso at POP Cinema thought my work was "too American" and instructed Nicanor to make his rewrite "more European." Nicanor is currently looking for financing for the project elsewhere.

Rapper X

While in pre-production on my short film *Gruesome*, based on my novel *Johnny Gruesome*, special effects artist David Gray put me in touch with a gentleman I'll call "Rapper X." Rapper X claimed he had a deal with Universal Studios to produce 20 low budget features under an urban horror label. "Urban" is a marketing code word for "African American," but the people who use it might just as well say "ghetto," because to them this niche market means a hip-hop audience hungry for blood and guts in their horror entertainment.

I was skeptical that Rapper X had a 20-picture deal with anyone. In fact, I never believed it for a second. He helpfully informed me that he was "the next big thing in rap music." He had very specific ideas about the brand of "extreme horror" he wanted to depict and I was intrigued enough to watch the "horror rap" videos on his My Space page. They were gory and graphic and showed a real disdain for women, but I found the images powerful and thought he had talent as a director. He had created a supernatural character he wanted to be the motivating force behind several other violent characters.

Rapper X said he already had a writer on the project, but he was unhappy with the writer's work. I told him I would write his screenplay for $1,000, made payable in thirds, the first installment due upon signing. He had no problem with my fee (Why would he? It was a bargain!), but he wanted me to submit a treatment to him before he would hire me. I don't work from treatments, and I wasn't interested in auditioning for the job. But by then I was interested in the project, so I reluctantly agreed to write the treatment.

Rapper X gave me much less material to work with than Nicanor did. He knew who his supernatural being was, and who a few of his other characters were, and what two or three scenes were, but that was it. He had no treatment and he never offered to let me see what the other screenwriter — if there was one — had written. I preferred it that way, because I didn't wish to be influenced by someone else's work. I interviewed him for an hour and a half and recorded the conversation for my notes. Rapper X wanted a lot of torture, a lot of murders, a fast pace, and an extreme point of view. He planned to have a digital effects artist process the entire film with "impact editing"—the ultra fast, in-your-face editing technique used in most contemporary horror film trailers ad nauseam.

Torture and outright gore are not my forte, so I decided that my treatment would concentrate on characterization and story — the elements he had the fewest ideas about — and I would worry about the gruesome details and mayhem when I was actually on the clock. For one week, I allowed the characters and story points to percolate in my mind, and then in one marathon 12-hour session, I pounded out the treatment and was very satisfied with the results.

Rapper X loved my work. Now he just needed to sign the contract I had drawn up and pay me. A month passed, during which we had numerous phone conversations about production matters such as casting and crew, and he hired several people here in Buffalo to work on his production. But he didn't pay me.

Another month passed. He decided to shoot the film in Buffalo since the crew was here. I spoke to the Buffalo Niagara Film Commissioner about obtaining a morgue and a police station for free. I started to feel like a co-producer (albeit an uncredited, *unpaid* one). The crew members started to grumble, including the digital effects artist who had edited an outstanding trailer for the project.

Rapper X asked me if I would settle for a first payment of $200 instead of $333.00. I agreed, partly because I wanted to believe he was for real, and partly because I had bills to pay. A week passed, followed by another empty promise. Two days later, I e-mailed him that I was withdrawing from the project and made it clear that under no circumstances was he to use any of my ideas in a script, or to use my treatment to raise money. Ultimately, that was his game: he had gotten a free treatment from me which he showed around to try to raise money. When that money never materialized, he was unable to pay me. He couldn't even scrounge up enough to pay me the $200. I wished him luck with his projects, and he wrote back:

"*I BETTER NOT SEE ANY OF MY IDEAS ANYWHERE OR WE'RE GOING TO HAVE A PROBLEM.*"

I realized that my first impression of him, when he put on his act of rapper bravado, had been correct, and I was angry at myself for allowing myself, and my talent, to be used. Too bad, because the treatment would have made a hell of a screenplay, and I believe he would have directed a hell of a film.

But this business is full of people who talk the talk but don't walk the walk. If you suspect that someone you're dealing with is full of baloney, he probably is. Trust your instincts when dealing with strangers.

Fees

After completing a recent project, I raised my rate for writing screenplays for films with budgets under $100,000. I now charge $1,000 for a treatment, $2,000 for a first draft, $750 for a polish, and $1,000 for a rewrite. I also ask for five (5) Net Profit Points, but I don't insist on them. I offer other services as well: I'll read and critique a screenplay for $750, and will rewrite a screenplay for $2,000. It's a living, but just barely.

What's a good fee to charge for writing a micro-budget horror script? I've seen $1,500 listed most often on budgets, but that doesn't mean you can't charge more. You don't want to price yourself out of a gig on a production with a shoestring budget, but if you don't value your ability, no one else will. I've never been offered a screenwriting job on a film in the $500,000 to $900,000 range, but if I was, my fee would start at $20,000. For a film with a budget of $1 million or more, I'd have an agent or entertainment attorney negotiate for me.

7

Devi Snively

TRIPPIN' FROM FESTIVALS TO THE AFI

Good contacts can be made at even the smallest horror conventions and film festivals. I met screenwriter-director Devi Snively and her producer partner, Augustin Fuentes, at the Halloween Horror Picture Show in Florida. We exchanged films, a common enough social activity at these functions, and I found myself intrigued enough by their shorts, the gory *Confederate Zombie Massacre*, the offbeat *Teenage Bikini Vampire*, and the gothic *Raven Gets a Life*, to stay in touch with Devi and follow her career progress. She and Augustin completed their first micro-horror feature, *Trippin'*, and she participated in the American Film Institute's prestigious Director's Workshop for Women.

Was Trippin' *your first feature length script?*
No, I've written 13 feature scripts. I made *Trippin'* because it had the lowest budget. I love screenwriting. It's cheaper than therapy. Some people go and talk to a therapist, I just sit down with my pen and legal pad and go for it.

You write by hand?
I can't create at the computer. I have to be spread out with a bunch of paper and books laying on a bed or a floor. But I do my second draft in Final Draft.

Where did you attend college?
I did my undergrad, although actually I was a dancer, at Sarah Lawrence, and then I got my film degree at the Academy of Art in San Francisco. I have a Master's of Fine Arts.

And now you teach a course on horror films at Notre Dame University.
It's called "Culture of Fear: the Horror Film."

I'm hoping to dispel the notion that you have to follow paradigms to write a good script.

I like to have fun when I actually write the script, and I like to have the voices in my head just go off and tell me everything I need to know, but in order for that to happen, and not just be a self indulgent bunch of mishmash, I need to know my story and have structure and have character development, and I do actually use one of those annoying paradigms for the very beginning, just to make sure my story has enough conflict and it's going to work. So I kind of see it like a roadmap. I get that roadmap out there, I have a safety net to fall back on, then I put all that stuff aside because by the time I'm done with all that I know my story so well that when I start writing I barely have to glance at it.

How often do you deviate from the map?

Always. I use a paradigm to a degree, but primarily because I also worked as a script reader. The reader will take your script, look at how many pages it is, see what happens on page 10, see what happens on page 30, and all of that, and if you don't meet the standards, they're going to toss it aside. So my thought is, "Well, okay, if they're going to do that anyway, I'll make sure that I can at least fool them into thinking I've done their little thing, but then go on and do my own thing."

How many points does the paradigm you follow incorporate?

Let's see. It's the Catalyst, Plot Point One, Mid-Point, Plot Point Two, Climax and Resolution. That's only six, at least the version I use. (Robert) McKee has ten points.

Do you create character sketches?

I actually do more character sketches now for the minor characters because I think about the main ones for so long before I put pen to page that I know them. I talk to them sometimes. I just come home and I'll be like talking to myself and Augustin will be like, "Oh, God, there she goes," and I'll be like, "No, no, no, no, I'm just talking to my character, it's not a big white bunny, I know they're not really there." It's all improv. I find where the problems come in are minor characters that a lot of people overlook, and those are the ones that sound very stereotypical and bad, so even if it's a cop with five lines, I'll usually give him more of a back story because I wouldn't have thought of it and I don't want him to sound like every other cop who has five lines in a movie.

You've got a film degree and you're teaching a class on film now. How necessary do you think it is to go the film school route?

I look at it this way: my brother taught himself to play the guitar. I could never do that. I could not just pick up a book, or pick up a guitar, and teach myself. I need guidance. For my personality type—I'm an academic—I love school, I love feedback. For me it worked really well. I do think that most people can't just pick up the camera and learn. With screenwriting, even more, I think most people need guidance, you at least need to be in a screenwriters' group and get feedback. I think a class or two never hurts. Even if it's a horrible class, you're going to learn what not to do if nothing else. The more approaches you hear, and the more of other people's work that you're exposed to, I think it really helps. Also, just the access you have to people, and equipment, and resources is incredible at school.

Who did you work for as a script reader?
I worked for a small company out of San Francisco but they were a freelance company that got work from L.A., so I got it kind of third hand. They'd send me scripts and I'd read them and give coverage back.

Did you ever read anything that went on to be produced?
Good God, no (laughs). At least not that was recognizable from what I read. I read a lot of bad scripts.

What were some of the most common mistakes you saw?
There was no method to their madness. I think people just think, "Oh, I can write a script" and don't put any thought or planning into it and start on page one. And by page 60, you've got a disaster. Some people obviously have talent and have some good ideas, but if you don't have structure and you don't do your homework before you "fade in" then I'm gonna "fade out."

What's the syllabus for Culture of Fear like?
I work from a historical, primarily chronological, perspective, starting with the silents, the German expressionists, and then the Universal monsters and so forth. Usually I go according to decade, but occasionally I go according to subgenre. I also talk about the evolution of gore, and how that came in during the 60s with Herschell Gordon Lewis, and how we started really freaking out, and obviously the 50s with the Cold War and McCarthyism. There are different themes that we cover every week, and I do some foreign units, but there's really not enough time to get too deep into any of it. So it's pretty much an overview of how the horror film has evolved over time according to how society has evolved.

Tell me about the female horror filmmaker community as you see it, and what it means to you to be a female director working in the genre.
I love it. And more and more females are getting involved, which is really cool. I think it's fascinating that, especially when people see *Confederate Zombie Massacre*, they look at my name they assume I'm a guy. In fact, when I got into New York to do the NYC Horror Film Festival I was the only female direc-

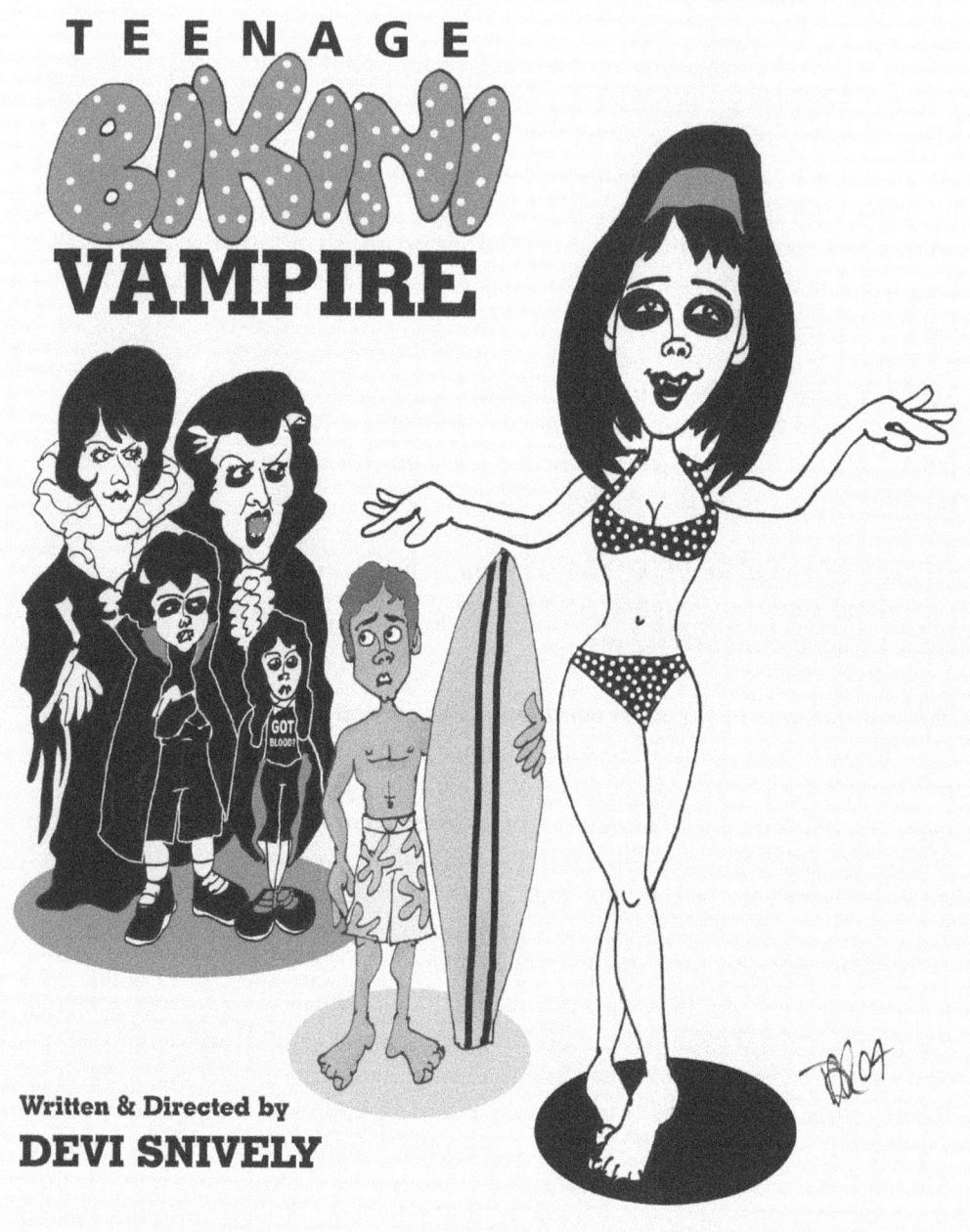

Teenage Bikini Vampire (2004), Devi's award winning offbeat short. Photograph courtesy Devi Snively.

tor there, and when I walked in — and that was for *Raven*, actually — they looked at me stunned and were like, "We were sure you were a man." So yeah, people do assume ahead of time I'm a man and when I go to these things I'm frequently one of the only females hanging out with the guys. But what I like about that is that it doesn't seem to matter. It's a very open community, for the most

Devi teaches "The Culture of Fear" at Notre Dame University. Photograph courtesy Devi Snively.

part. And I think it's because a lot of women choose not to do it, it's not because they're not invited to participate. On a professional level, I'm sure that's very different, but then that's the film industry in general, and it's just harder to break in as a woman. If you want to get into television it seems easier, but if you want to work on actual films women are just not given the same opportunities, so you have to make it happen yourself.

Of all the people I'm interviewing for this book, you have the most film festival experience. How did you get started and what was your plan of attack?

I got into film festivals by accident. I'd been a screenwriter and one of my scripts won at Slamdance, and I didn't know what a big deal that was until they called me and said, "You don't understand. You need to come out here." Producers started calling my agent begging me for my script, and so I went to Sundance and all that for the first time, and oh my God, that was so much fun. I thought, "Wow, I need to get a film in here next year because this is way too cool." It's like camp for adults, you know you hang out with filmmakers, talking about film, watching films, never sleeping, lots of drinking too, which isn't bad. It's such a great environment, and that really inspired me to want to make films. So then I started making films, and I was like, "Okay, you know, you submit it to Sundance, I get that." Well, of course you don't. Very

Echoing her short film *Raven Gets a Life*, Devi juxtaposes the classic Universal gothic imagery with contemporary goth culture. Photograph courtesy Devi Snively.

few people get into Sundance. Then I started realizing, "Okay, we got into a couple of festivals. Why did we get into these ones but not other ones?" And you start to figure out the relationship; you go the websites and find out what other films have gotten in and you form a strategy. And it's not that difficult, you just can't aim too high at the beginning. Then you get known, too. There are a lot of festivals I get into, I think, as much because I know the people who run them and they've got a legacy thing going on. As long as you don't produce something really, horrendously bad, and not up to usual standards, you're going to get that little extra "in" that someone who's never applied before might not have.

The list on your website of festival prizes you've won is pretty astounding.

That's at least six months out of date, too. We've attended over 100 now with the last three films.

Many of them aren't even horror film festivals. How do you separate festivals that aren't genre specific and will truly give genre films consideration from those that say they're open to genre material only because they want to scam as many submission fees as possible?

Go to their website and see what films got in the previous year. And I would make sure that they accept a number of shorts, because if they're only going to take 16 shorts, forget it. 1,000 entries, 16 shorts — no matter how good

The cast of *Trippin'* (2008), Devi's first micro-budget horror feature. Photograph courtesy Devi Snively.

your film is the odds are against you. A lot of times when I do the genre festivals I'm with the same films over and over again, so I take a look at those films and see what other ones they've gotten into. I talk to other filmmakers who have similar type films.

How many festivals do you attend each year?
    I haven't gone to as many this year. It's probably been like 30, maybe. I'm just tempted to go to all of them but I can't.

Tell me what you were thinking when you decided to tackle a feature.
    It just seemed like the right time. I get picked on a lot for doing shorts. "Well, there's no money in that. What's the point? It doesn't matter." Which I disagree with and I continue to make shorts and will continue to always because they're great and fun, and they do have, I think, a better life in some cases, they're going to get into way more festivals than most features. But of course I got into this to make features, I'm a feature length screenwriter more often than a short film writer. I've been dying to make a feature if for no other rea-

son to finally see one on the screen. I know enough about what I'm doing now that it's time to take it to the next level and learn what I don't know and make mistakes and go on from there. Many mistakes are made, but sure enough I'm in a completely different realm of filmmaking now.

It seems like the people who are the biggest know-it-alls really know the least.

It's true. Even when I was at my AFI interview, they asked me why on earth I wanted to do this program. "You've done nine shorts, you've done a feature, you have a degree, you teach. Why on earth do you want to go back to education and all that?" Socrates taught us, "Wisdom is knowing that you know nothing." I like to think I know a little bit, you know, a tiny little bit, and it's constantly growing, that's what's fun about this, I like to learn. Shorts are a good opportunity, but boy, a feature really puts it into perspective. Also, I wanted to know if this is what I actually want to do. I knew at the end of the film I was either going to be like, "I never want to do that again," or "When do we do the next one?"

What's the log line for Trippin'?

"Three couples go to a remote cabin in the woods and then bad things happen."

A cabin in the woods movie. Is the cabin the only location?

The first 10 minutes of the film actually take place in the van on the ride out, very *Texas Chainsaw Massacre*.

Special effects?

Oh, yeah. There's a fair amount of gore.

How did you raise the budget?

I'm a rebel with a trust fund. I grew into a trust fund and we took $10,000 out of it and said, "We're making a movie." And that was it.

Were you able to get everything done on $10,000?

We got everything that we set out to get. I want to do more pickups. We have to do some special effects pickups but that's already paid for and that's fine. There's one scene I really, really wish we could go back and get some more footage for.

What format did you go with?

24p, we used the Canon XL2. I love that camera. Obviously, when you do Mini–DV 24p you're not going to get a theatrical release. But we had a great DP and we had about $10,000 worth of lights donated, so it's well lit and it looks nice for 24p.

How long was your shooting schedule?
   16 days.

Was there a day off in there?
   Oh, no. In fact, for me it was 18 hour days, 16 days straight. That was a mistake. And there should have been days off. If I could have watched dailies I could have fixed a lot of stuff. And I had no sleep the entire two weeks. I had insomnia on top of everything, so I don't think I slept once.

That's what I don't like about these 10-day shoots, there are no days off, and the filmmakers seem to think that the little bit of money they're saving on rentals or catering is a good thing, but really it's much better for everybody, even on a 10-day shoot, if you have at least one day off in there.
   Yeah, it really would have been helpful. But with us it really wasn't even about the rentals, it was about the people. Everyone worked for free, they took two weeks off from work and a couple of extra days we tacked on because we couldn't do it in 14 days. We didn't have a choice, but I won't be in that position again. We'll do two separate shoots or find some other way to make it work.

Larry Fessenden recommends studying literary classics and learning to write rather than immersing yourself in filmmaking.
   I think that's 100 percent right. If you have nothing to say, then who wants to watch your film? And it comes through on so many different levels. I think some of the most valuable stuff I've been learning here at AFI is stuff I didn't know much about, like production design. Wow, I have such a better appreciation for production design. I didn't quite know everything it encompasses. It's really opened my eyes and I'm looking at all sorts of different levels that I've never even considered before. That's where your production value comes in, especially when you have no budget. I mean, we actually won an award for production design for *Raven Gets a Life* and there was no production design! We just found amazing locations that already had production design for us. But now I'm being more intentional about that and I've been interviewing production designers, and it's so great because of the details and the questions. I didn't realize they needed all these characters' back stories, but of course they do because they're creating their homes. Just like with the costume designer, you really have to talk a lot about the characters because they need to get into their heads. "What would this person buy?" It's not just, "Let's do something that looks pretty"—let's do something that adds to the story.
   I think one of the best things I've learned about pre-production is that you've got to go to every Goodwill in town. It's amazing what .25 can add to your production design. I think I spent $20 at one Goodwill, and I mean this was bags and bags of stuff. I'm just walking through looking at stuff and think-

ing, "Would this be in the cabin? Would *this* be in the cabin?" This really horrible, ugly, kitschy weird crap that weird people must keeping their homes that I would never in a million years want, but it adds so much and it's cheap. And then you can put it on e-bay: "Hey, this is that important prop from that famous film!"

How did you deal with the special effects on Trippin'*?*

That was actually a nightmare, frankly. There's always miscommunication between the effects artists and the camera team, then me, and reality (laughs). It just never seems to work well. That's why a lot of the pickups are effects that we just knew we didn't even want to try to do on set, and we didn't have to because they were all inserts. But a few of them didn't work and a few of them are amazing, and they all took longer than we'd hoped. We didn't allow enough time, and we knew at the time that we weren't allowing enough time. It happens. But it's funny because some of the best stuff is the little, simple stuff. Just getting some chitlins and mixing them up with the right color food dye or whatever, and throwing it in a shot adds an awful lot. Some of the best effects were just throwaway ideas that happened at the last second.

Would you call yourself a latex woman or a CGI woman?

Oh, latex, definitely. I usually hate CGI effects. They take me out of the movie. What I love is mixing the two. If it's the perfect blend, and I was really happy with *Raven* in that respect, we had digital and practical effects together. Ian Strandburg, the guy that I work with is really great at doing that, like when Death pulls the junkie's body out of himself, it was such a simple, simple thing, but Ian knew to direct the actor to do a slump in a certain way, so really there wasn't that much digital stuff going on. In *Trippin'*, in one scene we just didn't have time to do all the makeup because we had three dead characters, one's blown his brains out, the other two have overdosed on drugs and they're bleeding. There's no way we could have done it. Ian went, "Get me these three plates and I'm going to do it in post."

What made you apply to the American Film Institute Director's Workshop for Women?

I was ready to be rejected. This year my resolution was to turn things up a notch and think professionally. I've decided I don't want to be a hobby filmmaker. I will be if that's what happens, but I want to give it a real try. And I needed to be taken seriously. So I thought, "I'm never in a million years going to be accepted into this." It's easier to get into Harvard Business School than it is to get into this program, so I really didn't think I had a shot in hell. But I thought, "You know, if I don't start taking myself seriously how is anyone else going to?" So I applied, and go figure.

What does the program entail?

I had five weeks to get an apartment, pick up and move, come out here for the 3-week intensive program, raise $25,000 to make a film, and be out here to shoot through August and have picture locked by the end of August.

Is your AFI short a horror film?

It's a dark comedy plus horror. It's very reminiscent of the old E.C. Comics, it's totally one of those.

Once the film is finished, what does AFI do with it?

We have to have the premiere here in Los Angeles. They provide one theater for the single premiere and then they have the AFI DWW showcase in May of next year, where they show all the women's films. And then after that it's up to us to get it into festivals. We have maybe 18 months that we're allowed to do the festival circuit and then they get distribution. I don't know if they do compilations or if they distribute them individually. Some of them make money. Our actors get paid first, and AFI gets 50 percent, and then after the actors get paid I get 50 percent, which then I share with the producers.

If this leads to a career, do you plan to stick with horror do you immediately turn to a romantic comedy?

Oh, God, no, I'll stick with horror!

8

Development Hell

In Hollywood, "Development Hell" refers to an unusual state of limbo in which filmmakers sometimes find their projects sentenced. The project might be a highly regarded original screenplay, or a literary property, or a comic book. For whatever reason, the project is stalled: sometimes a studio rejects the first attempts at a screenplay adaptation, or finds itself without a suitable director or star. Sometimes numerous screenplays are commissioned and developed; Universal studios spent over $30 million developing *The Hulk* even before Ang Lee became attached — and started the process all over from scratch. And then they remade it just a few years later!

Development is the nurturing of a project from the first germs of an idea through pre-production. In Hollywood, the creation of a screenplay is often part of the development process. For an independent feature, this is usually not the case: the filmmakers usually require a completed screenplay to entice investors to finance a film — even if investors never even read the script, or understand how a screenplay should be read. Development entails raising production funds, which may require attaching certain talent, such as a "name" actor with "marquee value." It also requires a certain amount of legal legwork to ensure that everything is on the up and up, and that all parties involved know what is expected of them and are protected.

For an independent film — especially a micro-budget movie — "Development Hell" refers to a slightly different situation. You've assembled your three key players: a producer, a screenwriter, and a director; you've agreed on a concept and a format (digital versus film); and your writer has written a screenplay, which most of your potential investors won't even bother to read. You've attracted a name or two: nobody huge, or even big, but people with genre street credibility who may help garner the film some attention and respect. You've settled on some ideal locations; perhaps you've selected a cinematographer; you know when you want to shoot; and you have an attorney and an accountant standing by to draw up the necessary paperwork so you can start banking investor funds.

There's just one problem: you have no investors. All those people who told you they'd invest in your first film have fallen by the wayside. Either they're "not liquid," or that tax refund didn't turn out as large as they thought, or they owe money to the government, or their son is going to college or their daughter is getting married. Or maybe their accountant simply explained to them what a risky venture investing in a motion picture can be. The reasons for a potential investor backing out of a film deal are endless. The point is, you have a screenplay and no money with which to shoot it.

Unless you're independently wealthy, there is no magic formula for raising money. If I knew of one, I wouldn't have time to write this book because I'd be making a movie. But I can tell you how I've raised money, and how I've seen other people raise it, and I can show you the proper way to develop a property into a package suitable for presentation to your potential investors.

Making a Pitch

If you're lucky enough to get "face time" with a production exec, research what films they've released, determine which ones were successful and which ones weren't, and draw the appropriate parallels between the success stories and your film. If possible, learn which projects the person your meeting with was involved with, and acknowledge his past endeavors. You don't have to be a gushing sycophant — in fact, I recommend against that; people prefer sincere interest to flattery — but your lunch date will most likely appreciate that you've done your research and respect you for it. If the exec makes suggestions, don't discount them out of hand, but don't immediately bend to his will, either. Politely say you'll take his suggestions under consideration.

Prospecting

When I worked on *I Was a Teenage Zombie* I saw the prospectus that the filmmakers showed to their investors. It was typewritten, Xeroxed, and slipped into a plastic folder. It was minimalist at best and very sloppy. It included a budget for $35,000. At the time, I heard the director and producers discuss that was an arbitrary figure, which is why it only accounted for distribution of 25 percent of the Net Profits to investors in the film instead of 50 percent; they expected it to cost twice as much, but didn't want to scare off the investors they had. In reality, any investor with an IQ above 40 will investigate a film's budget — or have someone do that for him — and will conclude if a budget is too small to realistically accommodate a feature length motion picture. The *Teenage Zombie* team had a slightly different game plan, because they also wanted to raise a separate budget for the film's soundtrack, which ultimately included songs by Los Lobos, the Waitresses, and the Smithereens.

When it came time to develop *Slime City*, I originally modeled our prospectus on the one for *I Was a Teenage Zombie* because I didn't know any better. Frank Henenlotter arranged for me to meet with Edgar Ievans, his producer on

Basket Case, and that was one of the most valuable hours I've ever spent. At the time, Edgar lived in an office he rented in the Village. I remember cold cement floors, an enormous roll top desk, and caged light bulbs. He was trying to raise money for Frank to shoot *Brain Damage*, which they would only refer to as *Elmer the Parasite* because they didn't want anyone to steal their title (When I read the script, I guessed the real title was *Brain Dead*, which hadn't been used yet; we learned the actual title when we received our first paychecks from The Brain Damage Company). Before our meeting started, Edgar received a call related to their current project. I remember him saying, "You tell them $15,000 is not enough for *Elmer* in Japan." Wow — this little hole in the ground was where *deals were made*!

Edgar took out a piece of paper, drew a circle on it, and drew a line down the middle of that circle, halving it. He explained that when you raise money through investors, you form a Limited Partnership, and that the investors, or partners, were entitled to recoup their entire investment through the first monies received, and that no Net Profits could be divided until all of the investment capital had been recouped. After that, Net Profits were divided evenly, 50 percent among the investors and 50 percent among the filmmakers. So if a film costs $50,000 to produce, the first $50,000 received from the sale or exploitation of the film goes back to the investors. The second $50,000 received is divided down the middle, $25,000 to the investors and $25,000 to the filmmakers. In the event that the film goes over budget and additional funds need to be raised, the filmmakers must sell of some of their "points." It is entirely conceivable that the ratio could end up being 60/40 in favor of the investors, 70/30, or even 80/20. This is why Edgar cautioned me not to be too liberal with awarding points to people working on the film for free.

Edgar set me up with his attorney, Gerald Gold. If you're smart, you'll spend the money to get an experienced entertainment lawyer. Even if you plan to shoot a $10,000 film, I recommend you set aside money for a minimal package from such an attorney. Even a single consultation for a $5,000 film may spare you years of aggravation, missed opportunities, and bad deals. In Chapter 9, Jerry discusses legal challenges faced by indie filmmakers.

Wall Street Money

Somewhere along the line, I learned about two Wall Street types who were looking to produce a low budget horror film. We'll call them Abbott and Hardy. I submitted the script for *Slime City* to them and they immediately expressed interest. Peter and I met with Abbott first, a friendly enough guy who took us to Hardy's apartment. They showed us some unimpressive footage from a film they were supposedly producing, directed by someone I didn't like. We left that meeting with a strange feeling, but Abbott gave us a contract stating they would finance *Slime City* for $150,000, much more than we were looking for. I would

Promotional flyer created by Eric Maché for *Slime City*'s development.

Concept art by R.J. Sevin for *Deadly Rites*. Logo design by Julia Sevin.

receive $2,500 for my screenplay, and Peter and I would each receive $12,000 as director and director of photography, respectively. Needless to say, we were excited.

Jerry cautioned us not to let our enthusiasm overcome our common sense. The contract didn't specify where the film would be shot, and we were both East Coast filmmakers. It didn't guarantee us participation in sequels. And it didn't spell out the circumstances under which we could be replaced, or who would have creative control over my screenplay. I wanted to believe that Jerry was being overly cautious, because it seemed like Abbott loved my script, and why would he and Hardy go through the trouble of financing our project and securing our services if they didn't want to make the same film we did?

I relayed Jerry's concerns to Abbott over the phone and he took Peter and I out to lunch. He didn't have any qualms about the issues we raised. Many of these guys try to see what they can get away with, and fully expect you to take issue with their terms. It's a way of business for them, and in their eyes, if you don't demand changes, you deserve what you get. Our potential executive producers wanted to bring in another screenwriter to "punch up" my script. First, they didn't want the character of Alex, possessed by the evil spirit of Zachary, to murder his best friend, Jerry, because they felt Jerry was the most likable character in the script and they wanted him to survive. I explained that Alex had to kill his best friend in order to show that he had crossed a line and was irredeemable. The Wall Street wizards also wanted me to change my entire ending so that Alex would live and love would save the day, as it had in *A Nightmare* on *Elm Street 2: Freddy's Revenge*. "But *Elm Street 2* sucked!" I argued. "You can't argue with its box office," Abbott said. Now, *Slime City* is largely remembered for the extended gore sequence at its climax, which could never have occurred with the changes these guys wanted. I felt I had to make up my mind on the spot and not allow cooler heads to talk me into turning my screenplay into a pale imitation of a movie I hated. I stood my ground, Abbott said he would discuss it with Hardy, and we never heard from them again.

Partnerships

That was a tough call, but I did the right thing. Unfortunately, by the time the deal collapsed, we had missed our planned start date. Even though we'd commissioned a plaster head cast to be made of our lead actor, Robert Sabin, it took us an additional year to raise $35,000 to shoot the film. Peter and I joined forces with Marc Makowski, a customer at the video store where we worked, and Jerry set up a Limited Partnership for us. Peter kicked in $10,000 of his own money, Marc kicked in $5,000, I kicked in $5,000, and we each brought in two or three investors. Because we put up so much of the money ourselves, and we were not paying ourselves to work on the film, Jerry structured first tier deferments so we would receive fees for our efforts before any of the investors recouped their money. We received portions of those deferments, but none of us recouped our investment. The best we were able to do was write them off over a period of time.

For *Undying Love*, I formed a Joint Venture Agreement with Marc and Ed Walloga, a former SVA classmate, and we financed the $35,000 film ourselves. We went with a Joint Venture Agreement because it was simpler and less expensive than a Limited Partnership. Since the three principal filmmakers were also the principal investors, there was no point in going the deferred payment route again. When Marc and I co-financed *Naked Fear*, we went with a Joint Venture Agreement again. The budget for that one was $5,000, but due to numerous mistakes made during production, it ended up costing $7,500.

A Limited Partnership restricts you to using 25 Partners. Roy Frumkes went with a Joint Venture Agreement for *Street Trash* because he had 90 investors. Today, an LLC — a Limited Liability Corporation — is the most common legal structure for a motion picture partnership. We'll examine all three options, as well as what should go into your investor package, in our legal chapter.

Artwork

Although it isn't necessary, it's a good idea to use artwork to show potential investors so they can visualize a marketing strategy beyond reading your screenplay — as long as the artwork is well done. For *Slime City*, graphics

Eric Maché's concept art for *Johnny Gruesome*, the unfilmed screenplay that became a novel, a rock CD, and a music video.

designer Eric Maché photographed a blonde in conveniently tattered clothing running toward the camera; he superimposed this image over a photograph of a New York City street and added a bold logo. For *Brain Damage*, Frank Henenlotter had his special effects team sculpt a maquette of his monster, Aylmer, and photographed a close up of it with the title *Elmer the Parasite*. For *Johnny Gruesome*, I asked Eric to paint a "portrait" of my heavy metal zombie character reminiscent of Basil Gogos's *Famous Monsters of Filmland* work. Remember the adage, "A picture is worth 1,000 words"? I think an evocative illustration is potentially worth a lot more than that.

Trailers & Demo Reels

Some filmmakers like to shoot trailers or short demo reels to interest investors in their projects. I have mixed feelings about this approach. Your trailer/demo must look absolutely professional if it is to work; if it doesn't, it will have the exact opposite effect that you desire. A sloppy looking trailer or demo will turn off investors.

Roy Frumkes shot a demo reel featuring psychic Nancy Fuchs for *The Psychic*, a proposed feature in which Fuchs would play herself. Although he had a solid screenplay and an attractively shot demo reel, he was unable to get the film off the ground. However, Jimmy Muro shot a short 16m version of *Street Trash*, which led to a 35mm feature version. And Sam Raimi directed a 30-minute Super 8 film called *Within the Woods* that eventually became *The Evil Dead*.

Still, in the wrong hands I find this approach counter-productive. At film festivals, I regularly see trailers that filmmakers have shot for films that haven't been made, and judging by their poor quality, I don't believe they will ever generate interest in feature film versions.

Attaching Talent

In the filmmaking business, "talent" refers to actors. This is not a slight against writers, directors, or any of the fine technicians and craftspeople who break their backs making films. For the purpose of this topic — raising money — "talent" means one thing: bankable names. What makes a "name" bankable? The larger a production, the bigger the name attached to it should be. A low budget filmmaker is fortunate to have a recognizable face attached to his project, and a micro-budget filmmaker is lucky to even have a has-been actor attached to it.

When you pitch a project to Uncle Joe because he owns a used car lot and likes to wave around a lot of cash, Joe's first question is likely to be, "How much?" His second is, "Who's in it?" And his third will be, "Will there be nudity?" Depending on how you answer Joe's third question, his fourth will likely be, "Can I be there on the day that you shoot that?" Uncle Joe is predictable that way.

People invest money in films for two reasons: first, they are attracted to the perceived glamour associated with filmmaking; and second, they hope to turn a profit, or at least break even, on their investment. In their eyes—and they aren't stupid—this is much more likely if a celebrity is attached to the project, even if the celebrity in question isn't an actor; a name can be an athlete, a musician, a reality TV star, or even an accused murderess. How far you're willing to go to attract a name is up to you. Fortunately, SAG's Ultra low Budget Agreement makes it possible for any filmmaker working with any budget to attach one professional, recognizable actor to their production, even if it's only for a day.

Just remember: "talent" comes with additional expense and headache. Just because SAG says you can pay them $100 or $150 to do a day's work doesn't mean you'll get them for that rate. You may pay 10 times that amount, plus airfare, hotel, and a nice dinner. Still, if it helps you to finance your film, it's money well spent.

Reality Check

Raising money for a micro-budget film is extremely difficult. I can't tell you how many people I know who are looking for financing for different projects, and how many will strike out and give up. The worse the economy is, the greater your chances of failure. One way to get around this is to design your film as cheaply as possible and finance it yourself. Another is to take the exact opposite approach: increase your budget to $500,000, $750,000, or even $1,000,000 so people with real money will take you seriously. When approaching potential investors, remember that presentation is even more important than that screenplay and those storyboards you toiled on so hard.

9

Jerry Gold

BRIEF LEGAL BRIEFS

Throughout this book, I've noted several instances in which Gerald J. Gold, Esquire, has steered me away from bad business deals, or has made the terms of certain deals more favorable to me. Now you can benefit from his experience directly. This essential chapter is intended as a general guide, to give you an idea of what your options are and how to proceed. Different states may have different laws, and my whole point is to demonstrate the advantages of obtaining an actual entertainment attorney.

Let's start with your legal background.
My career in entertainment law began in 1973 in the business affairs department of a major talent agency, International Famous Agency, the predecessor to what is now ICM — International Creative Management. As a young lawyer I drafted and reviewed contracts and assisted agents in the negotiation of client deals. After about a year and a half, I was more than a little stressed, and decided to take a shot at working for myself. I've now been in private practice as a solo practitioner for thirty-three years, specializing in both entertainment law and residential real estate. They have absolutely nothing in common, but it's a nice mix. In terms of my work in your world, I've represented producers, writers, actors, personal managers, and investors,(mostly individuals, but sometimes small groups) that hire me to analyze investment opportunities in the entertainment sector. Most of my work has been in development, financing, and distribution, but surprisingly little activity during the shoot (principal photography), which I suppose is a good thing, because production related legal stuff are usually big problems, difficult to solve ... with extreme time pressure to boot.

Why should a first time filmmaker working with a low budget hire an entertainment lawyer?

Good question. I'm not going to say that it is absolutely essential, but it makes a lot of sense to hire a lawyer with industry experience in order to identify and properly deal with all of the issues involved. A lawyer with a general contract background can draft a professional looking contract, but, if he or she is not familiar with all of the aspects that should be included in an agreement, the client is not being well-served.

The germ of a film generally starts with the screenplay, so I'd like you to discuss the ways that writers should protect themselves and their work.

I'm far from a copyright expert. Generally, if there's a significant copyright issue, I refer it out. Most of the writer clients I've worked with over the years have submitted a copy of their work to the Writer's Guild of America, (even though they may not necessarily be a WGA member, the Guild will accept submissions). Or, in the alternative, a writer can file a copyright notice (Form TX)—with the Library of Congress. There's a $45 filing fee. Under present law, the length of the copyright is the author's life plus 70 years. An effective way for a writer to stay on top of his business is to keep a detailed paper trail of all transmittals of his material with brief file memos summarizing his meetings regarding the property, including noting everybody in attendance. Just an idea in and of itself can not be protected. Even a generally defined storyline is extremely difficult to protect. So, a writer should take the typical steps in an effort to protect the work without being overly paranoid.

On my first project you sat me and my key partners down and drew up a partnership agreement between us. I'd like you to explain why it's so important, especially for friends working together, to have a written agreement before starting a film.

I couldn't agree more… You have to look at the need for an agreement from the standpoint that something positive will happen, but it is probably even more necessary in the event that the project falters … to spell out who among the principals can move forward, and what they have to move forward with. So, an agreement between principals is of paramount importance, and the agreement should cover areas such as financial contributions, percentage interests, responsibilities, liabilities, control (creative control distinguished from business control)—what the plan is regarding the dilution of interests in favor of outside investors when … IF … outside. Investment capital is obtained, the administration aspects of a film project … all sorts of stuff. It should especially clarify from the writer's standpoint what the ramifications will be if the project dies. The people who customarily come together in a low budget development deal are producer, writer, and perhaps the director. Often, an individual can wear two or more hats, but, in any event, the writer needs to protect his property. The director usually doesn't come up with any seed money. He can take a casual position that if the production money is raised, he will be on board, and if the money isn't raised, he will move on to the next project. The producer is often the one who needs to come up with some early seed money. As investment capital is being raised, it is placed in escrow and can't be touched unless and until the required amount has been obtained. Again, the need for an agreement between the principals—especially if they have long standing relationships—is very important. It can be labeled a development agreement; sometimes it can be a joint venture; some prefer a partnership agreement. Whatever the chosen form of agreement, it has to clearly set forth the deal.

A lot of sample forms and contracts can be found on-line. Do you advise people to use those?

Well, to be perfectly honest, I'm not that familiar with the on-line entertainment agreements. I think it's a great idea for creative people to learn as much as they can about the business and legal aspects of filmmaking. I know that you personally have always been very, very up to speed and probably saved yourself a lot of money as a result. If the contract forms are comprehensive you can always use them as a learning tool. The key is to be able to flesh out issues. The problem with most non-lawyers is that although they might have both adequate drafting and negotiating skills, they fail to identify issues that may come back to haunt them. I suppose I'm not against using forms if they're comprehensive enough; but, if they're not sufficiently comprehensive, they can be dangerous. A little bit of knowledge can be dangerous.

Can you describe the difference between the various business entities filmmakers can choose to form?

We're probably talking about four different types of entities that low budget film producers typically use. Historically, they went with the Limited Partnership agreement to raise money (capital contributions). One of the downsides to a Limited Partnership agreement is the cost of complying with state laws requiring the publication in newspapers of notices identifying the name of the Limited Partnership and the names of the Limited Partners. Substantively, at least in terms of what's contained in the agreements, there's very little difference between a Limited Partnership and a Limited Liability Company (an LLC). The LLC is presently more popular. Why? Well, first of all, there's very rarely a state publication requirement, so the costs of formation are considerably less. When you're making a low budget film, you rarely have the comfort and safety of certainty that you have all of your investors lined up. The formation costs are absorbed by the principals, and they're hoping that the deal happens so that they get reimbursed out of the budget for these out of pocket formation costs. That's when the filmmaker is at financial risk; you want to limit your downside. If it's a Limited Liability Company, the name of the agreement with the investors is an Operating Agreement, and the principals are Managing Members; in a Limited Partnership, the document is called a Limited Part-

Actor Tommy Sweeney (with glasses) and producer Marc Makowski at the premiere of *Naked Fear* (1999).

nership Agreement, and General Partners run the show. As I mentioned, both entities and their respective agreements are similar in terms of setting forth the various percentages interests that are granted, the recoupment position, etc. The documents spell out all of the financial aspects of the arrangement between the principals and investors.

A third legal entity is a Joint Venture. The problem with a Joint Venture Agreement is that the individuals who don't have either business or creative control are not insulated (protected) from liability from the acts or omissions of the individuals making the decisions. A third party can sue any of the signatories to the Joint Venture agreement. In both a Limited Partnership, and a Limited Liability Company, for the individual investors, they are insulated (protected/shielded) from liability. It's a passive investment and they have no involvement at all in the making of the movie. If the film makers become liable to third parties for any reason, the investors are not personally liable. The worst that can happen is that they lose their investment ... their capital contribution. As I mentioned, in a Joint Venture, everybody's conceivably on the hook and potentially vulnerable in a lawsuit. The only way to soften or eliminate that risk is by making sure that the budget contains sufficient liability insurance, errors and omissions insurance and workman's compensation — so that in the event of a lawsuit, it's likely that the insurance will be sufficient to pay a judgment. I would only recommend a Joint Venture as a development agreement, which we've covered, or, in the event that the principals are contributing entirely their own money for the cost of the film, along with comprehensive insurance in place.

A fourth possible entity is a Subchapter-S Corporation. It is a corporation, but it's taxed as if it were a partnership. The operative document is the shareholders' agreement and one of the primary reasons for forming a corporation is that, similar to both the limited partnership and the limited liability company, it insulates the shareholder investors from liability. The corporate formation costs and franchise taxes vary from state-to-state.

Normally the agreement with investors, regardless of the type of entity, entitles the investors to share in the net proceeds derived from all sources in all media. Sometimes producers favor the utilization of what is referred to as " a mini-maxi" clause, which means that the producers have the right to activate the entity and spend money when a specified minimum amount of money has been raised, rather than wait for a larger amount of money to come in (which might never happen) Ultimately, the amount of money raised is divided by the interests of all the investors ad the participation (percentage interests) would vary depending on how much money ultimately is raised. This mini-maxi is a very useful investment tool. Another aspect that must be set forth clearly is the division of profits to the investors. Generally speaking, investors are entitled to between 40 percent and 60 percent of the net profits; 50 percent is most common. It depends on the leverage and the track record of the filmmakers. If they have a particularly enticing project, maybe they can limit the investors' participation to 40 percent. If they're desperate, and the investors are sophisticated, the investors might get 60 percent. Commonly the Investors contribute 100 percent of the cost of production. However, it is an effective sales tool for the filmmakers to invest some of their own money. It instills some confidence. The agreements usually provide for first recoupment by the investors, on a pro rata basis out of first monies derived from the commercial exploitation of the film. Until investment capital is returned to investors (recoupment), there is no profit. Profit, of course, is the amount remaining after all of the costs of production have been recouped, and a reasonable reserve has been established for future bills that come in, including general administration costs that are reasonably anticipated.

Net Profit formulas are tricky. There are concepts such "producers' profits," contrasted by concepts such as "100 percent of a film's profits." The definition of Net Profits must be set forth in the investor's agreement. Other areas that are addressed include deferments, finder's fees, reimbursement of costs expended before formation, the dilution of interests if additional capital is necessary, administration aspects and, statements, including auditing rights.

Another aspect which is not particularly significant in low budget films, but perhaps worth mentioning, is the area of multi-picture investment deals. Sometimes a producer will have two or three potential film properties and try to entice investors with the approach that it's a good idea to invest in the package because if one of the films is successful, the investor is going to make money. My feeling is that such an investment is not the wise way to go. More often than not losses eat up wins, rather than wins softening the impact of losses.

Let's talk about different types of deferments.
A deferment is compensation that is paid later, and is often contingent as opposed to certain. The main concern of an investor' is, "am I going to at least get back my investment?" When I look at deals for investors, I try to ensure that the individuals primarily responsible for bringing the film in, for delivering the film, within the budget, suffer some sort of a penalty if they fail to do that. If possible, some of their compensation is held back and used to cover at least a portion of cost over-runs.

But there is a different deferment philosophy when you're dealing with people who are only responsible for their specific job and not responsible for whether or not the film is completed on budget... So, in that particular situation, the investor might say, "Okay, we will allow certain deferments to be paid before we get back our money, because at least it allows the film to be made at a reduced cost." So, the investors will allow some people to get their deferments out of first monies derived from the exploitation of the film. As I indicted, others may not get their deferred compensation until the investors have recouped 100 percent of their capital contribution.

Then there's a third level, a bonus provision, where at some point following recoupment, and after a certain level of profits have been generated, there is a further deferment level, the theory being, "Well, the investors got back their money, the investors made a profit, now let's sweeten what was otherwise a not very attractive compensation package for the people who really made all of this happen." So we've got all sorts of tiers, but as I indicated, the main concern, of course, is dealing with issue of the investors recouping their investment. Nobody wants to lose money. Not even cousin Ralph.

What needs to go into the package that filmmakers present to potential investor, and what sort of representation must be made as far as how risky it is to invest in a movie?
We're talking about a concept called a disclaimer, where you're really spelling out loud and clear that this is a high risk investment. I've seen many investor packages where they use as an illustration successful films with a similar budget, and break down the specific sources of revenue that was generated. I always have a bad feeling about doing that, because it's misleading. Of course, every once in a while a low budget film generates tremendous revenue ... but it is a rare occurrence. What you want to do is to identify and approach poten-

tial investors who can afford to make an emotional business investment. Because if you look at this thing from a purely practical perspective, investing money in the entertainment industry, particularly low budget film, is not a great investment. Historically, it is not. So what you want to do is, you want to distance yourself from any kind of hype; what you're really looking for are investors who are willing (for whatever reason) to take a shot with you and then, if they make a few bucks you've got them forever. So, unless you already have deals in place, the disclaimer should state that there's no representation whatsoever that the film is going to be distributed or licensed let alone make any profit. In fact, I suggest that the disclaimer go so far as to set forth clearly that there's no guarantee that the film's going to be completed, let alone distributed, and if completed and if distributed, that it may not generate sufficient money to return capital. The disclaimer is something that you have to do. If you don't you're making a mistake. You're leaving yourself open to credibility issues and perhaps some legal issues. So ... it's painful, but in many types of investments—whether you're investing in real estate or the stock market, the investor reads the disclaimer language, takes a deep breath, and gets past it.

What should be in the investment package ... to kind of offset the risk factors ... are bios of the principals, track record, especially if they've done anything; you've got to cover the areas of both creative and financial control. I never recommend including the screenplay, simply a synopsis of the screenplay is sufficient. A budget summary is extremely important. You don't have to present all of the line items, but let the investors know what the film is (hopefully) going to cost to make, including post production. I recommend that the budget include a reserve fund of between 5 and 15 percent ... just in case.

The proposed personnel, actors, director, etc. ... that is a tricky area. If you are a filmmaker relying on investors, and you have well known people in your package, unless and until you know the money is in place, you cannot enter into a contract with these people ... because their representatives will want a pay or play situation, meaning that the actors or the director will get paid whether the film happens or not. You, the filmmaker, are not in a position to guaranty compensation if the money isn't raised. So, you mention key personnel in terms of, "they have expressed interest." But make sure that you don't misrepresent that you've entered into a contract with anybody, and you should say that "in the event that X, Y or Z are not available, we will attempt to get people of equal prominence."

Another element that's key to the investment package is the deal summary highlighting the significant aspects of the investor's agreement. You address areas such as over budget penalties; dilution of interests—what happens if additional monies are needed? What very often happens if the film is heading over budget is that the principles forfeit a part of their profit participation and some of their points are made available for sale to generate additional monies needed to complete a film. That brings up additional issues that need to be addressed.

How would such additional investors affect the investment and recoupment position of the initial investors? This whole area of over budget financing and dilution of interests to accommodate the "later money" is critical ... and sometimes complicated.

And then, of course, you have to include in the package the investment agreement itself, whether you utilize the LLC's Operating Agreement, the Limited Partnership Agreement, or the shareholder agreement — that's part of that package, too.

The question ... who pays for package? Since you can't spend capital contributions until you hit the minimum amount, you need a development fund. That development fund is normally covered in the development, Joint Venture or partnership agreement that I referred to before ... spelling out the agreement between the principals.

Once we decide what type of entity we're going with, what's the next step as far as opening a bank account? And related tot hat, let's discuss the mini-maxi a little more.

All of these agreements presuppose that you're going to raise the money. And all these agreements provide an out date, so that if an investor invests money, and that money is sitting in an escrow account, there has to be some kind of an out date enabling the investor to pull out of the deal if it remains in escrow too long. Investors won't tolerate having their money tied up indefinitely, waiting for you to raise the requisite amount of money. The mini maxi concept I mentioned earlier often comes into play to combat impatient investors. "Can we actually make the film that we want within a budgetary range? Hopefully we'll raise X amount, but what happens if we only get Y? Because if we wait for X, and we only have Y, the investors might send us a letter saying, "You know what? I'm tired of asking. Give me back my money." So, the mini-maxi has to be realistic. Normally there is a range. What you want to do is, when you set out to make the movie, you want to be optimistic, so you want to possibly say to yourself, "Well, let's not cut ourselves short. Let's shoot for a nice amount so we know we're going to be able to have enough production value to do what we want. On the other hand, what is the bare minimum we can do this for ... and do a good job?" The mini-maxi is a concept for the protection of the filmmakers, so that they don't lose impatient investors. And again, just by way of example, it's just a mathematical formula to determine, ultimately, what the capital contribution is worth in terms of acquiring points in the movie. If less money is raised, then the investors' capital contribution is worth more because their percentage of investment, relative to the whole, is greater. . So the investor might say, "Well, I'm glad that we're doing the mini, because now I've just bought 14 points instead of 10." Other investors will say, "You know, I'm afraid of the mini, because if this film is not made because they run out of money, then my investment isn't worth anything." So it's really a question of philosophy (if you're an investor), whether you want them to come in short (make the film on a reduced budget) or you want them to come in flush. In the low budget world, I believe that it's in the investor's best interest for the producers to raise the most amount of money they can. Even if it means that the investor's participation is less, I think it's advantageous to ensure there's enough money to finish the film. With low budget films, the biggest problem that producers face is that they run out of money.

In terms of how to do this, you need to create your legal entity and open a bank account, establishing an escrow account to deposit the investors' capital contributions. You can open up an escrow account and a checking account as soon as you've formed your entity ... once you've actually filed the papers. It is a simple process.

You cannot simply take investors' money and put it in your own checking account for safe-keeping.

As I've mentioned, the question is always, where are you getting the money to form the entity? Again: You cannot touch the investors' money. You may have to give it all back if your money raising effort fails. It often does fail ... more times than not.

If a filmmaker gets to the point where he's negotiating a distribution deal, he's very fortunate because he's finished the film and someone's interested in it. What should people have in the back of their minds that they should be looking for, in able to protect themselves?

The first thing you need to do is you need to research the distributor. Who are you talking to? What's their track record? What have you learned about how they've dealt with other filmmakers? Do they have a history of not paying? Do they have a history of being cheap? Do they have a history of waiting to be sued? So you have to arm yourself with as much information as you can regarding the company you're dealing with, and that's really, really important. One of the first items of business is to have a game plan concerning the extent of the rights to be granted. Are you giving up worldwide distribution agreement, or are you limiting it to United States domestic theatrical? Are you carving out foreign rights? Again, it's wise to create sort of a business plan, where you either do or don't want to put all of your eggs in one basket ... video rights, foreign sales, merchandising possibilities, cable. Theatrical distribution is becoming considerably less significant than it used to be. You might want to entertain six or seven different negotiations. On the other hand, sometimes if you're keeping it on a small, market by market situation, you lack sufficient leverage to get what's most important, and that is a guaranteed advance. My position has always been that unless and until the company you do business with dips into their pocket and demonstrate a financial commitment, they can put your film in a drawer. With a financial commitment, there's a greater chance that your film will be worked. You want to show your investors that a company is interested enough in your film to pay you some money upfront. And sometimes that advance, even though it's not big, is psychologically big. Other important issues to be addressed are prints and advertising, or cassettes and advertising, or DVDs and advertising. They could conceivably be even more important in the long haul than a cash advance. You try to create an environment wherein a company is making a statement that they believe in your film and they're willing to work it, and they have to work it to recoup the investment that they're making in it. If they're not willing to make any kind of an investment, and they're doing you a favor, chances are that nothing ever is going to happen to your film.

Another aspect of negotiation is performance. The amount of royalty or licensing fee that your distributor's going to get can be increased as the result of success. Very often people ask, "Well … how long should I make the agreement for?" Often you don't have much of a choice because the company wants to have enough life to recoup its advance. So, regarding the length of the agreement, when the distributor comes up with an advance, you don't have the flexibility and the leverage that you would if they were not making an advance. What you want to do is look at the overall picture understanding that companies are in business to make money. You want them to make money with your film. If they're going out on a limb by risking capital on you, you have to understand their needs. If they're not, then do not be short-sighted. Make sure you get your rights back if the company does not perform.

Another area of interest is the frequency of statements, and auditing rights. But very often, low budget filmmakers do not have the deep pockets to sue a distributor … and it can turn into a very difficult situation.

To sum it up, if you are unable to get an advance, you've got some real problems, including some disgruntled investors. That's unfortunately the state of the industry right now.

I want to step it down just a little bit, in terms of real micro-budget film; there are no filmmakers making features for $1,000. I'm surprised how many people are making them in 10 days for $5,000. The reality is that the market is so glutted now because people are making these digital video films that a lot of these filmmakers are lucky if someone will take a chance on them, and aren't paying advances. So for these micro-budget filmmakers, getting some kind of a deal is as much about being perceived as a filmmaker as it is about making money, whether or not that perception actually happens.

Here's the distinction, and I'm glad you raised that because I want to be clear that my comments apply to somewhat loftier projects. If somebody's making a film for $5,000, chances are that they don't even have investors. They might have a friend or two, but mostly it's probably their own money or family or credit card money. It can almost be considered as a resume, a demo, a way to put somebody's name out there. The emphasis on advances and revenue flows become inapplicable because the goal is just to be able to show you that you've got some creative skill, and maybe the next project will put some money in your pocket. My comments apply to films that cost, you know, at least $50,000. If we're talking $5,000 — in situations like that, as long as you're getting your releases from actors, and you're not infringing on anybody's literary rights — for that type of money, even hiring a lawyer is an extravagance you may not afford.

But on the other hand, I have a couple of friends who got into a situation where they wanted to make a movie for a few thousand dollars, they ignored my advice to sign an agreement between themselves, had a falling out, neither one of them can do anything with the footage, and then of course the cast and crew completely wasted their time.

Of course, that's what happens. Again, when film making becomes a business, then you need to address the areas we discussed in this conversation. How many of those low low budget films have you seen?

More and more! I have a friend here in Buffalo who's made films for under $1,000. All he has to do is have one screening, where he charges all his friends who come, and then there's a local TV show that pays him $200 to show them once, and he's broken even.

That's great. But that is not really a business ... it's an avocation.

Their problem is they stop there and move on to the next one; they don't try to reach the next plateau.

Again, it's because they're not looking at it as a business. They're looking at it as a creative release, which is a whole other world. There's nothing wrong with that, but people have to make a living, and obviously they're not making a living making movies. Their spirit might be enhanced, but that's a whole different world.

10

Making a Budget

Before you can approach private investors for money, you have to know how much to ask them for, don't you? You must determine how much your film will cost to make. The common mistake is to come up with an arbitrary figure — $30,000 or $300,000 or $3,000,000 — and then make your expenses fit that figure. A budget should be an honest and realistic breakdown of what you expect the film to cost, and expectation and guesswork are entirely different things, just as "How much will my film realistically cost?" and "How much do I want it to cost?" are completely different questions. Of course, you can have a best case scenario and a worst case scenario, the "mini-maxi" that Jerry just referred to.

The first step toward budgeting your film is to do a breakdown of the script. This means examining every scene, identifying which characters need to be present, where the scene must be shot, what props, costumes, and special effects are required, and how long you estimate you'll need to shoot the scene. You make this determination based on how many pages and setups (or camera angles) you anticipate shooting, how many actors are involved, whether or not you need a dolly or a Steadicam, and if action or special effects are involved. A dialogue scene between two people sitting in a café will take less than time to film than a foot chase on a crowded sidewalk that moves into a street, stopping traffic, and ends in gunfire.

Paying Yourself

How much should you pay yourself? If you're making a micro-budget movie, the producer, director and screenwriter will probably make the same thing as everyone else on the film — nothing. But they'll each own a piece of the film. On a low budget film in which people are being paid, the fees for all three of these top dogs may account for 10 percent of the total budget. I was looking at a sample budget for a $1.5 million film the other day and it broke down like this: Producer — $20,000; Screenwriter — $20,000; Director — $120,000. That's quite a disparity, isn't it? I've also seen scripts for $500,000 films that paid the director $8,000 and the writer $2,500. But there are no rules.

On *Deadly Rites*, a $1.5 million project I'm developing, the producer, director (me), and screenwriter are equal partners. We're asking for $50,000 each and will share any profits equally. On this same project, an actress who wishes to be involved has approached a woman who may raise 50 to 75 percent of the budget from her investor base. If that happens, the actress will be entitled to a 5 percent finder's fee (but only for the money she is directly responsible for raising), and the woman actually raising the money will be entitled to a cut of the film's profits as the executive producer. As more and more people become involved in the financial end, we may end up cutting down our fees to make sure there's still enough money in the budget to make the film we want.

Food for Thought

Once you've completed your breakdown, you can make up your shooting schedule, which will enable you to calculate how much you're going to spend on cast and crew. Even if they're working for free, you can now estimate how many meals you need to pay for and possibly much hotel fare you should anticipate paying. Don't just guess what your food budget will be; call a caterer and get an estimate based on a head count and schedule. You won't like the answer you get, and you'll probably decide to use the caterer for one meal and supplement that with snacks. Traditionally, cast and crew will find coffee, juice, fruit and bagels waiting for them when they arrive on set or at location. "First meal" is served six hours after set call. On most shoots I've been on, a second meal—usually pizza—was served whenever it appeared we would shoot beyond 12 hours, which is common. Of course, each meal slows down production; even if everyone eats fast, they tend to get sluggish. In my experience, every one-hour meal really means almost two hours of down time.

When the Assistant Director calls "Lunch," he will either set the meal break as a flat hour, or an hour from the time the last person on line is served his food, which guarantees that person will have time to eat and digest his meal. Occasionally, you may request that the crew take only a 45-minute break, or even a 30-minute break, but this must be an exception, not the rule. Some people on your crew will thrive on junk food; others will prefer healthier food, like fruit. You have to take all of them into account.

You must feed your cast and crew. It doesn't matter if you're paying them a lot for their services, a little, or nothing (although a person who is working for free might argue that he is even more deserving of sustenance). On *I Was a Teenage Zombie*, we shot for one month. I remember one day when we shot outside Brooklyn College and there was no money for food. Most of us didn't have money in our pockets for food because we were working on the film for free—and we were paying to take mass transit to location every day. The assistant director brought the director, John Michaels, a big sandwich. John didn't ask for the sandwich, but he didn't refuse it, either. In fact, he called for a break and we all sat in a circle and watched him eat his sandwich. I could tell he felt uncomfortable with the situation, but it didn't occur to him to break the sandwich into bite sized morsels, like they do on *Survivor*, and share the wealth. It was demoralizing, and I vowed my people would never go hungry.

Plutonium Baby was filmed in Connecticut woods. The cast and crew were put up in a hotel and paid $50.00 a day. This was a "cabin in the woods" movie, and the producer hadn't rented lights, so it was a *daylight* cabin in the woods movie. The night before the last day of shooting, the filmmakers ran out of money — and didn't bother to inform us that they expected us all to go the night without eating and then give them a full day of work. I witnessed the producer trying to make an actress feel guilty for complaining about the situation. We united, delivered an ultimatum, and ate KFC that night. When the producer later realized the director had only shot half a film, and he needed us to shoot for another week, we asked for a $25 daily raise and insisted on two meals a day. They hired a great caterer.

On *Slime City*, we had plenty of cold cuts for lunch but we always had hot food for dinner; sometimes pizza, maybe some Chinese take-out, a McDon-

Johnny Gruesome (Ryan O'Connell) demands star treatment in his next production (2007).

ald's meal or two, and home cooked food. On *Brain Damage*, Anita Muro—Jimmy Muro's mother—cooked our meals in the production facility's kitchen, and I don't think I've ever eaten better on a film (although Anita cooked a lot of pasta, which led to a lot of on set flatulence!).

Come up with what you feel is a realistic food budget for principal photography, pickup days, and re-shoots—and then double that amount.

Other Expenses

What other expenses can you expect to incur on a micro-budget level? Do you or your DP own a camera, or must you rent one? A sound mixer, boom pole, and microphone? Lavaliere microphones? A slate? Tripod? Dolly? Gels? Gaffer's tape? Don't forget raw film stock, Mini–DV tapes, or Hi Definition digital memory cards. And extra batteries!

What about costumes? Props? Art direction? Photocopying scripts? On *Gruesome*, a music video I shot to promote my novel *Johnny Gruesome*, I needed a big black car to serve as Johnny's Death Mobile. I found a 1960 black Cadillac with fins, just what I wanted. Unfortunately, it cost me $300 for two shoots. That's $300 I hadn't anticipated when I drew up my budget, and I've been doing this for a while. That amounted to about 8 percent of my total budget, a large overrun for a single item.

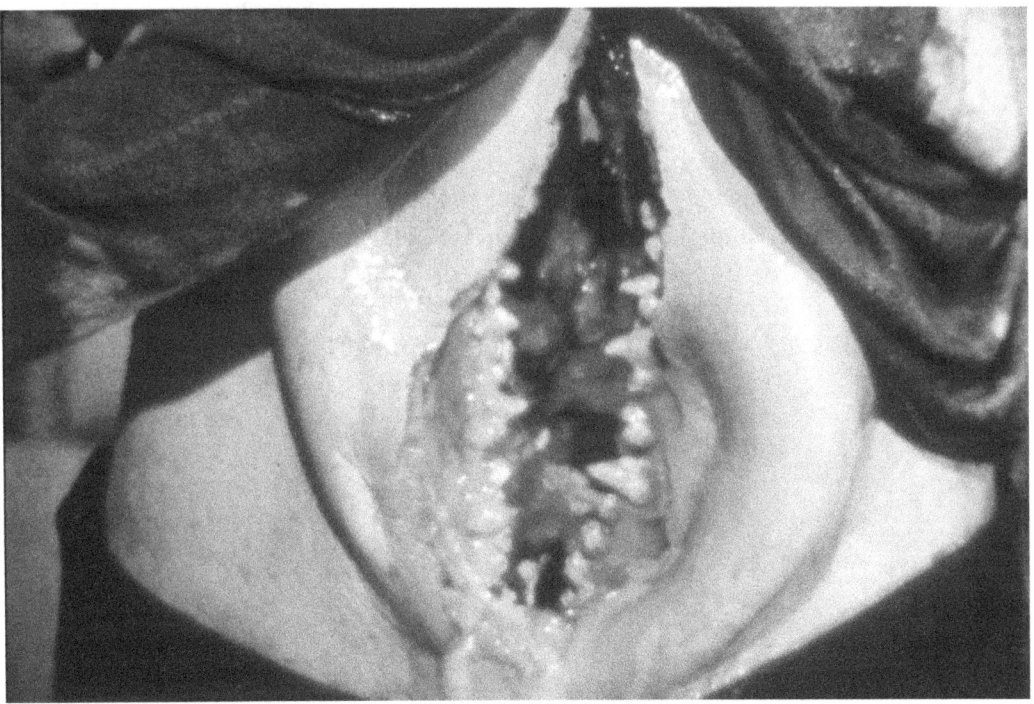

The "stomach mouth" from *Slime City* (1988). You must feed your cast and crew!

Gas money: production vehicles don't run on enthusiasm. Tolls. Parking tickets. You need insurance to obtain shooting permits. Even if you decide to shoot guerrilla style and forego permits, you should have insurance for your cast and crew members. The last time I checked, an insurance carrier was willing to give me 12 days' worth of production coverage for $600. That fee was the same whether I shot for one day or all 12. But that means $1200 will buy you 24 days of coverage, enough for a decent shoot. The courier I spoke to was willing to allow me to spread my 12 days out over multiple weekends—good news for micro-budget filmmakers who are weekend warriors. Be sure to shop around.

If you're making a horror film, you probably need special effects. If you want the effects in your film to help sell it, they'd better be good. Remember: you get what you pay for. On *Slime City*, an effects heavy picture, I paid Scott Coulter and Tom Lauten $7,000 to do all our effects and straight make-up. That covered a full month of pre-production and a month of production. Recently, the cost of foam latex has doubled. Do you expect your SFX artist to shoulder this burden? Of course not. Even if an effects artist is working for you for free because they're building a portfolio, or for points or a deferred salary because they believe in your project, you're still responsible for the cost of their materials, and that can amount to a tidy sum.

The score. Maybe some of your friends are in bands and have agreed to let you use their songs for free. Great! But you still need incidental music. Maybe someone will do a good synthesizer score for free, and maybe they won't. For *Slime City*, I hoped to get a cheap synthesizer score. I met with composer Rob Tomaro, discussed what I wanted musically, and danced around the cost because I was inexperienced. He came back with a demo tape featuring some horns and other instruments that blew me away—and because of studio costs, a $1,800 quote that also blew me away. I'm a sucker for quality, so I bit the bullet. It's a wonderful score, many reviewers and viewers have commented on it over the years, and for the film's 20th anniversary in 2008, Rob and I released the remastered soundtrack on CD.

Here is what a budget may look like on your 10-day micro-budget epic:

Producer	0
Director	0
Screenwriter	0
Actors	0
Camera man	0
Sound Man	0
Boom Person	0
Legal	$1,500
Insurance	$600
Special Effects	$2,000
Food	$1,000

10. Making a Budget

Tape stock	$400
Editor	0
Music	0
Screenplay copyright	$40
Motion Picture copyright	$40
10% Miscellaneous	$558
10% Contingency	$558
Total	**$6696**

Your total proposed budget is $6,696.00, or $6,700.00. Can a film really be made for this much money? Yes, it can. But for argument's sake, let's throw in some additional expenses. After all, we want to make a quality production!

Wardrobe	$500
Art direction	$500
Set construction	$500
Gasoline	$500

Now we're up to $8,696.00, or $8,700. But as our budget increases, so do our miscellaneous and contingency figures, which are percentage based. Due to the nature of this business, which is plagued by variables impossible to predict, that money will be spent before you even shoot a frame of film or video. Consider it gone. So now your budget looks like this:

Producer	0
Director	0
Screenwriter	0
Actors	0
Camera man	0
Sound Man	0
Boom Person	0
Legal	$1,500
Insurance	$600
Special Effects	$2,000
Food	$1,000
Tape stock	$400
Editor	0
Screenplay copyright	$40
Motion Picture copyright	$40
Wardrobe	$500
Art direction	$500
Set construction	$500
Gasoline	$500
10% Miscellaneous	$745
10% Contingency	$745
Total	**$9,070**

See how much our budget has increased, purely on a theoretical basis? Let's say you finish your film for the preceding budget. What's next? You may decide to hold a screening or local premiere for your production. A theatre will charge anywhere from $200 to $500 for such an event (it's always cheaper on a weekday), but you'll probably want to make flyers to stick up around town. And you probably want to sell this film, or at least get it distributed, right? Distributors aren't going to fly to Boise, Idaho to attend your screening, so you'll have to produce screeners to send them. Ideally, these will be DVDs with menus, in DVD cases with color packaging inserted into the sleeves. Don't send your DVDs in jewel cases or paper sleeves; use this opportunity to show how your film might be marketed and might stand out. It costs approximately $3.00 to mail a DVD if you include the expense of a padded envelope.

Congratulations! You've just entered the $10,000 club. And if you plan to spend $10,000, don't be surprised if that figure becomes $12,000 to $15,000. Of course, there are determined — and hopefully talented — individuals who will make this same film for $4,000 or $5,000. They'll do this by eliminating the legal and insurance figures and cutting everything else in half. It can be done, especially if you're working with your own money and shooting 10 to 15 days. But if you're presenting a budget to an investor for consideration, don't be surprised if they disbelieve your estimate. And pray that none of your cast or crew are injured on your shoot, because you'll be liable.

Budgeting a Bigger Film

A budget like the one above is fine on a micro-budget film, but when you reach a bigger arena — say a film in the $500,000 range — you're better off using a movie budgeting software program for a detailed budget. Or, better yet, hire an experienced production manager to do one for you. They will typically charge $500 for such a service, but everything is negotiable.

11

Roy Frumkes

PRODUCING SCREAMS AND LAUGHTER

During my sole year as a student at the School of Visual Arts in New York City, my Film Production instructor was Roy Frumkes, who had directed *Document of the Dead*. Roy brought in Tom Savini and Stan Winston as guests, fresh from their respective successes with *Creepshow* and *The Terminator*; he showed us *The Projectionist*, a film he helped produce, which introduced the world to Rodney Dangerfield, and *Burt's Bikers*, a docudrama he directed spotlighting a special program for children with Down Syndrome. It was a fun class, for which I shot the Super-8 shorts *Cult Figure*, starring Robert Sabin, and *Bad Worms*, the genesis for *Slime City*. Two years later, we were classmates in a SVA night class on Production Management: I was there to learn how to pre-produce *Slime City*, and he was doing the same for *Street Trash*.

Roy was born with arythroblastosis, a blood disorder more commonly known as the "RH Factor." As a child he suffered from polio, before the Salk vaccination, which required him to be quarantined on the second floor of his family's New Rochelle home, and Tourette's Syndrome, before it had a name. He controlled the latter by filling notebooks with his thoughts, a process he continues to this day. And he was regaled by the show business tales of his grandfather, who was Harry Houdini's booking agent at the end of Houdini's career. I've often thought that Houdini may have inspired Roy's interest in special effects. It's easy to see how being quarantined fueled his imagination and writing a lifelong, epic journal helped inspire his career as a screenwriter.

Roy attended Tulane University in New Orleans, where he was the entertainment editor of the college news paper, *The Tulane Hullabaloo*. When he got out of college, he joined the National Board of Review of Motion Pictures. Decades later, with profits from *The Substitute*, which he created and co-scripted, he bought *Films in Review*, the country's first film magazine, which he currently operates as a website. In typical Frumkes fashion, when director

Jimmy Muro asked him to pen a *Street Trash* sequel two decades after the film's run, Roy numbered it "3" instead of "2" because so much time had passed.

You worked as a theatre manager for United Artists, and then for a publicity company called Great Scott. How did you actually break into filmmaking?

It was in 1968 that I did *The Projectionist*. I had taken some classes at NYU after I got out of Tulane in '66, where I met a fellow named Harry Hurwitz, who was six years older than me, and a frustrated filmmaker. He was teaching at NYU and he and I really got along well. If one were to print the legend, then I dropped out and he quit his teaching position to do *The Projectionist*. If one were to print something closer to the truth, perhaps he got fired, and maybe I wasn't getting good enough grades. Whatever the truth of the situation was, we left. And I raised the money to make *The Projectionist*.

I teach a class now called Finance and Distribution, and I bring in lots of people from the industry, indie-filmmaker-distributors like Bill Lustig, documentary filmmakers, music video filmmakers, feature filmmakers, every kind. And what becomes clear is that on one level, whether you're independent, or in Hollywood, it's all the same — there is no one formula for raising money. A lot of it has to do with building contacts, with structuring your career properly so you don't start out by making a film that's doomed to failure so that you lose all your initial contacts and have to start over again. That's what we did. *The Projectionist* is a good film. The Museum of Modern Art called it one of the three best films of the year it came out, which was '71. That, *Death in Venice* and *McCabe and Mrs. Miller* were their top three choices. They put $60,000 into a medium range restoration of *The Projectionist* about five years ago. They really love the film and because of that it's kind of survived. But it was utterly inaccessible to a mass audience; it was experimental in form. It got a cult following, but in those days "cult" was a euphemism for "financial failure." I really believe today that if you've got some strange film in your head, don't make it your first one. Make the first one something where, marketing-wise, it has a solid chance at success, so that you can then build a career on it and do your *Being John Malkovich's* later.

We did four films together, Harry and I. And what happened with *The Projectionist* was that I'd raise money, and then we'd use it all, and then Harry would blithely say, "We need more money." And I'd go dig up somebody new and get money out of them. One of them was a guy named Michael Osterer, who'd been a year below me in high school. He got very excited about film, but he didn't want to put money into *The Projectionist*. He was willing to finance a horror film. We agreed, and our plan was to shoot the film in one week, edit it in three weeks, sell it, and put that money into *The Projectionist*. The film was called *Shriek Out*. It was an anthology film, which Harry and I wrote and co-directed. We had two camera people. He would take one, I'd take the other, and we'd go off and shoot. We had Judd Hirsch starring in one story, before he became well-known, and I was in it, too, co-starring in one of the other two stories. Well, we ran out of money before we finished it, so it didn't serve our purpose at all, outside of giving us a respite. And then, years later, when Harry went down to Tampa to teach, a lab down there had the negative and eventually, after he couldn't bail it out financially, and didn't let me in on it so that I could have possibly raised money to cover the costs, the lab destroyed the negative, and that film is completely gone. There's nothing left except a few stills

Then Rodney's place opened in '71, so that year we did two films. One was a TV special at the opening of his club, called *An Evening at Dangerfield's*, which I directed. The other I wrote with my same friend whose girlfriend appeared nude in *Shriek Out*, Robert Janes Winston, although Harry didn't let us go past the treatment stage; he believed that actors should improvise, as they did in *The Projectionist*. The difference was, there was only 18 minutes of dialogue in *The Projectionist*, and this film was *all* dialogue. It was called *The Comeback Trail*. And so the actors had the structure created by us, but no dialogue, and a few of them — Buster Crabbe and Ina Balin — were not really skilled at improvisation, so scenes wandered, imbalanced by the awkward and often endless improvs. Harry wasn't able to cut it into any kind of really smooth shape because of improper coverage during shooting, and his chief skill, outside of being an idea man, was as an editor. The film never came out. And then, several years later, he was able to get some more financing and he re-shot part of it. The new footage featured Henny Youngman, Professor Irwin Corey and Hugh Hefner, and the title was changed to *That's Adequate!* In that form, it made it onto TV, distributed by Max Rosenberg's company. I thought the new cut was less amusing than *The Comeback Trail*, which wasn't good. There was a theatre in New York called the Thalia, and they got in touch with me at some point and said, "We're doing a festival of films that were never released and we'd like to show a double bill of *The Projectionist* and *The Comeback Trail*." So I helped arrange that. Harry was living out in L.A. at that point, so I went to the theatre and spoke before each show. My son then was maybe 10, and I said, "Christopher, they're showing *The Comeback Trail* for the first time." And he said, "Really? Where?" I said, "At the Thalia Theatre." He looked at me and said, "The Failure Theatre?" I said, "Well, yes, but that's not what I said..." (laughs)

How did your partnership with Harry wind down?
Well, after four films that didn't do well —

—you both figured one of you was doing something wrong?
(laughs) Well, we both had to resort to teaching, and I guess Harry couldn't go back to NYU, so he went down to the University of Tampa. And I started teaching at SUNY Purchase. While I was at SUNY I became dismayed by the teaching films that existed about filmmaking. They were all about big budget

films like *Butch Cassidy* or *Star Wars*, there was nothing that students could relate to. So I tried to get a series of films off the ground, films on filmmaking, shot on the sets of independent films. They didn't go for it at SUNY Purchase, which was just too big of an organization to care, so while I was there the only film I worked on was something I initiated called *Tales That Will Tear Your Heart Out*. That didn't get finished. But then when I moved to the School of Visual Arts, which is a privately owned school, and I sent a letter to the Rhodes family, suggesting that if this series of films were made, they would say "Produced by the School of Visual Arts," and would be shown in high schools all over the country, it would be good promotion. Unlike a big place like NYU or SUNY, where a letter just goes into the ether, this letter was read and considered, and one week later I received a check from Silas Rhodes to go shoot the film. It was really something.

This was 1978. I had to find an indie feature being shot outside New York, because New York was still a union state. Not only could you not combine right to work and union people on a crew — there were no student PA's, working on features like there are today — you also couldn't shoot a non-union film in New York. They had union guys stationed at the equipment houses and if they saw a non-union group picking up stuff they would follow them to where they were shooting and would actually cause trouble. So I had to find a film that was being shot outside of New York. I had seen *Night of the Living Dead* and had later seen George speak at the Museum of Modern Art, but I didn't know him. However I did know Richard Rubinstein fairly well socially, and I learned they were starting *Dawn of the Dead* in Pittsburgh, so I checked on that. And *Document of the Dead*, which is what came out of this, marked a really unique moment in history because they were not doing making-of documentaries about independent features. This may have been the first. *Dawn* was a three-month shoot and there were no other crews there except us (and a brief visit from a German TV crew). It was amazing. In recent years I've visited the sets of *Land of the Dead* and *Diary of the Dead* and they've got three film crews a day on those shoots.

It was a major turning point in my career when *Document* finally came out, and it didn't come out for several years because after the school's money ran out, I raised additional funds, and I cut together a feature length film, which was useless for high school classes. They have 50-minute classes, so no schools were going to rent it. I had effectively shut myself out of that market. Video was in its infancy, and no one was offering us the kind of money I thought was worthwhile for that market, so I put the film away. 10 years later, an ex-student named Len Anthony approached me. He had a company called Off Hollywood, and he remembered the film and asked if he could release it. He offered me good money and, more importantly, an ambitious marketing plan, so I agreed. And he asked, "Can you do an update? Because this is already old." I called George, and he was working on *Two Evil Eyes*. It was 1989, 11 years later.

So I went back up and shot the second part, and Off Hollywood funded it. The first *Document of the Dead*, which was 66 minutes long, shot on 16mm film, cost $33,000. And the second part, 24 minutes long, shot on video, cost $50,000. That's how much costs had gone up, even with the shift to a cheaper medium.

You shot Document **with a student crew. What were the conditions like?**

I had a small crew, there were seven of us, we were in two cars—two camera people, a still photographer, one sound guy, and I guess a general grip, and then there were me and Sukey. Sukey Rafael was my co-producer on that and on *Burt's Bikers*. The DP was a key element, because that was Reeves Lehmann, who in later years became the Chairman of the Film Department at SVA. At age 19 he'd been in the Tet Offensive, which was the worst year in Vietnam. He was a marine commando and he brought back with him his military skills. Richard Rubinstein had very rightly quarantined us, we were not allowed to get with 100 yards of George, so we brought up long lenses which would enable us to shoot from across the mall. And it made sense to me. George had only made little films, like *Martin*, in 16mm, and here he was doing a big film in 35mm with hundreds of people in a mall and on a sizeable budget for him. We went up there and Reeves said, "Man, I'm not gonna stand for this." He would take his crew and they'd be crawling on their bellies across the floor, using marine commando tactics. George caught sight of it out of the corner of his eye and he was really amused. And if you think about it, *Dawn* is a military film. It's a horror film, but it also overlaps into the war genre—these S.W.A.T. guys barricaded in this place—and in fact at times he and his DP, Michael Gornick, were worried that it was drifting too far away from the horror genre. So George obviously likes that kind of movie and he liked seeing us do this guerrilla stuff, and within hours he lowered the barrier, saying, "You guys are great, do anything you want." That I credit to Reeves and his shenanigans.

Did you have any idea what George was achieving?

No. When we arrived, as soon as we had gotten our stuff into our rooms, we joined them and looked at what they'd done. They were down-converting the 35mm to 16m because his company was geared up for 16m, shooting commercials and TV docs. I'm looking at this stuff and it looked like pop art, all bright colors—the complete opposite of the look of *Night of the Living Dead*. Also, when we arrived, they had finished shooting everything they needed to at that point, and they were improvising, so they had bikers swinging off the rafters, and George was playing a zombie in a Santa Clause outfit. It was hard to imagine where this brand new vision had come from. Also, I was really concerned about getting the stuff that I needed for my film. I treated *Document of the Dead* as if it was a narrative. George was the star, and both my camera guys needed to get 10 close ups each of him, 10 mediums, 10 longs, and then Savini was a co-star, and I needed 5, 5, and 5, and they had little graph charts and my assistants were looking over their shoulders and checking off when they got each spatial design. I felt if I got all those spatial designs I could cut together an interesting film in the same way I would use space in a narrative — long shots for objectivity, close ups for emotional punch, etc. I ended up being lucky in the same way that I'd been lucky with *Burt's Bikers*, in that my cast was good. I think documentaries are like narratives in that way, too. If the characters aren't sympathetic, the audience loses interest. But George and Savini were wonderful, and Rubinstein was kind of menacing. It was like a real movie, you know, giving characterization a lot of weight, and the same is true of *Burt's Bikers*. And that's why it expanded to feature length and still worked.

Did you ever dream Document *would have the life it's had?*

No, I didn't. Even when *Dawn of the Dead* became the huge and enduring hit it was. I just felt that I'd be lucky to get *Document* on VHS, maybe on TV one day on a cable channel that could leave in the violence. I didn't foresee what was coming, which was this incredible love of Romero and devotion to him and the genre, so that everyone had to have *Document of the Dead*, and whichever company distributed *Document of the Dead* just cleaned up. Then, when the DVDs came along, they started doing these collector's editions with three, four discs in each country, and it was very clear, either through pre-marketing or whatever, that the fans would not buy these big collections without *Document* being included, so suddenly I was re-licensing the film over and over again, for more money than *Street Trash* ever earned. Really, *Document* and *The Substitute* have been the big winners for me in my career. I'm doing a final chapter, which is about *Night 2*, *Land* and *Diary*, so it's going to come out again, and every fan — just like they always have to buy any film that they love over again if there's one new thing added to the disc, they're just going to buy it again. It's going to go all over the world again, and even if distribution companies have *Document of the Dead* out now and have a license on it, they don't have the license on *The Definitive Document of the Dead*, which is a new film even though it contains much of the footage from the earlier incarnations.

How did your friendship with Wes Craven begin?

I saw *Last House on the Left* when it opened in New York. I went with Bob Harris, who is the world's foremost restorationist, and a very close friend of mine, and with Robert Janes Winston, who wrote *Comeback Trail* with me — what there was of a script ... it was actually a treatment. Harris walked out, he was really offended and he couldn't take it. My other friend stayed and liked it, as I recall, but thought it was the only film he'd ever seen that made a case for censorship. I just loved the thing without any qualifications, and I took down Wes's name, and the name of the company that released it, and I wrote him a letter and said, "Wes, you don't know me, but I loved *Last House*, I could tell it was your first film, I can tell it was shot in 16m, and I think you have so much talent, it was so powerful." Two weeks later this sizeable box arrives, and I open it up and it's all the outtakes, and all the scripts, starting from when it was called *Sex Crime of the Century*, filled with his notes on them. And included is a note in which he says, "If you like it, you can have it. My crew spat at me as they walked out of the screening. I'm not putting it on my resume." I got in touch with him and we became friends. Later, during the shooting of *The Hills Have Eyes,* he was having a very difficult time, and he was writing me and I was writing him back, trying to keep his spirits up.

And he was involved with Tales That Will Tear Your Heart Out?

At SUNY, what I did get off the ground was this feature—an anthology comprised of several little stories—and I brought in professionals from the East coast, because there wasn't much going on on the East coast, and each of them either directed or wrote a segment, and acted as a mentor to the otherwise student crew, and I produced the whole thing. I invited everyone I knew to participate: DeWitt Bodeen, who wrote the original *Cat People*, with Simone Simon, wrote one of the stories; Al Kilgore, who created *Bullwinkle*, was writing one; Chuck Hirsch, who produced *Greetings* and *Hi, Mom* with Brian De Palma, wrote and directed one. And Wes Craven, who I'd become friendly with, was sitting around not doing anything, so he joined in. Everybody got 1 percent of the film. All the students got 1 percent, all the guest professionals that I brought in got 1 percent.

The thread-story was mine, and I didn't know that I had ripped it off from *Kolchak: Night Stalker*, it was just something that had sunk into my unconsciousness and mutated into this. It was about a graveyard, where some cult is doing an incantation, and all the corpses get up and leave, to finish doing what they were doing when they died. So each writer or writer/director created one of these unfinished stories, and you would see them come to their conclusions. I gave everyone one day of sound; no matter how many days they wanted to shoot, they had to get their sound done in one day. And they all had to start in the graveyard, so the location for the beginning of every story was the same. Seven people conceived seven different versions of rising from the grave.

Anyway, I had purchased a bunch of Styrofoam, out of which the art department was going to carve tombstones, and we had a fog machine. I was not there all the time, I would come and check how they were doing. And the night before we started shooting, I came by the graveyard location and said, "Gee, those tombstones look great." They were on a hill, and everything's looking atmospheric. And I noticed some people, townspeople visiting SUNY Purchase just to check out the campus or whatever, and I notice that they're scrutinizing the tombstones. I walk over and one of them is saying, "You know, this tombstone is for one of the guys who founded White Plains." And suddenly I'm seeing that these are real tombstones. What the overzealous students

Roy and wife-to-be Puincie sitting on Ashbury Park theatre stairs watching filming of *The Projectionist* (1971). Photograph courtesy Roy Frumkes.

Chuck McCann and Ina Balin cavort in *The Projectionist* (1971). Photograph courtesy Roy Frumkes.

had done was to bypass the Styrofoam, they'd gone to local graveyards and just took the tombstones and brought them to the location. And I have to say, in the years since, having worked on ten films, I've been through some really harrowing adventures, I mean some of the most terrible instances of amoral film behavior imaginable, but I never got a chill like I did that night, realizing that I was actually a party to grave-robbing, and that a citizen had spotted it! I grabbed one of the crew and said, "Get these things back where you found them!" They pulled up with station wagons and loaded the tombstones in, weighing the station wagons down. They drove away and I really don't know if they put them back in the right places. That was really horrifying.

It's ironic that you saw Last House on the Left **with Bob Harris since you were largely responsible for restoring it.**

You're right, that really is an odd coincidence. I still feel it's a very powerful film. At one point, when the VHS came out, and it was an R-rated version, I said to Wes, "We've got to restore this thing." He said, "Really?" There was an uncut 35mm print off the Super 16 to 35mm blowup negative (it was shot in Super 16) in Sean Cunningham's office, up on a shelf. We took it down and went through it, and we found a lot of stuff. Local communities had

Judd Hirsch and David Holiday in the *Shriek Out* segment co-directed by Frumkes and Harry Hurwitz. The film was never completed and a lab destroyed the negative — only rare stills like this remain. Photograph courtesy Roy Frumkes.

cut that thing to pieces, and very few release prints came back untouched, but this was one of them. It had material in it that's never appeared in any of the various versions that have been released around the world, but Wes didn't believe a lot of that stuff should be in what he considered this to be: which was his final cut. He was feeling differently about the film by then, that not everything he'd left in back in '72 still belonged. So we picked out about three minutes of interesting, non-'R' material, I made 16m reductions on it, I got it to the company that was releasing it at the time, they reinserted the stuff, and so his sanctioned version was released. Other countries have released longer versions, but they're not the cut that he wanted. I'm continuing to release the outtakes. I've just done a deal with the UK distributor of *Last House*, who apparently has worldwide rights outside the U.S., and they're giving me a very lucrative deal. They asked if I had anything more, so I went back into the archives (aka my closet), and found another five minutes of simulated sex footage, and they were thrilled.

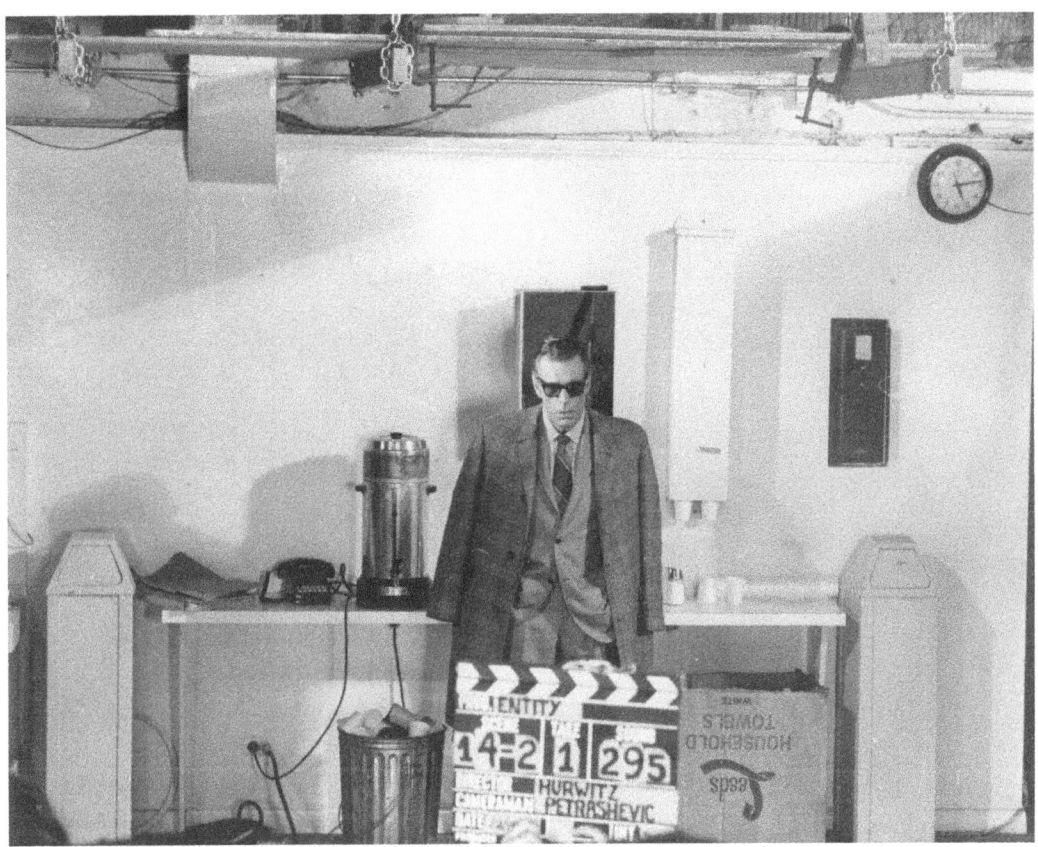

Buster Crabbe readies himself for a take in *The Comeback Trail*, released in an altered form as *That's Adequate!* (1982). Photograph courtesy Roy Frumkes.

You have a real appreciation for Chaplin, and you've said* Street Trash *is a black comedy more than it is a horror film. I was going to go out on a limb and suggest that comedy is your first love, not horror.

It certainly is the one consistent thread through all my work, I have to say. Slightly-to-exceedingly dark comedy, even in a film like *Burt's Bikers*, which is about handicapped children. For me, what made that film exciting was daring to be comedic about those kids.

I remember when Jimmy Muro and his gang started wearing the T-shirts for the* Street Trash *short around the SVA dorm. How did you become the screenwriter and producer of the feature version?

I had Jimmy and Mike Lackey first year, in Production. And then I had them again second year, for Screenwriting. It was in second year, around that transitional period, that they did the short. I did visit the set and I wore a beautiful navy peacoat in a scene where I'm raiding the liquor store at the end and I run out with a crate of bottles. I tripped and flew out-of-frame, nearly rolling across the street, but I'm in the final cut.

Mike Sullivan (in tux) in Chuck Hirsch's tale from *Tales That Will Tear Your Heart Out*, the never completed zombie anthology film Frumkes launched while teaching at SUNY Purchase. Photograph courtesy Roy Frumkes.

Two things were happening then: first of all, an uncle died and left Jimmy some money, and he invested it in the beginnings of a Steadicam apparatus; and the other thing was that one of the people who visited the Dive was Terry Levine, who saw the short, went up to Jimmy, and said, "I will give you $50,000 if you'll soot another 60 minutes to add to this 15, and we'll have a 75-minute film." Jimmy came up to me in class and explained what happened. He said, "You know I'm not a screenwriter. I can't do that. Would you be interested in writing the script?" I thought about it for just a few seconds and I said, "I'll tell you what. You have a much more elegant feeling about what you want to do in the future, so why do something shabby, a rush job in 16m and cut around this footage you've already shot, which is fun but not good-looking, and very cheap in terms of its makeup effects. Why not let me write a script for a larger budget that would give you a better-looking film, and I'll produce it and raise the money. And he said, "Great, man!" It was like instantly that was the deal. I wrote the script, and I would send him pages, which is something I didn't do with the new one—*Street Trash 3*.

But anyhow, back to the original. He said, "You can write anything you want." I used some stuff from the short, enlarging a few of the gags, but he didn't really care whether I used anything from the short. There were two things, however, that he insisted on being in the script: one was a scene where a guy gets his head taken off by an oxygen tank, because he'd worked at his father's collision yard and had discovered how dangerous those things were; and the other thing was a scene where a bum sticks his cock through a hole in the wall and pisses on someone else and the guy he's pissing on cuts his cock off. I said, "Well, that's not particularly funny, but I'll think of a way to make it work." And then, when I was writing that sequence and sending over the pages, he called me up and said, "Man, I don't know what you're smoking, but please send some over immediately!" So those were the only two things he insisted on.

We printed up about 300 business plans, and it took about a year to raise the money. We had raised half of our original budget of half a million by the time we had to either shoot or wait. We'd put together a crew of 55, and 35 of them were students, so we had to shoot during the summer, while they were out on break. We initially had an eight-week schedule planned. There was about $220,000 in the bank, and it was up to me to make a decision whether we should go or not. And I thought we should go. The way the money was coming in, slowly but surely, I figured we'd be able to keep up with the needs of the production, and so we launched. This again was an experiment in producing. I was always looking for ways to enable students to cross over from the academic to the professional world; that's what I did with *Tales That Will Tear Your Heart Out*, even though it didn't get finished; that's what I did with *Document of the Dead*, even though it didn't lead to a series of films, which I wished it had; and that's what I was doing with *Street Trash* as well. I made it two-thirds students and one third professionals, hoping the professionals would mentor the students. What I hadn't counted on, and the whole Iraq fiasco reminds me of it in a very malformed, analogous way, is that the students weren't up to it. They weren't professional yet. So for the first week, or week and a half, they were really cooking and then they started losing it. They didn't have the energy, they didn't have the skill, and they started dragging the production down. That was the main reason that it went more than a month over schedule. It ended up being about 13 weeks of shooting.

That may be the most audacious aspect of the whole production.
And I think it really shows, even though so much of the film was cut to give it an appropriate running time for an exploitation film. (A lot of those scenes that were cut made it into the documentary, *The Meltdown Memoirs.*) Jimmy had everything he needed: he had a producer whose only role was to protect him, not to say, "Hurry up," which is rare; and he had enough money, even though it was coming in bit by bit, to do everything he wanted, everything he had devised in terms of shots, and to go back and do them over if they didn't come out right. There were scenes that were shot several times. We just bought the time, and kept on going and going. And then we went into September and faced a real crisis because the students all had to go back to school.

Eddie Garcia and Lydia Kassak in one of the never completed *Tales That Will Tear Your Heart Out*. Photograph courtesy Roy Frumkes.

One by one we lost them, and we were scrambling to fill the gaps, plus we were short on money by then and hiring more professionals to replace the students was a difficult task.

Who was most responsible for the look of that film?
That's interesting, too, because Jimmy came to me toward the end, when we were getting ready to do the titles, and asked, "So what should it say, 'A Roy Frumkes Production/A Jim Muro Film'?" I said, "Jesus, no. This was a group effort. I understand that in Hollywood those titles add to your salary value on future projects, but everybody contributed to this film and we should just be part of that creative group effort." And he said, "Okay." So, to your question, the look of the film for me was the art department and David Sperling, with some help from storyboard artists and a lot of other people. The art department created this other world, a kind of *Road Warrior* world, that was hyper real, and then David Sperling, who was the DP, made the choices, undoubtedly with Jimmy's help and all, but based on storyboards and meetings with

Tales That Will Tear Your Heart Out : John Mobray as a hardhat fighting off protestors at a local cemetery. Photograph courtesy Roy Frumkes.

everyone, for lenses, for polarizing filters, etc. Somebody, maybe it was me, it was so long ago I don't remember, made the decision to hire the two best graffiti artists in Brooklyn to put colorful graffiti all over so it wouldn't just be this bland-looking collision yard; there'd be color that could pop out at you with the right lenses.

When Jimmy did some Steadicam shots for me on Slime City the following summer, he already knew that the school wasn't going to allow him to use the film as his thesis.

I have enjoyed my years at the School of Visual Arts, and I feel that as schools go, they're very student-friendly and extremely alumni-friendly, compared with schools like NYU, which are more like corporations, where one sends a letter to the board of directors and never hears a thing. I've always found SVA to be pretty open. But that was, in my 30 years of being there, the biggest mistake they ever made, because he's become a real industry star—one of the few highly visible ones the school produced—and yet they didn't graduate him. They didn't accept the film, which they originally said they would, so he didn't bother graduating. And every year I bring it up: "You should give him that degree. He's an alumni that you really should be proud of." And it has not yet happened. I don't personally remember how upset he was, but I certainly feel he was betrayed. I think that the then-chairman, was, I don't know ... jealous, perhaps? But yes, that was Jimmy's thesis project.

What was the faculty's reaction toward you regarding the film?

There were some faculty members that were neither fond of me nor of the fact that I was doing the film. When it opened and *The New York Times* said, among other things, that "Had our forefathers anticipated *Street Trash* they would have re-thought the First Amendment," and then added, "The film was produced by Roy Frumkes, a teacher at the School of Visual Arts. Some recommendation."—one of the teachers there who didn't like me strode into David Rhodes' (the president's) office and slapped the review down on his desk. But I never heard a thing about it. And I really took that to be a measure of the school's liberality and their good attitude. I never got any flack from the administration, and I really was impressed by that.

You booked two back-to-back screenings of the film at the Ziegfeld, which had 1,500 seats, so everyone in the New York film community was invited.

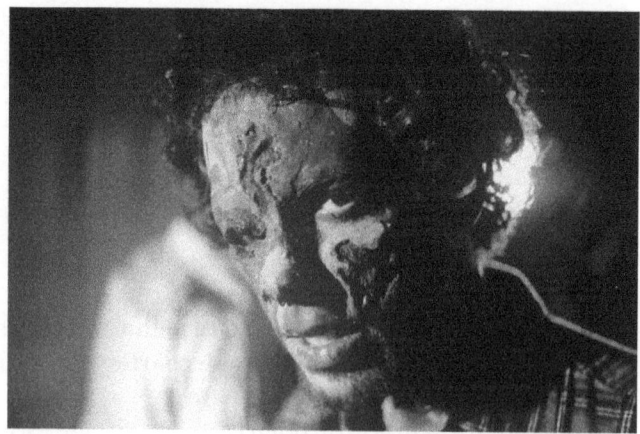

Roy Frumkes — writer, producer, director, and zombie in *Document of the Dead* (1985), re-released as the appended *Definitive Document of the Dead* (2009). Photograph courtesy Roy Frumkes.

Director Jim Muro (left) and screenwriter/producer Frumkes on the *Street Trash* (1987) location. Muro was Frumkes's student at the School of Visual Arts Photograph courtesy Karen Ogle.

We had money left at the end to do this correctly, and it cost $3,000 to rent the Ziegfeld for the night. And then the theater booking agent, probably seriously regretting their decision to rent the thing, insisted on charging us another $300 to put the name on the marquee, which we went for. I've always been of the opinion that we seriously wounded the Ziegfeld's aura, that the theatre was never the same after that night. The whole student body was invited, and then all the studios were invited to come and see it, so they'd see it with an audience. And that's really how the film was sold, because David Whitten came from Vestron, and was so impressed that he corralled me out in the lobby. There was a huge train of well wishers coming by and shaking my hand, and he was just hovering around like a little gnat, saying, "But listen, I know how to market this..." and I didn't know who he was, and I was replying, "Great, give me a card, I'll call you." He desperately wanted the film, he saw instantly that it had to be cut a bit for the U.S., but also he knew exactly how to market it. And he was eventually frustrated in his attempts to do so. I believe that had he had his way, it would have been a hit. I think it would have made the difference, because he really understood the marketing strategies of the exploitation genre.

I was thrilled to see our film projected in the most elegant theatre in New York, on that screen, looking as good as it did. A lot of things happened there that I was greatly amused by. I walked out into the lobby, oh, about 15 min-

Frumkes as a zombie in Tom Savini's *Night of the Living Dead* remake (1990). Photograph courtesy Roy Frumkes.

utes into the film, I just couldn't sit still, I was pacing, looking at people, watching the thing, listening to the audience. So I walked out into the lobby and I see Reeves and Jimmy Callahan, who shot *Burt's Bikers*, on the stairway, and I said, "C'mon, guys! The film is started." And they said, "We know." They were sneaking out! And I cracked up. Nothing could really hurt that experience. It was so much fun.

Street Trash veterans Frumkes (left), Nicole Potter, and James Lorinz reunited for *The Sweet Life* (2003), directed by Rocco Simonelli. Photograph courtesy Roy Frumkes.

It's up in the air whether or not the Street Trash *sequel is going to happen. What can you say about the story?*

When I was done with the script I sent it to five readers, which is standard practice in the industry. I waited for their comments to come back, and if three or more people agreed that something was not working I would address it. In addition to that, all their little comments, if I thought they were useful, I'd incorporate into the polish, so the film changed from 90 pages to 96 by the time I sent it to Jimmy. However, one of the readers said that it most reminded him of *Lost Highway*, in the sense of it being so much like the original and yet on another plane, like in another dimension. I really took that as a great compliment because that is what I was intending and I didn't know if anyone out there was going to get it just by reading the script. I didn't want to do a sequel, and I didn't want to do a remake; I wanted everyone to come back. A friend of Jimmy's put up a website and asked fans to contribute, to say what they wanted, and I was not surprised at all that they wanted to see everyone from the original return. They wanted the original filmmakers back, and they wanted the original cast back. And most of the cast died in the original, so the challenge was how to bring them all back? Some of them come back as themselves and some of them come back in new roles. But they all have kind of vestigial memories that this went down once, yet none of the memories are clear. Like Bill the Cop is taking his shirt off at one point, and someone says, "What's that scar on your back?" indicating the place where he was stabbed by Bronson's femur knife, and he says, "I think I got stabbed a long time ago." And then some of them use lines that they used in the original, but the responses are completely different. Like Bronson says to a winette, "I used to make women like you parade around the village bare pussy," and she fires back, "Was that the East Village or Greenwich Village?" So it'll be fun for fans of the original in that respect, and also just for being really strange by playing with what the concept of the film really is. It's very tight, it still has the *La Ronde* structure of the original, where there's an ensemble cast moving the narrative around, but the way it's passed from character to character is much more organic this time. Rather than allow for serious improvising on location, on the set, I brought the actors into my apartment who improvised on the first shoot—Lorinz, Vic Noto, Nicole, people like that—and I had them work with me here on tape so that I could get their improvs into the screenplay initially, rather than wait for them to do it during the shoot. I'm very happy with it, but who knows what's going to happen with it?

The Sweet Life, *which your former writing partner Rocco Simonelli directed, was the first feature you produced in a digital format.*

It was amazing, but low-budget digital just wasn't all there. It is now. Even by the time we completely finished the film it was better, because we wrapped shooting 2 weeks before 9/11, and we lost a full year due to that. Our editor was out in Brooklyn, Rocco was in Jersey, traffic was snarled for endless hours for many months, we just gave up on it for an entire year, we got very little done. The foreign sales had been so affected by 9/11 that it's never recovered. It affected how much money territories would spend acquiring product, and it affected them in what genres they would pick. Before 9/11, romantic comedies were selling. After 9/11, the genre was eradicated in terms of any foreign market potential. So that's been a terrible uphill battle and I've kept the investors appraised of it, I've cut out articles from *Variety* and other magazines that make it very clear what happened, and sent them to the investors, to let them know that had I anticipated 9/11 I would have done a horror film instead. Because horror is still the one market that is universally salable, the one genre that works in every territory. Obviously, things like action films work, but we couldn't have afforded something like that. Horror films don't need big names, or tons of money, just a unique idea, extremely well done.

You've advocated Syd Field's original Screenplay *book. Do you adhere to that, or are you pretty much on automatic when you write a screenplay?*

I've always been on automatic, but when I write a script for Hollywood I make sure that it — it tends to just happen—follows the paradigm. It's ingrained in me. But I do believe that distributors look for it. They've all taken his class or read his book. There's nothing more dangerous than a little bit of knowledge. The development process is a morbid one in respect to artistic integrity. And the Syd Field stuff has had both a positive and negative effect because the story department people and in-house producers are all waiting for us with this short-hand knowledge, to make sure that they can show their superiors that they know what makes a script good and, by making often-counterproductive notes, justify their paychecks. But balancing that, I think that American audiences are trained, unconsciously, to respond to the script structure Field and his cronies have promoted. For a foreign film it really doesn't apply, and for an indie film it doesn't necessarily apply.

The SAG Ultra Low Budget Agreement now makes it possible for even microbudget filmmakers to cast actors with some marquee value in their films. Do you recommend going that route?

Yeah, I do, for a couple of reasons. First of all, the reason SAG did it — and this is not one of the reasons for recommending it — was that they realized that they were losing out on a huge and growing market, that the industry was changing, that the indies were coming into their own, that the new "foreign film" was now the "indie film," and that they could get a piece of that market if they could only drop the severity of their contractual obligations, which were inappropriate for indie endeavors. So they created these different entry-level agreements for SAG, but didn't increase their staff. On the bigger budgeted film agreements, $2 million and up, SAG still sends people to visit sets to make sure that the actors are getting treated properly. But for the lower ones, even the "Limited X," the one I used for *The Sweet Life*, which is for bigger films [up to $200,000 budgets through post] than the super low budget one you mentioned, nobody checks up on you. They just want a report each week, and their little piece of the action. So you literally have this deal where you can use union people without supervision. You can see where that's great for us. We found there was only one person in the New York office dealing with all of the Limited X films, and that person was stretched too thin to really keep on top of us. I made sure that our assistant director was making the weekly reports, that every week they would get what they wanted so that they would never have reason to be concerned. Having attended to that, there was no follow up by them. So that is a huge positive. The other huge positive is that you can use all these gifted SAG actors. 90 percent of them aren't working regularly. And if you can write a one-week cameo performance into your screenplay, and fit it into their schedule, they'd love to do it. They prefer to be working. The agreements allow them to do it. It does get tricky if you happen to have a hit, because even on the "Limited X," for instance, stipulates (a) that any deferred portion of the SAG actors' salaries the rest of their salary, is placed in a first position, ahead of the investors, and (b) and worse, is that for each market you sell, you have to repay them the entire amount. So if I made a DVD sale on *The Sweet Life*, they all get about $12,000 worth of deferments out of first monies, then if I do a TV sale, $12,000 again, and if I do a limited theatrical, $12,000 again. Every market is a new total repayment to the SAG actors. So that, down the line, was a potential problem. We haven't done a TV sale yet, or a limited theatrical, (laughs), only an "incredibly limited theatrical," so it's not been a problem yet. But they get you in that way, if the film earns money, they're first in line, over and over again. They used that when I went in, as an argument to try to convince me to go for the larger, "Low Budget," two-million-and-under deal. They said, "Look, on the back end you're going to have to be doing this, and doing this. Why don't you just get it over with now?" But I couldn't because on the "Low Budget" deal, had we done it, everyone would have to have been SAG, even the extras. I couldn't afford it. I really couldn't afford it. Going "Limited X," we only had six SAG actors out of 35. It made a big difference financially in terms of how much we had to raise to shoot the film. And by allowing us to use just a few SAG actors, we added great and otherwise inaccessible talent to the cast, and name value as well. Joan Jett — it was really important to get a name. And on your super low budget film now, you can also get a name.

What are some of the basic business tenets you think micro-budget filmmakers need to follow to protect themselves?

The idea of using an entertainment lawyer is still a primary thing. Even if they're only looking over stuff that you've cribbed from the Internet or books, for contracts, releases, music licensing, options agreements, etc, they nonetheless have to be involved. And there are a number of them who will strike package deals. On *The Sweet Life* our lawyer did a package deal for a certain amount of money which got us all the way to distribution, including negotiating the music rights to two pieces. Unless you are protecting yourself from the very beginning, and doing things correct legally, you'll end up with a film which can't be released, and that's devastating. Most licensors look to see if all the legal stuff is in order, and if it's not, they can't touch your film. So you've gone through all this for nothing. That's one thing.

The other thing, which has become much more important since 9/11, since the turn of the century, is an understanding of marketing. That didn't use to be as necessary. Eventually, when you approached the distributors, you would all discuss it. But now, in order to raise the money, you have to have understood your markets, you have to be able to convince investors that there is a market, showing other, similar films that have done well, what you've done to guarantee them a market, and what things you left out of your script on purpose, so that the market will be satisfied, what you put in on purpose, that sort of stuff. I think they should be teaching pre-marketing now at all film schools. The extent to which pre-marketing is imperative is a really recent development, just because the market has shrunken so badly in the wake of 9/11, and investors now have a limited understanding of the importance of marketing that didn't exist when we did *Street Trash* and the other films before 2000.

You've been teaching for over 30 years. It's got to be a wonderful feeling to know you've had an impact on so many people's lives.

I love it. I really do. I didn't always feel that I was giving my best, I always felt that, even with teaching, I could have done better or found a better way to communicate knowledge, but I also knew I was combining entertainment and enlightenment in a way that other teachers weren't. I knew that a good way to get information across was to make it fun rather than just going by the syllabus. And it was nice to see that a lot of my ex-students remembered me, and used my examples—I saw things crop up in Spike Lee's early films that he had clearly gotten from my class. I went to a screening of *Never Die Alone* by Ernest Dickerson and he came in as a guest speaker. I hadn't seen him in 20 years, since I taught him at NYU's Graduate Film School. He just walked in and said, "Roy!" and ran over and gave me a hug. That's really nice stuff, I agree. It's been more gratifying than I expected it to be. I started teaching and for a long time taught because I needed a backup for filmmaking. The films were few and far between. But I've grown to really love it and today I teach more for fun than for money, and I look forward to it, to seeing reactions on their faces when I tell them the stories, when I print the legend, you know. I tell the stories my way and work up to a certain climactic surprise and hear the whole class gasp. Really, really great fun. Mainly I'm enjoying International Cinema, which is Film History as opposed to Production. The first class I do concerns post-holocaust films; I show *Hiroshima Mon Amour* and *Godzilla*, and after that, they know what they're getting into with me. They cannot believe I'm combining two films like that. So yeah, teaching has been more and more rewarding as the years went on, even though I'm doing it less and less.

12

Preproduction

Preproduction is the period following development of a motion picture and preceding its production. It is the phase of *preparation* for production, when you start executing all those great ideas you've been formulating in your mind. At this point, you should have two-thirds to three-quarters of your budget raised and in the bank if your production is dependent upon investor capital.

On a professional shoot in which you are paying your cast and crew, the accepted formula is that every week of production requires two weeks of full time preproduction. On a low budget film, this is probably unaffordable, but you will need at least one week of prep for every week of filming, and your special effects team may need longer. On a micro-budget film, your preproduction may only consist of weekday evenings after work and weekends preceding your shoot. There is nothing wrong with this, as long as you start early enough to put in the necessary time.

I shot *Undying Love* during a two-week vacation from my job, which means I worked right up until the first day of shooting and returned the day after filming. You make do with the time you have. But I spent my days off preceding the shoot painting my apartment for filming, meeting with production personnel, and making runs for equipment and expendables; I auditioned and rehearsed my actors at work. Needless to say, I had no time for anything else.

Getting Started

You have a completed screenplay and at least two-thirds of your projected budget in the bank. If you're smart, you've taken care of the necessary legal work to get this far. You've broken down your script and made your shooting schedule. Now you must cast your film, line up your crew, and lock in your locations. Some of these things will take all of your preproduction period to accomplish and some will even overlap production. So you'd better get started right away.

Casting

If you have a sizeable budget — say, anything over $150,000 — you may want to hire a casting director. This is especially useful when dealing with SAG actors, and if you want a SAG star. If your project exceeds $200,000, and you want a SAG star, then your entire cast must be SAG as well. A good casting director has already auditioned many of the actors who will show up at a casting call, and will recommend people to you they have worked with before. They know who is reliable and who is difficult, who delivers and who doesn't.

Anyone reading this book will probably do their own casting. I wrote *Slime City* with Robert Sabin in mind for the lead role; *Undying Love* for Tommy Sweeney; and *Naked Fear* for both of them. For each film, I took out a casting ad in *Backstage*, a weekly production trade paper, to fill other roles. When you take out such an ad, you must specify if your shoot is SAG or non-SAG; if you are paying your cast; and whether or not your film includes nudity. The ads I've taken out have resulted in thousands of headshots arriving my doorstep, many of them completely inappropriate for the characters I listed. They have also resulted in potential crewmembers submitting their resumes. That's how I found Scott Coulter and Tom Lauten, who did the special effects on *Slime City*, and John Rosnell, my DP on *Undying Love*.

When I received Mary Huner's headshot, I knew she was perfect to play Lori, the innocent female lead in *Slime City*. Even though there was no nudity, I had a harder time casting Nicole, the gothic vamp who seduces Robert's character and plunges him into a world of darkness. When you audition actors, you don't give them the whole script, but "sides"— pages containing one or two scenes featuring the role you're attempting to fill. I gave a complete script to one actress before auditioning her, which resulted in this message on my answering machine: "Mr. Lamberson, I read your script — what I *could* read of it — and I'm not interested." Remember what I said about artistic discrimination? Even if you specify "*Low Budget Horror Film*" in your ad, a certain number of actors who despise horror will waste their money and your time by submitting their headshots anyway.

I auditioned another actress for my heavy metal seductress, and thought she was perfect for the role. After reading the script, she called me in person: "I'm sorry, Mr. Lamberson, but I'm starring in a heavy metal exercise video for kids that I'm producing, and I don't think your film would be good for my image." I'm not making this up. We went into production without our Nicole, and I was too overwhelmed with 18-hour shooting days to lose sleep over it. When I saw how committed Mary was to the project, I said, "How would you like to play *two* roles instead of one?" She leapt at the opportunity, and Ivy Rosovsky, my costume designer, found a long black wig for her to wear in her new role. Add some long red fingernails and fetish costumes from Troma's *Class* of *Nuke 'Em High*, and Mary was unrecognizable as Nicole. It's a testament to her ability that most viewers and reviewers didn't realize she played both roles until seeing the end credits. This was not a brilliant move on my part; it was an act of desperation. And it happened again.

I wrote *Undying Love* for Tommy Sweeney, and I cast Julie Lynch as the girlfriend of his character. Once again, I had trouble casting my femme fatale. Scream queens were only just becoming popular with horror fans. I mentioned the possibility of Julie playing both roles as Mary had, and Julie loved the idea. But I didn't want to repeat that gimmick, so I cast Julie as the villainess and asked Mary to help me out by playing the "good girl." At least this time I was able to come up with a solution during preproduction rather than production. Unfortunately, the night before shooting was to commence, I received a call from Julie, whose agent had taken another look at my screenplay.

In *Undying Love*, Camilla sucks Scott Kelly's blood by performing oral sex on him. Even though my films contain little or no nudity, as a storyteller I've always enjoyed sexual themes; *Slime City* is about sexual frustration and AIDS more than anything else. In the *Undying Love* script, I had Camilla recline on her bed, hike up her skirt, and spread her legs. Looking down between her raised knees, Scott says, "You're bleeding," and Camilla answers, "I'm bleeding for *you*." Then Scott gets down on his knees and leans forward, presumably drinking Camilla's blood.

Julie said, "Greg, is he supposed to be drinking her discharge?"

"Yes," I said, "but it's all off screen."

"My agent says there's no way I can do that, and you can't edit in footage of another actress to suggest it's me."

My back was against a wall. If I'd said no, we'd either have had to postpone shooting, which wasn't a possibility, or hope we could cast the role with somebody else before the shoot was half over. I caved. Julie was professional to work with, and I thought she delivered an excellent performance, but I've always felt the film lacked "bite" without this scene.

When casting a micro-budget film, be sure your actors are committed to your project — and to your vision. On *Slime City*, I cast Terrence Spivey as a mugger. He was so dedicated to the project that I wrote vastly different roles for him in *Undying Love* and *Naked Fear*. I look forward to working with the same actors on my films, but it's more fun for them if they have something different to do each time.

For *Gruesome*, a short film/extended music video based on my novel *Johnny Gruesome*, I cast Erin Brown, aka "Misty Mundae," star of many POP Cinema sexploitation films, as Johnny's girlfriend. Her fee, airfare and hotel fare ate up half of my $2,800 budget, but I wanted an actress with a fan base for that role. My wife Tamar, who produced the short, agreed it was a justifiable expense and put up the money. Erin was always difficult to reach by phone, but she was a pro on set; money well spent.

The Crew

I liken hiring a film crew to those sequences in mercenary movies like *The Wild Geese* in which the perfect team is assembled. Sometimes these folks have worked together before and sometimes they'll meet for the first time at one of your production meetings. Let's identify some of the key roles you need to fill (unless you're a jack of all trades, like Scooter McCrae or J.R. Bookwalter).

The Director of Photography is probably the director's greatest collaborator during production. The D.P. helps the director frame shots and determines lighting schemes. Usually, he is one of the most experienced individuals on a film set, and the rest of the crew takes his opinions very seriously. I wrote *Slime City* knowing that Peter Clark would be my DP, and he turned out to be one of the most gung ho people I've ever worked with. I was saddened when he died in 2000.

On *Undying Love*, I hired John Rosnell, a "tinkerer" and one-man army who owned his own equipment. Mere days before production started, John's van was stolen, with most of his equipment — including his 16m camera — inside it, and he tried to back out of the production. I told him that was impossible, that he and I had already planned too much of the shoot together and I couldn't find such an important replacement on such short notice. He agreed to stay on, and we rented a camera — several, in fact. We used at least four on that shoot, and sometimes we didn't know where the camera for the next day was coming from. Because John was a tinkerer, every one of those cameras went back to its owner in better shape than it had come to us. Several months later, he got his camera back; the thief had taken it to a rental house for servicing, and the service person recognized the modifications on the camera as John's distinctive handiwork! Like Peter, John was a real workhorse. In 2002, he died from cancer while sitting at his editing console, working on *Town Diary*, a mystery film he co-produced.

The Sound Recordist is as important to a film as its DP. This is a critical lesson you would be well advised to heed. Many low budget films have been sunk by poor sound recording. *Naked Fear* has the best sound of any of my films — because we had to dub the entire thing! Get a good sound person with their own equipment and you'll be set. They'll be able to recommend an experienced boom person, or will work with a PA. If you're shooting a micro-budget film on Mini–DV, you might get by with a minimalist crew consisting of yourself, a producer, a DP, and a sound person. If you're shooting on 16m, you'll also need at least one assistant camera man (AC), and if you're shooting on 35mm you'll need two. Matthias Saunders, my DP on *Gruesome*, has sometimes worked two-camera shoots with a camera crew of five. It depends on your needs and budget.

Once you have different departments that need managing, you'll need an assistant director and a production manager. An assistant director actually runs

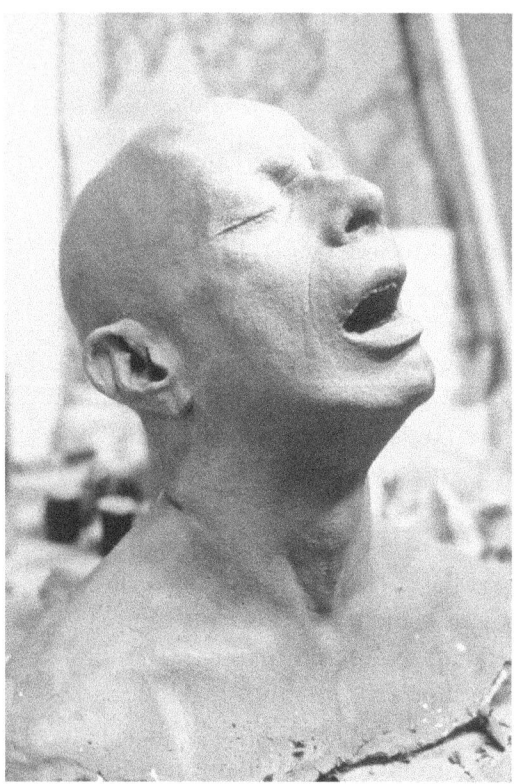 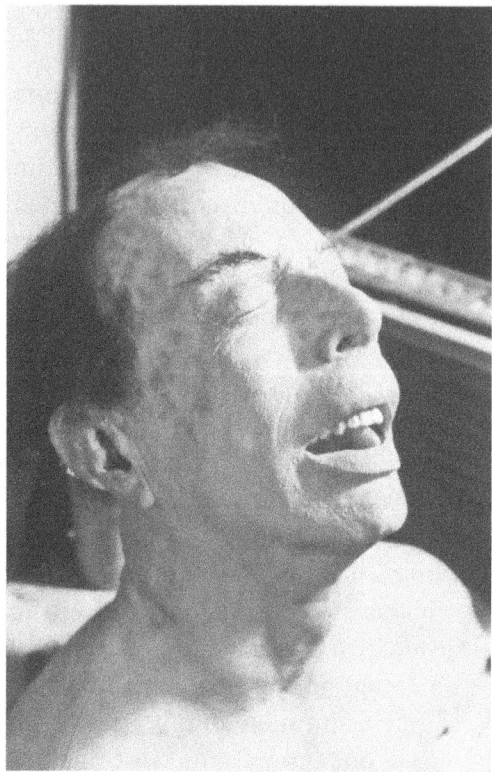

Above, left: Bust of actor T. Clay Dickinson as Hagard, a bum whose head gets smashed with a pipe in *Slime City* (1988). Photograph courtesy J. Scott Coulter. *Above, right:* The finished bust of T. Clay Dickinson for *Slime City* (1988), painted, with hair and teeth. Photograph courtesy J. Scott Coulter.

the set, not the director, and the production manager — who is usually the first person to arrive on set and the last to leave — is in charge off set; he is the person who dispatches production assistants on runs and makes sure other locations are ready for filming. When you have a SAG cast, you'll need a 2nd AD just to walk the actors to set, keep waiting actors in the loop, inform actors of upcoming set calls, and fill out daily SAG paperwork.

A *production designer/art director* and a *costume designer* will also add a lot of production value to your film, and production value will help you sell it. On *Slime City*, Bonnie Brinkley — who went on to be the art director on *The Daytrippers* and *Independence Day* — was my production designer. She made sure that all of the sets and props were colorful and consistent, and transformed a friend's apartment into an urban cave dwelling for Nicole (we later discovered that she used plaster to do this, rather than paper mache, which led to trouble with the landlord). The one time she was unavailable to come to a location was a complete disaster: in the dinner scene with Lori's parents, you'll notice that the walls are bare and white — and look horrible. Had Bonnie been there, she would have hung pictures on the walls or asked the DP to throw a gel on one of his lights. Never use blank white walls in your film — unless, as J.R. Bookwalter did in *The Dead Next Door*— it's to make a blood gag more effective.

Ivy Rosovsky was my costume designer on *Slime City*. I'd met her on the one day I worked for Troma, as a PA on *Class of Nuke 'Em High*, and she was the one positive thing to come out of that miserable experience. She purchased outfits for most of the important actors at thrift shops, and bought multiple copies of the costumes Robert and Mary wore during the film's gruesome climax — I believe five versions Robert's outfit Robert and 10 of Mary's. Anytime an actor is performing in a special effects scene involving gore or slime, you should plan on duplicate outfits. A good costume designer will also keep track of what costume an actor should be wearing in each

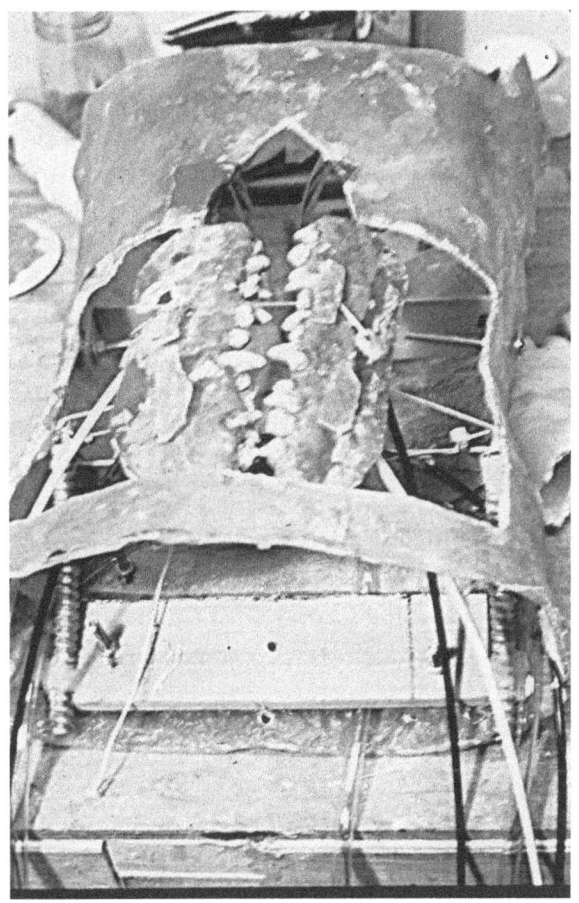

Full sized "stomach mouth" armature built by Tom Lauten and Scott Coulter for *Slime City* (1988). Photograph courtesy J. Scott Coulter.

scene, and will wash clothes not being used. Ivy also choreographed Nicole's "exotic dance" in *Slime City* and played the role of Lori's best friend.

There are, of course, other crew members, some of whom you may be able to do without and some of which you can't: a continuity person; drivers; grips and gaffers (hiring them is usually the DP's domain); set builders; and so on. How about straight make-up? You want your actors to look good, don't you? Especially that scream queen you shelled out good money to hire? Having your actors do their own make-up is a sure way to slow production, and you want them to spend their down time thinking about their performance, not their eyeliner.

There is one other essential person I want to discuss, who is potentially as important to a film's success as the DP and the sound recordist: the *still photographer*. You must have high quality stills of your production if you hope to sell and promote it down the line. You need scene stills and behind the scenes stills marketing purposes. This is crucial. On *Slime City*, Scott Coulter took a plethora of photos, many of which appear in this book.

On *Undying Love*, the only good still we took was of Julie Lynch biting off Robert Sabin's tongue; for everything else, we took actual strips of 16m footage to a photo lab and had them blown up. When E.I. Cinema licensed the film, they had to create video box art using an actress who isn't even in the film. On *Naked Fear*, we made an even more egregious miscalculation: we relied on computer "frame grabs" from the digital footage, but since we shot the film on Hi 8 video, they were practically useless.

You must have a set photographer, preferably someone whose sole purpose is to shoot photos. On *Gruesome*, I thought I'd learned my lesson: I assigned Jason Mager, my 1st AD and editor, to shoot stills. He got some good ones, but we shot in an enormous haunted house attraction, and it took us so long to move around the place that there was never enough time to grab all of the stills I wanted, particularly of Erin Brown. If the most important advice I give you in this book is to sign agreements with your partners and collaborators, and the second most important is to pay as much attention to your sound as to your picture, the third most important is to have a set photographer.

Eric Maché, who has created excellent graphics for me over the years, was the still photographer on *Frankenhooker* and *Basket Case 2*. Karen Ogle, who lived on the same floor as me at *Sloan House*, took the stills for *Street Trash* and *Brain Damage*, then parlayed her work on those films into a career. The photos that Eric and Karen took for these films are still used to promote them two decades later.

Soliciting Crew

When seeking crew members, you're best bet is to use people you've worked with before, or who have been recommended by people you trust, rather than strangers. When I was seeking crew members for *Gruesome*, I received the following e-mail after placing a casting ad:

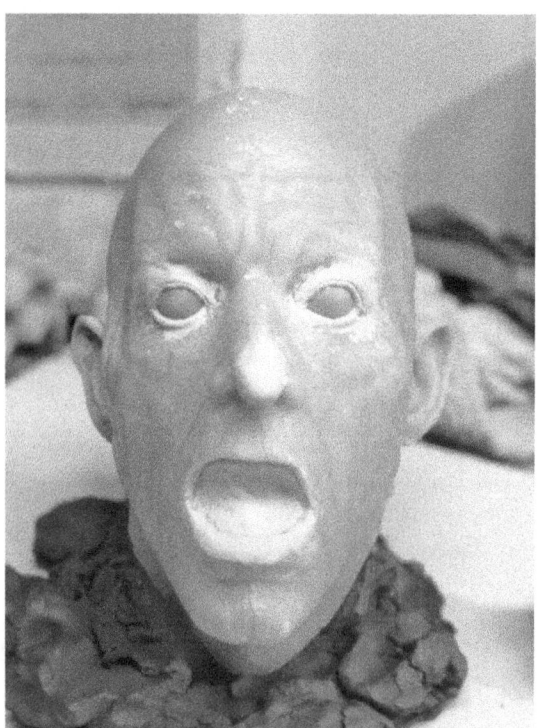

Tom Lauten's mechanical head of Robert Sabin for the climax of *Slime City* (1988). The mouth opened and closed, the eyes rolled up, and the head split open. Photograph courtesy J. Scott Coulter.

> Hi
>
> About me.....I am 50 years old. I made my first super8sound film when I was 13 "The Brain Suckers"......Made my last film in 1982.."Bad Dream....The Creep 2" It would be cool to work on another ....I'm a head banger from way back. I still have the camera and lights...Lighting is most inportant..even with video Contact me if your are intersted
>
> Fellow horror fan,
>
> Donald
>
> PS........Cool web site.

Unable to resist such a tempting offer, I e-mailed Donald a copy of my 10-page script, and he responded:

> GREG.....
>
> I think your project is too filled with sexual overtones.
> I thought you were gonna make a horror flick?
>
> GOOD BYE

I was a little offended that someone had accused *me* of writing sexploitation, so I sent Donald an e-mail explaining that sexuality is often a major aspect of horror, whether overt or as subtext, which resulted in this communication:

> Hey Greg
>
> I am sorry.....I got the wrong impression.
> What dose surreal mean?....I would still like to be part of your project. If you need costums..I have some.....Well......Anyways....Good luck in your venture.
>
> Yours truely
>
> Donny

Costumes?!? I decided to pass.

Special Effects

If, like me, your love of horror stems from a fascination with monsters, your project likely features special effect. There are many different kinds of special effects— Computer Generated Imagery (CGI); practical effects, optical effects, animatronics, stop motion animation, cell animation and rotoscoping, and latex make-up effects. I will admit to a bias against CGI; I don't like how it usually looks, even in most big budget productions, and it's extremely rare for low budget films to pull it off well (Ty West's *The Roost*, executive produced by Larry Fessenden, is one notable exception; those bats looked damned good). One of the reasons for this is that CGI is extremely expensive if you're not able to do it yourself. I also find that CGI effects are easy to identify, which prevents a sense of wonder on the part of the audience. Give me some latex appliances, miniatures, and stop motion any day. As Devi Snively points out, CGI can be used effectively to enhance these techniques.

Due to the nature of horror films, it's easy for me to hypothesize that your film features latex appliances and possibly some simple animatronics. On *Slime City*, Scott Coulter was in charge of doing the make-up appliances, while Tom Lauten created the mechanical effects. To achieve the three different stages of make-up that Robert Sabin wore, Scott and Tom first did a life-cast of Robert, and then they sculpted the appliances on the likeness of his head that emerged from the mold. To enable our "crawling brain" to work — and for Robert's decapitated head to continue speaking — we built a fake kitchen floor which was elevated two feet above the real floor. We cut a hole in the stage floor and Robert sat beneath it, his head protruding through the floor. Tom operated the rod puppet of the brain from a similar position. There were many other effects — a prosthetic of a chomped off arm for Terry Spivey to wear; a gelatin-like yogurt that "breathed" when Mary picked up its container; a "stomach mouth"; and various traditional gore effects. It took time for Scott and Tom to create these effects, sculpt the appliances, and paint the various severed limbs. We paid them for a month of pre-production, and they worked hard. The most exciting period I've ever experienced as a filmmaker was when I rode my bike from my Brooklyn apartment to theirs, where they did all this work, a mile away. It was the first time I saw my creative ideas brought to life by other people. You must allow ample time for your effects to people to design and build the monsters and props for your film.

Undying Love and *Naked Fear* required only simple blood effects, so Craig Lindberg needed very little preproduction time. On *Plutonium Baby*, the actress hired to play the mutant creature freaked out during the headcasting process, and Daniel Frye (who handled straight make-up chores on *Slime City*) stepped into the role. It's a good idea to shoot test footage of effects whenever possible, but I have to admit I've never done so.

Storyboards

It is up to each director whether he wants to use storyboards. On *Slime City*, I storyboarded every shot in every scene of the film — and threw the storyboards away after the first day of filming. On *Undying Love* and *Naked Fear*, I didn't even bother. *Plutonium Baby* barely had a script, forget about storyboards. I remember Frank using shot lists on *Brain Damage*. A shot list made up by the director and the DP is very useful. I do believe that action scenes and scenes involving complicated special effects should be storyboarded.

Location, Location, Location

You need a place to set your film, don't you? Unless you're shooting your actors against a green screen and creating your backgrounds in postproduction, you need a physical location to shoot. Hopefully you kept this in mind while writing your screenplay. If you have some money to work with, you may hire a location scout to search for your locations, and a location manager to make sure that utilities are working and parking spaces are reserved when the crew arrives. Most likely, you'll do your own location scouting. It's a good idea to visit each location with your DP, sound recordist, and production manager so that your key people can identify issues and concerns which need to be dealt with prior to shooting. You need signed releases for most locations, just as you do for cast members (and crew members, so you can utilize behind the scenes stills in which they appear).

When I wrote *Slime City*, Peter Clark and I lived in Astoria, Queens. By the time we made our movie, I'd moved to Bay Ridge, Brooklyn. We filmed the exterior of the building outside Peter's Astoria apartment; the hallways in Marc Makowski's Bronx apartment building; and the interiors in my apartment, which was on the bottom floor of a two-family house. We also used my porch for a psychic's parlor and the living room — which we walled off with a swinging bookcase — as another character's apartment, and the basement as The Basement. When SVA wouldn't allow us to film at the school, we filmed three scenes outside a Brooklyn high school, and Peter applied Vaseline directly to the lens to obscure the school's name on the building.

For *Undying Love*, we used the same apartment for the hero's crib, the vampires' lair — and a French restaurant! We also used the basement for a drug den and a morgue. When we needed footage of Tommy riding the NYC Subway, do you think we spent thousands of dollars on additional insurance and permits? Of course not; as guerrilla filmmakers, we simply "stole" the shots we needed. By the time we shot *Naked Fear*, I'd moved to a studio apartment in Manhattan, so we shot that one in the New Jersey apartment of my assistant director, Ed Walloga.

On *Plutonium Baby*, the producers shot in the Connecticut woods owned by the Rockefellers — without the Rockefellers knowledge. They were unable to find the cabin called for in the script, but they did find a children's playhouse which was at least the right height — which is why you never see more than one corner of the cabin in any scene. When they had to shoot additional scenes because they only had half a movie, we shot in Central Park, near Harlem. Surprisingly, the footage matched — because in both the Connecticut footage and the Central Park scenes, you can see cars in the background that shouldn't be there!

Roy Frumkes wrote *Street Trash* around a collision yard because Jimmy Muro's father owned just such a business. On *Brain Damage*, Edgar Ievans and Frank Henenlotter rented three floors of a warehouse on 9th Avenue and 33rd Street. We converted one floor into our production headquarters — a soundstage, a stop motion animation studio, Edgar's office, a production office, and the production coordinator's office. On another floor, we built the special effects lab, and on the remaining floor we built living quarters for the effects crew. We built all of the apartments seen in the film, as well as the apartment building courtyard and the nightclub. The only locations we visited were streets, a restaurant, and the Muro collision yard. We also spent three hours on the NYC subway, which I'm sure cost a pretty penny. *Brain Damage* had a $900,000 budget, and that was in 1986 dollars.

There was one other location: the exterior of a sleazy hotel that actor Rick Herbst had to enter for an establishing shot. Frank wanted to use the Sunshine Hotel, down on Bowery, and he dispatched me and Joe Warda to get it. Through some minor investigation, Joe and I discovered that the building was owned by the Bari family, of Ray Bari's pizza. After spending a few minutes at another Bari establishment — where a guy walked in off the street and tried to sell us scuba diving equipment! — we were directed to a storefront which reminded me of a real estate office. Inside, after stepping over the resting figure of the largest Doberman I've ever seen, and past a very tall man with very large biceps, straight out of Central Casting, we stood looking up at a gray haired man in a dark suit, who sat behind a desk on a level three feet higher than the one we were on. I explained to him what we wanted, and that we only needed an hour to do it. I told him we didn't have much money, but would gladly give him screen credit in addition to a small fee.

The man shook his head. "No screen credit. The Bari name mustn't appear anywhere in the film. You can shoot at the hotel for one hour for $75.00 — but every additional hour will cost you $200."

We got the shot in an hour.

Shooting days can be 18 hours long — or longer. If you're going to use anyone's house or apartment besides your own, don't give false impressions to the people you're imposing on. Film crews tend to be large, with people coming and going; anyone who says, "You won't even know we're here!" is a liar or a fool. The last thing you want is to be told you can no longer film at a location before you're finished with it.

13

Larry Fessenden
THE ART OF HORROR

Earlier in this book, I dismissed the auteur theory, which supposes that the director is the "author" of a motion picture. But there are exceptions and Larry Fessenden is one of them. Larry takes horror and filmmaking very seriously, and there are reasons why he is such a respected figure in indie circles. He is a true artist, but he's also a supporter of independent filmmaking, and has helped many other filmmakers, on his own and through his Scareflix production company. Like Dr. Frankenstein, he is meticulously constructing a body of work intended to enlighten more than terrify —*thinking man's* horror films.

Did you grow up in an artistic environment?

No, no, my parents were liberal Republicans in the 70s. My father was a banker, my mom worked for committees, she worked for a hospital and the Museum of Natural History, she busied herself with three kids and with this volunteer work, and my dad was nine-to-fiver, though in those days it was eight-to-seven, of course. And he would do banking deals with China, so he was off and away for months at a time.

Did any artistic adults influence you as a child?

Well, I went to an amazing grammar school which had a lot of eccentric teachers and it seemed to be modeled on somewhat of a British styled school, an all boys' school, on the upper East Side (of New York). I have to say a lot of the teachers inspired me in one way or another. And, you know, I was the only one in my family who took piano lessons and I was always a drawer, so it's an interesting thing, you have to say, that artistic impulse may in fact be innate to the character.

Were you a Super 8 filmmaker?

Absolutely. I made *Dr. Jekyll and Mr. Hyde* with a dear friend when I was in 7th grade. It's one of the few movies I didn't finish but there's still existing clips. In fact, we shot in the house we would film *Habit* in years later, you know the country house on the beach. By 1985 I'd made about 50 Super-8 movies a few of which are still watchable.

Did you enroll in film school or determine your major later?

By then I was completely obsessed. I did, though, want to be an actor more than anything. I went to a prep school, the same one our fearless leader George Bush went to, once again steeped in the privileges and feeling completely like an outsider. The focus was on sports and I was, you know, not the nerd, but the goth, if you will, it wasn't really goth in those days, but as far as there were cliques like any other period in life and I was that guy, basically the arty guy, because what happened was I did branch out from horror into other interests. I loved Marty Scorsese and some of those guys, basically the whole 70s oeuvre. I was kicked out of Andover and I showed the admissions guy at NYU three of my Super 8 movies that I'd made by then and that got me into the summer program and I did well enough in this writing course and then went on to get into the school, which, by the way, was hardly an accomplishment because we paid the full tuition, darn right they'll take whoever. (laughs)

Did you know you were going to turn your college film* Habit *into a feature some day?

Maybe in the back of my mind. It seemed to be my life story, the pathos of not getting the right girl and being basically pathetic and a drunk has dogged me my whole life. Years went by, and in fact some of it came true, I met this French girl I became obsessed with, that's who I was with when my tooth got kicked out. I followed her to France, she humiliated me more, you know, it was all just life draining. Anyway, it seems to be the story of my life, and I always say I'll make *Habit* again, some version of the same story, but anyway, maybe I'll just do something similar. Speaking of this interview, I just find it utterly incredible how similar our vampire movies are. In a way, it's an exquisite celebration of how two guys from different backgrounds basically going for a similar thing and making sort of the same observations and having an appreciation for melding horror traditions and some kind of realism.

I call yours the art film with some horror conventions and mine the horror film with some art film conventions.

Yes, fair enough, I like that, we've got to do a double feature before we're too old.

How did you decide to make* No Telling *your first feature?

I hooked up with Beck Underwood and she loved the idea of *Habit*. I think she saw the original and we started writing a new version that would be my breakout first film. And then an unfortunate thing happened which really

David Van Tieghem and Miriam Healy-Louie in a dramatic moment from *No Telling, Or the Frankenstein Complex* (1991). Photograph courtesy Larry Fessenden.

changed my life, quite literally. My old comrade, ironically, the cameraman from the original *Habit*, gave me *Silent Spring*, which is a famous tome on environmental concerns and I became very possessed, it seemed to touch on this melancholy nerve in me about the way people treat the environment and just the basic human arrogance which I fought against all through my fancy prep school, and it really crushed me and we veered away from making *Habit* and we started writing this animal rights movie called *No Telling*. Me and Beck wrote it and we would go to animal rights meetings, all this kind of thing, and just became immersed in all the real facts about animal experimentation and pesticides in agriculture, all this stuff which no one wants to hear about, certainly not in an entertainment. But we wrote what seemed like a pretty fun script because it was still in the horror realm, it was a Frankenstein story. I believed in it and I was very excited and I tried a lot of different ways to raise the money with different kinds of producers. It was a very exciting, time consuming process.

Eventually I hooked up with an old friend who wanted to be a producer; she'd worked for Dino De Laurentiis. We basically conspired to get money from more private sources, basically, family members of mine and what I could pull together, and then we embarked on this indie film adventure in upstate New York. And you know, when it was finished I thought, this is a very accom-

Larry Fessenden stars as Sam in *Habit* (1997), his semi-autobiographical vampire exploration. Photograph courtesy Larry Fessenden.

plished piece, and I was very excited about it, and we went to The Independent Film Market in New York and there was sort of a buzz and I felt I had arrived. Then it became very clear that this was not a commercial thing at all and I became quite bitter over the next few years as it got no traction, and I think it's kind of a cool movie, and very heartfelt and kind of evocative, but none of this seemed to matter. I thought Sundance would take it; I thought, Robert Redford's an environmentalist, he'll understand. But of course he doesn't choose the movies. We went to some festivals and it had a small life, had foreign sales but it was a great disappointment. It took seven more years to get a video distribution deal.

Basically what happened is I stopped, and it just shows the dichotomy in my life, I pulled back and I eventually ended up being an actor in Kelly Reichardt's film *River of Grass* and just put my entire operation on the shelf and back pedaled and just left my ambitions at the door and ended up editing her movie for a year and serving her, and I got some nice notices about acting in that, but it was really about serving another vision and it was a way to lick my wounds and pull back. Then what happened is, working on her little film and seeing that it was well received gave me the courage to return to the *Habit* script Beck and I had started and I wrote it while in Sundance with Kelly's movie, and in subsequent weeks, but very quickly, and it was so intuitive, it

Sam (Larry Fessenden) and Anna (Meredith Snyder) exchange bodily fluids in the vampire drama *Habit* (1997). Photograph courtesy Larry Fessenden.

Wendigo **(2001) is told from the point of view of young Miles (Erik Per Sullivan). Photograph courtesy Larry Fessenden**

was everything I knew, writing *Habit*, and I hooked up with my buddy, this crazy maniac Dayton Taylor, and we produced the movie and that, to me, is still the true expression of what I have to offer as a filmmaker, because it was shot with seven people, just very succinct.

Habit *was shot by seven people?*

We just had seven people on the entire movie. It was just a very raw, true, guerrilla production shot for sixty grand all over New York, out of a Honda. You know, the lighting was incredibly spare; I don't even remember movie lights. We worked with practicals, and Christmas lights and kino flos and it was so artfully done by Frank DeMarco. It was just a great converging of talent, me, Dayton, and Frank.

That surprises me because one of the things that shocked me while watching the "making of" on the* No Telling *DVD was the enormity of the crew.

That's the point, dude. That thing became the most political, preposterous nightmare, with people back stabbing and complaining, people at all levels of ability, all of these attitudes, people who shot rock videos who thought they therefore knew how to make a feature. I loved my DP, David Shaw was wonderful, but he was overwhelmed by his crew, the politics of trying to do it environmentally, the souring there, some of my old friends involved who seemed to be jealous for my attention. In this effort to make a "real" movie I gave up all my principles and instincts, which is why *Habit* was a real return to who I am as a filmmaker. I'm fond of *No Telling* but it was a bad experience.

What was the budget on No Telling?

It was like seven hundred grand. So that's why when I say I believe in low budget film, it's because right from the start I've done big budget — obviously that's not big budget but in 1990 there was money there to play with. I mixed at Todd-AO and had a wonderful, award winning mixer, Rick Dior. It was, somehow, the climate that you could do things like that at this budget, but I question all of it, you know? It was no way to begin my career, and then the irony was realizing that the subject matter was so obscure and so repellent to people, and maybe my handling of it, but in any case, it was very humiliating. And I felt silly that I had spent that kind of money on something when I could have made that movie with a Bolex, which was how Beck and I both pictured it, much more raw. So it's a movie that got too big for itself.

And then *Habit* was really more to my taste. And then *Wendigo* was a matter of climbing back up the ladder with a new producer who brought a little money to the table, and of course this time we had wonderful actors and that scale worked for me, although to be honest I still bristled at some of the politics. I don't like the egos involved in film. I find them extremely disconcerting.

The scores for your films are very well thought out.

If not a musician, I'm deeply fond of music and opinionated about it. With *No Telling* I was in a Michael Nyman phase, which is the guy who scored all the Peter Greenway films, and my old musical friend and collaborator Tom Laverack was too, and so we went in that direction. It was his first score, and I think it's totally successful, there's a real Nymanesque minimalism. And then of course there's a couple of songs in there by him where I played sax and we did our thing, we'd played together and recorded as Just Desserts since the 80's. And then with *Habit* I went to another old friend who was a legitimate classical composer in the blossoming and he did that score, and once again Tom Laverack contributed to some of the songs, and then *Wendigo* was a whole new and exciting collaboration with a woman named Michelle DiBucci. But as you say, each time I spent a lot of time with the composers and to me it's an essential part of the movie. You'll notice, at the same time, that considering it's a horror movie, none of these scores have particularly scary scores. And it's something that I sometimes regret. Can't I just entertain my audience? (laughs) Why can't I make them scared? But really it's so obvious that my agenda is to address the melancholy of life, the loss. What's frightening in the world is when that thing you love is taken away from you, be it life's breath, or trust, or an ability to believe in something or losing a loved one through violence, but always — it's about the melancholy. So that's my curse.

The worst evil is human (John Speredakas) in Fessenden's mystical *Wendigo* (2001). Photograph courtesy Larry Fessenden.

There's a level of micromanaging required to direct a film that some people don't possess. They just don't seem to care about all these different details.

I do micromanage, that's just my nature. I basically edit my films, and if I'm told I can't I'll hover and re-edit whatever's been done. I have to intuit the film and in the end every thing has to make sense to me. There's still things that exist in parts of my movies where I haven't been able to accomplish either what I wanted or, the ones that haunt me the most are when I sort of gave in to make somebody feel good…

I know exactly what you're talking about.

They really wanted that shot in there, or they thought it shouldn't be a dissolve but a cut and I guess in the moment it seemed like the nicer thing to do and now I'm like, "Oh, my God, I'm the only one who has to live with this movie the rest of my life and I'm the only one who notices it. Why did I allow a moment of social generosity or waffling to basically keep me up at night the rest of my natural life?"

For many years I couldn't watch* Slime City. *And then when it came out on DVD I was able to appreciate it for what it is. But there's always those moments that send chills of regret through your body, that you wish you had done differently.

Fessenden approves a shot on location for *The Last Winter* (2007). Photograph courtesy Larry Fessenden.

Oh, God, dude, it's true. I'm notorious for re-cutting my movies after they screen and just never being quite settled with anything. I just watched *Wendigo* recently. Typical of me, I never give myself space to actually watch it properly, I just caught part of it, and then another day I thought, "Oh, I just want to see how it plays out," and I watched another part, and I was quite pleased with it until the end, and then I was quite confounded by my choices (laughs).

Like what?

To be honest, just the image of the monster continues to elude me, and this obsession, like Lucas, and it's not to make it more real or CGI, but just to sort of correct the angle. You know, it's a very elusive, mysterious image that I'm after, something from my childhood that I can't even draw: I don't know what it is, it's maddening. And you know, it serves a purpose in the story, I actually stand by that movie in every regard, in terms of its strange, truncated storytelling. But just the imagery itself I—and I'm talking about four shots, so you'll see, I will fix it! I'm going to go in there, I can't take it anymore! I was actually depressed for several days after I saw it recently. I thought, "That was a total mess. What did I do?"

While you were seeking distribution for Habit, and I was doing the same for Undying Love, Michael Almereyda came out with Nadja and Abel Ferrara

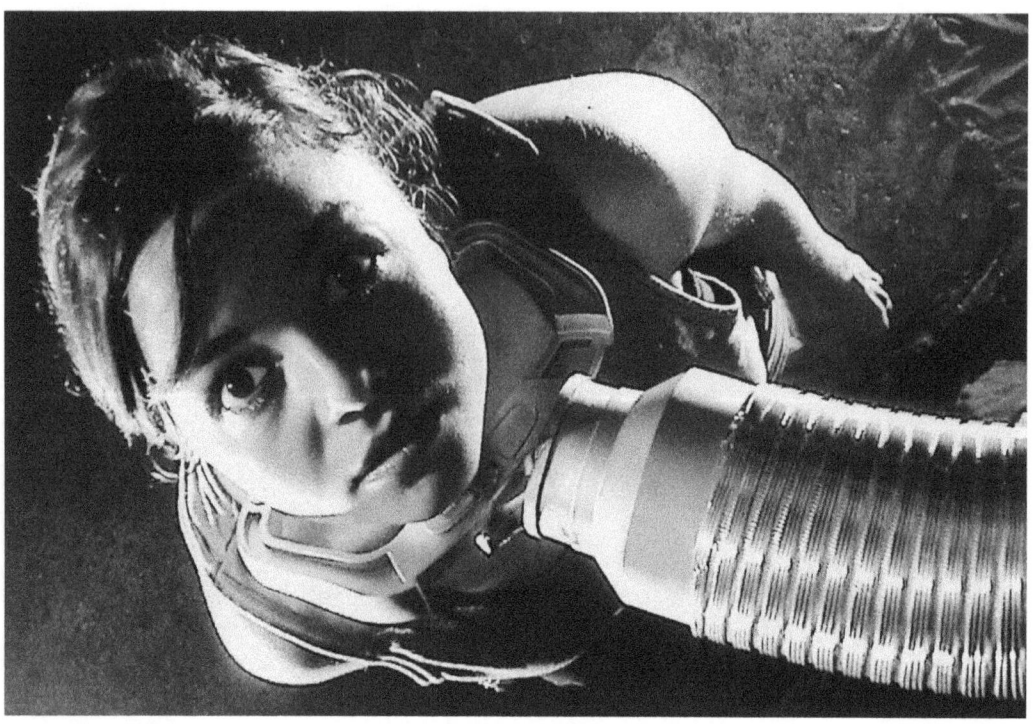

James McKenney's *Automatons (2006)*, a somber science fiction film produced under Fessenden's Scareflix banner. Photograph courtesy Larry Fessenden.

with* The Addiction. *Both were downtown vampire films shot after our films but released before them.

Oh, yeah, dude, there's no getting over that, to be quite honest. I love Michael, he's a beautiful character and I believe in his pure vision, but the fact is *Nadja* and *The Addiction* were made after our movies, and then furthermore, in my case, both of them were at Sundance the year before my film was ready for presentation and America said, "We've had enough of that." I credit that with my entire career arc because I think — and forgive me for not including you in this particular moment — but I have to say, I think *Habit* was a good enough film that it should have been in there and I should have been recognized and things should have happened for me. But, in fact, the opposite was true. I was left with this movie that I thought was a pariah, and I was like, "What the fuck?" And it took me months and months to figure out how to go forward, I was quite devastated. 'Cause believe me, I'd already made *No Telling* and that had been rejected, and I said, "Well, I understand. Nobody gets that movie." But *Habit* seemed to me to be a solid independent film by an auteur, which I thought was what Sundance was all about.

Did winning the Indie Spirit Someone to Watch Award for* Habit *generate any Hollywood interest?

Yeah, in fact it did. It was a year after those initial disappointments. So after the award I was in the trades, and I ended up taking all these incredibly cool meetings in Hollywood, James Cameron's company and some others, and I had a new script, but it wasn't a horror movie, and therefore a whole new level of absurdity and embarrassment entered into my world. I was trying to pitch this movie called *Hector Dodges*, about a guy who thinks the world is going to end and everyone makes fun of him, and one day something happens and everyone joins him in his paranoia. It was going to be my Millennium movie. I wanted to make it in '99, and finish it, and have it be my comment about entering the 21st century. Call me pretentious, but dude, it anticipated 9/11 because it was really about this urban dweller who was totally paranoid, he hated to fly, he hated tall buildings, hated everything, felt that the sky was going to fall down on him, and everybody makes fun of him and then one day it happens and the world becomes as paranoid as him. And then in the end it was about the power of love and it was supposed to be Frances McDormand and Benicio Del Toro. It was beautiful, lovely. So I was pitching it all over town on *Habit's* coattails, and everybody was like, "We thought you were a horror guy!" So they sent me home, packing, humiliated, and that's when I thought, "You know, fuck this. All right, fine. I'm going to write *Wendigo* because it's always obsessed me." So I wrote *Wendigo* in three weeks and started pitching that, and had much better luck, no longer with Hollywood, but in the New York scene again, and eventually hooked up with Jeffrey Levi-Hinte, who said, "You're so well prepared, you have every drawing, every concept, you've got the location — sure, let's do it. I'll find you the money." And that's how that happened.

I remember you were dissatisfied with the monster in some of the early test footage. Were the effects you ultimately used — the sped up imagery and stuff — part of your original plan or a reaction to some of these early tests?

Now that was very much my plan and I'm very happy with that stuff. It's beautiful, shot by Jay Silver. And speaking of getting a little distance from a project, when I watched the movie again just a month or so ago I thought, "Damn, that stuff is just what I want it to be." The issue was the monster suit I had made. I'm a bit of a literalist, you know, with monsters, as well as into the metaphor of it all. I loved the creature as it was designed by Tim Considine, but then I left town, and when he showed up on set with the finished suit, it was covered in this shag rug, and I said, "What the fuck, what happened to my monster?" It used to be this beautiful, svelte rubber suit that James Godwin fit into, now it was a shapeless wookie. I never recovered from the shock. And this is what you and I were talking about earlier, that moment when you don't assert yourself. And I still have this problem as an artist and a person. I just couldn't figure out how to tell him the suit was all wrong now, and so the monster we filmed was this big furry creature and I was very unhappy with it.

So even after I got this completely cool review from the Slamdance screening, from *Variety*, I basically went out and re-filmed the monster and this time I tore all the fur off, and because of a series of circumstances there could no longer be a person inside. So now it became a whole other thing. And that's not quite right, either. It's kind of closer to what I wanted. But all I'm trying to tell you is, I still don't have it. There's all this weird imagery in the movie and you can actually see the furry creature, and you can see the one that's got no fur on it. Obviously what I'm going for is this sort of impressionistic, sort of weird glimpse of something, and I think it's close to working, but it's not what I wanted. And it's not that I wanted a perfect CGI monster, it's just that I wanted the right kind of abstract imagery. And that's very, very subtle, and I don't know how to have gotten it once it went wrong, I was constantly trying to catch up, you know, never got my footing back. There are a few moments in the reshoot that are perfect, with the music and sound, so the mood of the film does work for me.

When you see the unvarnished latex appliances, they seem startlingly realistic. And then the moment they put the finishing touches on them, suddenly they're not real. When they make it not look rubbery, it looks more like rubber.

Yeah, there's an image in the "making of" where the puppeteer is inside the rubber and he does this move, and I edited it so it's exactly the moment that I want to look at, and to me that would be so cool if that thing was running around. But that's not what I got. I got this thing with a rug on it. This is why I worry about my future. I just don't know if I was making the right decisions. You see that that guy is really cool when he's walking on those legs in the office area, you're like, "This is awesome!" But it wasn't a practical way to make a movie about a stag monster. I should have gotten dancers on stilts, or something—I should have gotten something else. But I failed to do that. These are the regrets that I live with. I actually like my films to the extent that I believe in the themes and I like the sense of the camerawork. In other words, I can live with that. But I can't understand why I keep fucking up some of these managerial things of getting artists to shine under my tutelage.

It makes you appreciate and long for the perfect producer, who can come in and push you in those directions and then be the heavy fist.

You said that so well, dude. In a way, Dayton was that on *Habit*. In a way I don't think *Habit* could have been much more realized than it was at that budget. I obviously have regrets, but they've faded somewhat. Jeff Levi-Hinte has been an enormous supporter and he loves a great deal about what I'm trying to do, but he doesn't really understand the monster element, so those parts have been left to me. I need somebody who really understands that element of my work and how to push those elements to get them right. So when Guilermo

Del Toro teased me and said he wants to produce something I went, "Well, there's a producer who might save me from myself." Because he would know how to keep saying, "Are we getting what we're looking for here, in this fantasy element?"

***Wendigo* is very subjective from the boy's point of view.**
 Exactly. That gave me an excuse, for one thing, in that movie, to just go hog wild with crude effects. That was part of the premise. That's the whole set up.

And yet, the emotional connection that I felt was to Jake Webber's character, the father who fears that he won't be around for his son.
 Ah, I'm so glad you say that. I wrote it right before I had a kid, and filmed it when I had a kid. And when the two of them, Jake Weber and Erik Per Sullivan, are talking on the hilltop before he gets shot, and sort of talking about what philosophy is, when we filmed that I was so moved by the frailty of the father-son relationship. You know, you try to teach your kid that things are what they are, but you know, lurking, perhaps in the next moment, is disaster.

You push the real action back almost as far as possible.
 Many people have said, "Hey, how about *Wendigo* without that silly monster?" But that's always been my curse. It's the same thing with *The Last Winter*. It's going along as this relatively well observed character study and then somehow it veers into the supernatural. I think what obsesses me is structuring my movies so that they enter into the world of the mythic, because my feeling is that when things get truly chaotic, the mind starts to create mythic tropes to even understand where we are. It's almost like we have to reduce things to a mythic narrative when things go wrong. That's just the human instinct, the instinct for the story, which is what we're talking about when I say you can have crude effects and yet still tell a story. And similarly, as life un-frays and becomes more chaotic, there's this need to assign archetypes. So that's what happens in my movies: the archetype takes over, the mythology takes over, almost a cliché starts to take over what I've tried to lay down in a very realistic framework.

When you bump the logos for Glass Eye Pix and Scareflix at the start of a film, does that mean the film is a joint venture between two companies that you own?
 That's right. Of course it's relatively arbitrary, there's no legal binding going on, the films are copyrighted by Glass Eye Pix. That's the umbrella company. The idea of Scareflix is just to kind of give it a little bit of a brand name — it's branding, dude. And what Scareflix is supposed to indicate is a very low budget, perhaps unusual genre fare that seeks to celebrate ingenuity and resourcefulness over gloss. I don't call my films Scareflix. If I make a cheap film,

which may very well be my fate in the future, if I make something for under half a million dollars, or under a hundred thousand in fact, I might call it a Scareflick.

How did you decide to create this other brand within the company to help other people make these films?

I enjoy stepping back from the driver's seat and helping other filmmakers realize their vision. It gives me an ability to recharge. In fact, I often gain a sense of confidence because I realize I have opinions and something to offer other people. Often my own films have not been immediately embraced and I always come away a little battered, *Habit* being an example. And you know, finding the money and getting it all together takes years and years, so I've always talked about just encouraging these young folks to make really cheap movies the way I used to, meaning *Habit* and the movies before *No Telling*. And then James McKenney, who was working for me then, sort of challenged me, he said, "You say you want to do this, you want to be a Roger Corman, well here's a script I've got, wanna make it?" The reason Jim's proposal was appealing was that it was exactly what I wanted: He already had basically a whole team of collaborators ready to work on it. What he needed was some money and an umbrella company and some encouragement, and that's exactly how we did it.

This was *The Off Season?*

That was *The Off Season*. That was the first Scareflick. Let's face it, I think Jim was smart, he could see I was restless, I was sort of in between projects, trying to figure out what I was going to do next. *Habit* and *Wendigo* had both brought in a little money, so it felt like there was some money that could be applied toward a very small film. So he challenged me to do it. So he took me out for a few drinks and I said, "Okay, let's do it. Here's a tiny amount of money." And that's how the whole thing was born. And a couple years later that film made money for us, so we tried it again.

Ti West is a kid that I had known through Kelly Reichardt, she taught him at SVA (School of Visual Arts) and he had interned for me even before I knew Jim, and I had said to him "I like your short horror films," and you know, "If you ever write a script, kid, come and see me." So he waited a couple of years until he graduated, and I think the day after he graduated he came over and he started pitching me all these ideas. It was funny, he has that kind of mind. He didn't have a script that he wanted to make, he wanted to make a movie and he was willing to pitch me anything til I bit. He pitched me a voodoo movie and I was like, "The voodoo thing just doesn't work for me." And maybe it didn't make sense at that budget. And then he pitched me rabid bats that turn people into zombies, and I said, "Now we're talking." I think he went away and wrote it in three days and came back. I really admire Ti's drive. And once again, here's a guy who essentially did a lot of on the ground producing. And then I hired a producer to help him out, Susan Leber, who had done *Margarita Happy Hour*. She was the producer who was around New York and I said, "You got to go down and take care of these kids and make sure they don't blow the bank, you know, give some of your expertise." So she went down to oversee the production and *The Roost* worked out well. And there again, the sale of that film was very lucrative for us.

Next up was Jim's movie, *Automatons*, which is eccentric enough that it was not a sure thing that it would get picked up. But we were so happy with the reviews when we released it theatrically, so many periodicals and newspapers really got the movie and then it was picked up by Facets and so it's done well for us too.

When these are finished is it a communal approach to finding distribution or are you the main force?

One thing about Scareflix that needs to be said is I own them. It's kind of the bargain. And the reason I justify that is not that I want to rip off the artist, everybody is given points and the hope of sharing all the wealth but the reality is I need to support my little operation and that benefits everybody because we always put the money back into the work. So I have the say on who sells them, and I've used a couple of different sales agents when it shows at a festival, and when the contracts are being drawn I do all that talking with my lawyer, so the filmmaker isn't bothered with all that. And once again, this earns me my producer's stripes because it's just a pain in the ass. And you know I spent a year delivering *The Roost* and Ti was off touring and meeting Tarantino and Eli Roth and then eventually scheming on his next stuff and I'm sitting back in the office with Jim trying to figure out whether there's a Beta master of the three shots of the textless background and if there's a dialogue list and the music cue sheet and you know this kind of unspeakable hell.

How do you generally cultivate your ideas?

I usually wait until something strikes me and then I kind of ruminate on it, and I see how it fits into my thinking. It is important to me to have some kind of theme that will last longer than any kind of storyline, some theme that will kind of be important to me for the next five years. And then I generally try to put it out of my mind and I find that if it insists on staying there, if it keeps coming back to me maybe it's gonna be something I'm gonna work with and live with for a while and that just starts to percolate. And sometimes I'll write notes in longhand in a book, often about themes and characters and images. And all the while I'm collecting visual stuff, images and postcards and building a scrapbook. And then eventually I'll start writing, right in Final Draft, I'll write my notes and then that thing becomes my script. I'll just write helter skelter notes and keep reshaping them and reshaping them, in the way that some people use index cards, I suppose.

I am writing a new thing, and I keep saying, "Goddamn it, why can't I do a normal movie?" But what I realize is my process is more about mood and pacing and themes than it is about some sort of plot. It's like a mis-formed piece of clay that I keep on massaging until I find that it's about 95 pages, and then, how does it feel now? So I just build up from a basic series of scattered ideas. Now when I write with a writer, which I've done — *No Telling* was written with Beck Underwood and *The Last Winter* was written with Robbie Leaver — you know that was a little more where we sat down and we did notes and then he would go and write stuff down, and then I would take what he had written and rewrite it and we kept going back and forth that way. But it was essentially the same thing, where we'd just slowly massage it and slowly get more and more detail, more refined. And with *The Last Winter* script, because I had hired him, I still had the last word.

How closely do you adhere to these screenplay paradigms?
The three-act business?

Yeah, one guy advocates a ten-point structure.
I actually don't adhere to that at all. I've not even read those books. Now you'll find I give a lot of advice to other filmmakers and that is when I use these things more than when I'm writing for myself. It's a way to talk about what's working and what could be improved. It's a tool but it's not an end. The only time I use that for my own script is when I read it afterward: I try to see if that stuff is in there at all. So I don't dismiss it. I just don't build my piece with those things in mind. And furthermore this isn't advice I would give to someone else because I don't write scripts that should be made by other people. I'm creating a blueprint for my own type of movie, which is not necessarily a generically plotted film. Nor is the script necessarily a literary work that will stand on its own. I would like to believe that my films have a certain intelligence, which might make the scripts worth reading. But ultimately I'm driven by imagery; when I write something down I spend a great deal of time on the description, trying to capture a mood. The location I'm going to be shooting in is as important to me as the so-called plot.

I have my own rules about writing a script: I never refer to the camera; I try to get in there and have it be a read in which you're experiencing the film as a viewer might. I never write, "Camera zooms in on the window." I have all sorts of theories about how that can be phrased to convey exactly that but not by saying it, so you're never aware that you're reading a film script. So that's my process and I don't know how much of it I'd recommend to someone else.

Some screenwriting programs have functions that prompt you when a formula calls for you to cut back to a character, or when you should do this or that.

I'm so naïve I wasn't even aware they'd gone to the extent you're describing, but of course it makes sense that they'd have a writing program that would tell you what to do next. It's exactly the problem with the entire world. We're talking about the manipulation of emotions to reach the appropriate ending at 100 minutes, and therefore sell popcorn, and the same with the poster, that's got to have the three stars on the front. I mean, this kind of monotony that comes from this kind of thinking is so debilitating as to seriously cause a shock of depression across my entire being. It's the different rhythms in a film that become the film, these things you remember. Look at *Straw Dogs*, that probably has a fairly straightforward build and you could probably map that out, but surely it's other things going on that make that film special. Or look at Kubrick's pacing. Obviously writing theories can help you, but I only do it afterwards to sort of check what my intuition came up with and ultimately it's like, "Okay, fine, so I'm from Western culture," you know? I think this way. Aristotle and Shakespeare. I fit in to some degree. But to be guided by rote to make those choices is just appalling.

14

Production

I'm often asked which I enjoy more, making movies or writing novels. In truth, I'm always more satisfied with my novels because they're closer to my original vision and I never have to worry about budget — my dreams can be as epic as my imagination allows — or whether or not other people will deliver on key elements. But there is nothing like the all consuming adrenaline rush that comes with making a feature film. Several of the other filmmakers in this book discuss their productions in detail, so I'm only going to provide you with some brief anecdotes in this chapter. But let me offer this: how smoothly your production runs depends entirely on whether or not you've done your homework and made proper use of your preproduction time. Have you taken the necessary legal steps to cover your ass? Have you assembled a solid team of craftsmen and performers to realize your vision? Have you ensured that you have the right equipment and locations to stage your film? And do you have food to feed your people? If so, let's make a movie!

Slime City

I will never forget my first day as a feature film director. We loaded up our rented production van in Brooklyn and drove to Alphabet City in lower Manhattan, where we filmed all of the scenes set in Lori's apartment. We moved with the precision of a well orchestrated military unit — only to realize that I had forgotten to bring the raw stock. The soundman, Joe Warda, and I sped back to Brooklyn to fetch the 16m film. We were behind schedule before we'd even started.

The Brooklyn apartment I rented with Robert Sabin and another friend, Nelson Wakefield (who's acted in all three of my films, as well as *West New York* and *Law & Order*), was the production headquarters as well as its central location. Robert was the first roommate to be exiled — Ivy Rosovsky commandeered his room for the costume department — and Nelson soon followed; we needed one room solely to store the junk that we removed from the other rooms we were shooting in. Bonnie Brinkley took over our enclosed porch and turned that into the art department. Every night, crewmen slept on top of and below the elevated kitchen floor we had built.

On days when Robert needed to be in his possessed make-up, he reported to Scott and Tom's studio three hours before set call when we were filming at our apartment, and four hours beforehand whenever we filmed in another borough. Scott and Tom soon realized there wasn't enough time in the day for them to make our slime (methylcellulose, used as book binding glue — and a thickening agent in fast food milkshakes!), so Peter and I took responsibility for that duty — for one night. After our first 18-hour day, we simply couldn't stay up an additional two hours, mixing and coloring slime, and function the next day. So we brought in another production assistant, Kurt B. Davis, and quickly dubbed him "Slime Boy."

When we dropped our exposed footage off at the lab, the guys there shouted, "Slime!" This eventually became "Slime Guys," which is why my website is SlimeGuy.com. We rarely had time to watch dailies at the lab's screening room, so we borrowed an old 16m projector and watched them in our living room late at night. We cheered Peter's cinematography, and when he acknowledged my directorial skills, Ed Walloga, my AD, said, "We won't know how good a job Greg has done until we see everything cut together." I remember thinking, "Wait a minute — *that's* how you judge a director's work? I don't remember covering that in Production class!"

I auditioned Eva Lee for the role of Heather, a prostitute Alex brings home and murders. The audition went fine, but Eva seemed skeptical when I told her there was no nudity and she insisted on bringing a bodyguard with her. I sometimes think I'd have had an easier time casting actresses if I lied and told them nudity was required. On the night of the shoot, Eva showed up with her bodyguard, Anthony, a real hulk. While Eva struggled through her scene, unable to act because she was terrified of the filed down straight edge razor Robert was supposed to "kill" her with, Anthony was in my kitchen, wolfing down our craft services. No matter how many times I demonstrated to Eva that the razor couldn't cut, she was incapable of emoting in the scene; had I used the prop in the audition, I'd have known to cast another actress. In the end, Anthony literally ate all of our food, and Eva's deadpan delivery of "You crazy bastard!" will forever be the most quoted line of dialogue in my film, for all the wrong reasons.

We shot the film's climax, involving most of the effects in the film, over five days and four nights, and all but the last day lasted 20 hours. When crew members fell asleep — or passed out; suddenly they were just unconscious on the floor — we simply covered them with plastic to protect them from the slime and continued shooting. I would send Mary to take a nap, then wake her up when we needed her on set and stick a prop meat cleaver in her hand.

The first of two memorable incidents from this marathon stretch occurred when Robert had to throw Mary on top of the art easel which Alex used for his dining table. Robert and Mary — who later worked together in an improve group — choreographed the moment so Robert would grab Mary's shoulders,

Mary would leap off the floor, and Robert would guide her safely onto the easel. They carried it off like a charm, except that Mary landed on the easel with such force — and she only weighed something like 95 pounds — that the whole thing collapsed beneath her. After a stunned moment of silence I asked Mary if she was okay, and after she said she was the crew burst into laughter. Fortunately, Tom Lauten was able to repair — and re-enforce — the easel so shooting could resume.

The other incident occurred when it came time for Alex's brain to emerge from the mechanical version of Robert's head and crawl across the floor. The head split open on cue, and slime poured over the brain. Unfortunately, the methocelullose also *dissolved* the brain! Tom ordered me to bed and woke me when he had solved the problem. By freezing the brain, he was able to salvage it long enough for Mary to hack it to pieces with the meat cleaver.

One effect that didn't turn out well involved Robert's hair: Scott came up with the idea of Alex's hair gradually turning gray over the course of the film, so it would match Zachary's hair at the ending. Unfortunately, as soon as he poured methylcellulose on Robert's head, the gray ran out of his hair! Because we'd already shot most of the film when we discovered this, there was no way to un-gray Robert's hair in the previous scenes.

Plutonium Baby

We had only been editing *Slime City* for a few weeks when Scott Coulter called to see if we could travel to Connecticut to finish this 10-day production after the original crew, comprised of NYU film students, walked away from it. Peter Clark, Britt Petrucelly — who was editing *Slime* with me — Joe Warda, our sound recordist, and I made the Amtrak trek. We were all put up in a hotel, along with the cast and remaining crew, and the four of us stayed in one room. Because the producer hadn't rented lights, we could only shoot during the day, and we partied every night. This was our first paying film job.

As we proceeded to shoot this movie in the woods, we started recognizing certain special effects props. Our deal with Scott was that he would physically keep the props, but could not use them in other productions. And yet, there was our headless body, now hanging from a tree with bloody entrails hanging out of it. As we neared the last day of shooting, Dan Frye grew increasingly apprehensive, so I knew we were in for a surprise. In the film, one of the characters is bitten by a radioactive mutant rabbit (a hand puppet!) and becomes a mutant himself. When the actor playing the character emerged from the trees, we saw that he was wearing Robert's face from *Slime City*!

On the last day of filming, I went to director Billy Zarcha (*South Bronx Hero*) and told him he only had half a movie. We were willing to stay for an extra day without pay to shoot additional scenes. His response: "Nah, I'm tired." So we all went home. The producer, Ray Hirschman, hired Britt to edit *Pluto-

Terry Spivey models a prosthetic arm stump during *Slime City* (1988). Photograph courtesy J. Scott Coulter.

nium Baby, so *Slime City* went on hiatus for a month. When Britt's cut came in at only 37 minutes, Ray was forced to order additional shooting to protect his investment. He told Billy he had to forego his participation in the film to cover the extra expense, and Billy walked — taking the film's 12-year-old star with him. Ray and the screenwriter, Wayne Behar, contrived the remainder of the film as a "10 years later" sequel to the first portion. This allowed them to replace the 12-year-old with an adult, and give the character a sex life — even though the other actors from the film clearly hadn't aged a day! We had one week to complete two-thirds of a feature film, which is why the follow up footage is full of meandering shots "discovering" rooms, lengthy dialogue scenes, and interminable montages with no action but plenty of narration.

Ray took the director's credit on the film, but he was never even on set when we were. Billy, Scott Coulter, the stunt coordinator, Peter Clark, and Ed Walloga collectively directed about half of the film and I directed the remaining half — and my credit was "assistant director." My favorite bit is when the female leads escape from some yahoos who kidnapped them for no apparent reason other than to provide the movie's monster with additional victims. After the gals reunite with their boyfriends in the middle of the road, you can actually hear me directing them off screen: "Now move closer together... That's good... *Cut!*"

Sabin spent hours sitting beneath this stage for the filming of *Slime City*'s grueling finale (1988). Photograph courtesy J. Scott Coulter.

Brain Damage

Brain Damage was a six week shoot, following a couple of months of pre-production, which merged crew members from *Basket Case*, *Street Trash*, and *Slime City*. We shot in a warehouse on 33rd street — my old stomping grounds — in the middle of winter. My credit was assistant director, but I spent a lot of time watching what was being shot on a small videotape monitor. I wore a dress to double for actress Lucille Saint-Peter in the scene where she and Theo Barnes tear apart their apartment searching for the creature Aylmer; my made up hand doubled for Theo's in a shot where Rick Herbst wrestles the gun away from him; I actually second unit directed and shot a couple of the extras on the subway car, when Elmer kills Jennifer Lowry — and shot the unintentionally cinema verite close up of Jennifer as Elmer munches on her brains. For the gag when Rick hallucinates he has pulled his brain out of his ear, and brains gush all over the floor, I stood on a ladder and poured a barrel full of gore over the top of the set. Best of all, I got to operate the animatronic Elmer's eyebrows during the scene when he sings "Elmer's Tune" to Rick in the hotel room set, because Dave Kindlon, who built and operated Elmer, needed to concentrate on the puppet's lip movements (Frank: "What's wrong with his eyebrows?!?").

My worst memory of that shoot is of the two or three nights we spent at the Jim Muro Sr.'s collision yard, where *Street Trash* was filmed. It was freezing cold, and even the offices had no heat. We had these big jet heaters outside, but unless you stood directly in front of them, they didn't do any good. I developed a sore throat and an ear infection, and I've never been so miserable on a shoot. When it was over, and the sun was rising, we still had to pull cables out of the frozen, oily mud. We later learned we'd have to buy all of the sandbags that got oil on them unless we cleaned them, and scrubbed them one by one. Shooting in the winter isn't fun, even if working on a 35mm horror film with cool monsters is.

Undying Love

On the first day of *Undying Love*, we shot the opening and closing scenes that bookend the film, in which Tommy Sweeney's character, Scott Kelly, fails and then succeeds in committing suicide-by-razor blade in his bathtub (I call it "the first pro-suicide vampire film."). I wanted to do one shot with the camera aimed between Tommy's legs as the razor blade slices the water and lands on the bottom of the tub, and then a cloud of blood spreads through the water. There was no magic way to control where the razor would land once it hit the water, and it kept sliding out of frame. Every time we shot a take, Tommy got out of the tub, we drained the water, scrubbed the fake blood, re-filled the tub, and tried again — *19* times!

Tommy was an inexperienced actor, but was incredibly dedicated to the project. When he said, "I'll do anything you need me to do," he meant it, before the camera and behind the scenes. Julie Lynch was quite experienced, and a method actor to boot. When they started rehearsing together on their own time, I saw signs their relationship imitating the one between their characters — nothing more than a feeling, and all for the production. In the film, Camilla seduces Scott and turns him into a vampire so she can manipulate him into destroying her sadistic vampire master, Evan. I pictured Evan as a creature of the night in the mold of Lestat from Ann Rice's *Interview with a Vampire,* and I cast Andrew Lee Barrett in the role partly because he was tall and had long hair. Like Julie, Andrew was a method actor, and when he started rehearsing with her, the dynamic between Tommy and Julie challenged. The romantic triangle from the script had somewhat spilled over into real life — or at least into "rehearsal life." When we shot a bit with Scott slamming Camilla against a wall, Julie's back made a pretty loud slap. And on the day when Scott was supposed to slay Even, Tommy kept glaring at Andrew, psyching him out. At one point he even said: "I'm going to kill you, motherfucker!" Andrew actually became somewhat unnerved by Tommy's "method." During a rehearsal for the climactic fight in which Scott stabs Evan with an Indian Sikh assassin knife, we choreographed the action so Tommy would drive the knife into empty space

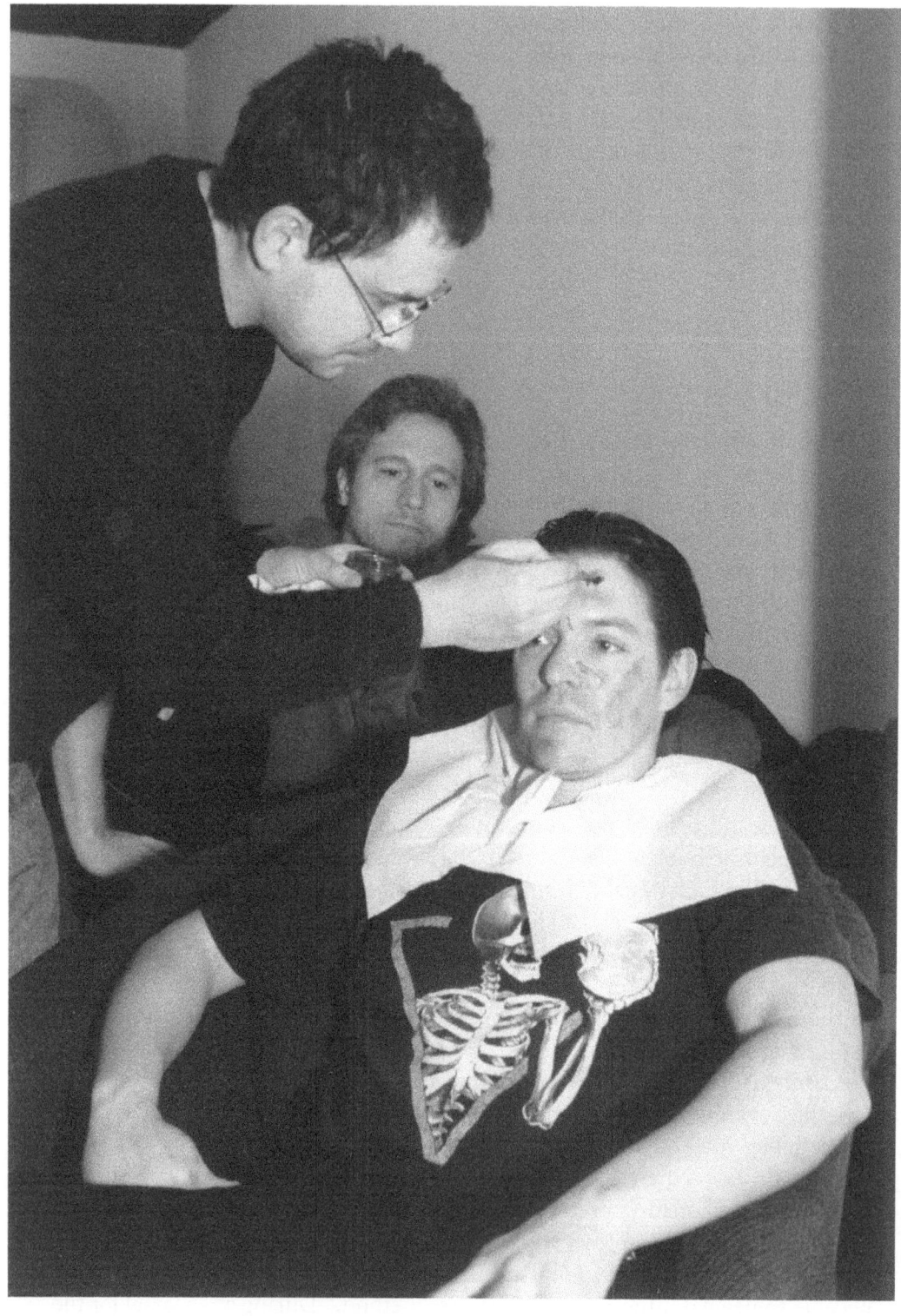

Special effects artist Craig Lindberg makes up Tommy Sweeney for the climax of *Naked Fear* (1999). Photograph courtesy Eric Maché.

below Andrew's armpit, hidden from the camera's view. We shot the scene, and when I called "Cut!" we saw that the knife had actually pierced Andrew's shirt, the blade pressing against his ribs. From that moment on, Tommy seemed perfectly relaxed.

After we wrapped shooting, Tommy missed our wrap party: he'd run a red light in the vehicle he'd purchased for the production, and had been drinking, and did not have his license on him — and spent the weekend in jail. The night should have been "ours," and everybody kept saying, "Where's Tommy?" The glamour of low budget filmmaking!

Naked Fear

For once, I was the one who lived at someone else's apartment during shooting, in this case, Ed Walloga's place in Weehawken, New Jersey, where we shot the film. It was the smallest crew I ever used, maybe six people including myself. The first day, we shot the pivotal murder scene in which Randy (Tommy) stabs to death a mugger (Nelson Wakefield) to protect his roommate, Camden (Robert Sabin). Because the script spent 20 pages developing the relationship between these psychologically dysfunctional roommates, I knew that this scene had to be powerful. My concept was that the dark living room would be lit by a glowing red lava lamp. Specific shots included a close up of Tommy with the a sheathed knife in his mouth; Robert watching in horror as Tommy's shadow raises and swings the knife over him; and the "bloody crotch shot" in which Tommy sheathes the knife in front of his bloody underwear and stands. I was pleased with my shots — but not pleased with the footage. This was one of those 12 hour days that became 20 hours, and when we watched the footage on the TV the raw impact I wanted just wasn't there. The camera was never quite close enough to the action to have the impact I desired, and the lighting was flat. After a brief meeting with Ed in the kitchen, I announced to cast and crew that we were scrapping the first night's footage. Because we shot way past our estimated time, we lost two days instead of one on a projected 10-day shoot. It was a demoralizing beginning.

And because Tommy had moved to Colorado, and had come to New Jersey just to shoot this film, we had to shoot all of his scenes in the span of one week, which became impossible after losing those days. He agreed to stay an extra week, which cost him his job back home, his apartment, and his girlfriend. I'm glad he's so good in the film!

In the climax, Camden beats the hell out of Randy and throws him out an apartment building window. We rented a studio space, put up a blue screen, mounted a candy glass window pane between two C-stands, and had Tommy take a running dive through our $500 prop. He had to nail it in one take, because there was no money for an additional fake window. As always, he delivered. Later, Phil Gallo, who edited the film, added the edge of the apartment building to the foreground and a night time skyline to the background, completing the illusion.

The payoff to the scene is a close up of Randy laying face down on the on the sidewalk, covered in blood and shards of glass. We didn't have a permit to shoot outside, so we left our few lights behind and walked searched the largely Cuban neighborhood for a bright street light. When we found one that looked decent, Tommy got down on the sidewalk, Craig Lindberg covered him with blood, and I threw fake glass on him that we'd saved from the studio shoot. Unfortunately, the footage was still too dark — until we heard a siren and a police car drove up onto the sidewalk, blasting us with its headlights and strobes. A neighbor had reported that a gang had beaten someone up and was videotaping the crime! When the cops got out of the car, they actually had their hands on the butts of their guns. As soon as we explained the situation, and they ascertained that Tommy was was not oozing genuine blood, they took off without even asking to see the permit that we didn't have. Fortunately, Tommy stayed "in character" and remained face down through most of the incident, so we had usable footage while the strobes lit the scene. And that's why the Weehawken Police Department receives special thanks at the end of the film.

15

Scooter McCrae

MICRO-BUDGET MAVERICK

Scooter McCrae grew up in Middletown, New York, on a steady diet of science fiction and horror TV shows like *Star Trek*, *Lost in Space*, and *The Outer Limits*. After graduating from SUNY Purchase, he worked on a pair of Frank Henenlotter films before directing his first feature, *Shatter Dead*. The film is a rarity: a low-budget zombie film that successfully turns horror conventions upside-down. His follow up, *Sixteen Tongues*, is as original and indescribable a narrative film as I have ever seen. Scooter and his handful of collaborators managed to create a convincing future world on a minimal budget, and with extraordinary production design. I honestly can't wait to see what he comes up with next.

Did you make Super-8 films as a kid?

I did indeed. Back in the day, when *Starlog* magazine bought *Cinemagic*, the underground Don Dohler publication. I was kind of getting interested in film at that point, so I immediately subscribed. It came out four times a year at best. I remember waiting desperately for this thin little 32-page magazine, but there were no ads so it was pure articles and listings of the films that people were working on. I remember finishing my first Super 8 movie and sending it in, and the thrill of the magazine coming and seeing it listed as part of their coming attractions.

Did you know before you went to SUNY Purchase that you wanted to be a filmmaker?

Oh, yeah, and it's specifically why I wanted to go to SUNY Purchase. I enrolled in the film program there, which I was very lucky to get into, and luckier still to be rejected by NYU, which is why I went to SUNY. NYU would have bankrupted my entire family. What's hilarious about this, of course, is that SUNY Purchase is a much more difficult film school to get into, even though it's a much cheaper school. It was a ridiculously beautiful price, and even then my family had to take out a student loan. It was the happiest accident that could have happened. Do you want to spend the money on the school, or do you want to save a little money so you can actually put a decent film together by the end of it? And that's what happened to me: the money went into the final project.

After college, was* Basket Case 2 *the first feature you worked on?
I took a job at a place called New York Flash, a photographic equipment rental place. I remember my boss taking me out to lunch one day saying they were going to "groom me up" for a better position, have me rise up a little bit in the company, blah, blah, blah. Two days later, on a Friday, I got a call from my friend Dan Ouellette, who was working on *Basket Case 2*. He said, "Do you know who this guy Frank Henenlotter is? Should I take this job?" And I was like, "Oh, God, oh, yes, take it." And he made me an art department PA. He said, "You seem like the perfect guy for the job. Can you do it?" And I said, "Uh, yeah. When does it start?" He said, "Monday." And I said, "Okay, I'll be there." Then I had to march into my boss's office after that whole lunch thing and say, "Listen, thank you very much, I really appreciate that. Um, this is my last day here and I apologize for no notice," and explained it to him, which made him no less angry, which is a whole other story. And then I went on to work on *Basket Case 2*, although I overlapped with the last day or two of *Frankenhooker*, which was finishing up; they shot back-to-back. So my first day there was helping mop up purple liquid and goop off the floor when they shot the last scene of all the little human bits in the refrigerator coming out and attacking Zorro.

***Working on those films, you must have known Peter Clark, who was my DP and co-producer on* Slime City.**
God bless him, I sure did. Jeez, he was just a beautiful guy. I loved hanging out with him and Frank when we were working. Just so funny, such a no-bullshit, no-nonsense human being. I know it put people off sometimes, but I immediately found him interesting and accessible. To me it was just, "What's not to like about him? You know, he says it like it is and he's got a sense of humor about filmmaking."

And now you're editing Frank's new film,* Bad Biology. *Is it safe to say he's been a mentor to you?
Oh, absolutely. Frank is, at this stage, the king of the independents. Who's left, really, that's independent anymore? Romero's got his big budget films under his belt at this point, Cronenberg is Oscar nominated, and Larry Cohen has written screenplays for some fairly expensive movies. They've all found their way of compromising. And compromise doesn't necessarily mean selling out, because I still think *Land of the Dead* was great, I think Cronenberg's work

DVD box art for *Shatter Dead* (1994), Scooter McCrae's brilliant little zombie film. Photograph courtesy Sub Rosa Studios, Inc.

Scooter with the cast of *Sixteen Tongues* (1999). Photograph courtesy Scooter McCrae.

is fantastic still. But they've found their way of working within the system. And Frank hasn't, to his credit, because his stuff shouldn't work inside the Hollywood bullshit system; it doesn't play nice with others, and if it did it wouldn't be Frank.

What drove you to direct your first feature?

My cinematographer on *Shatter Dead*—my friend Matt Howe—and I would get together every couple of weeks. One of us would walk into a video store, basically find enough tapes to fill an arm, five, six, seven movies, whatever looked like the worst pieces of horror film exploitation garbage, and then we'd get together at one of our places and just sit there and put in one after the other. Some of these things looked like they had actually been shot on VHS and put into a box, and we were like, "*We* could be doing this." And you know, *bing*! Light bulb goes off in the head kind of a moment.

At that point I had written one or two feature length scripts and I was getting very good feedback on them when I showed them to people, but they were concerned or curious about the overall tone of the pieces. "Well, are these supposed to be campy? Are they supposed to be funny? Are they supposed to be horrific?" And I was like, "No, they're horror films but they have a very black, dark sense of humor to them." So what I thought would be a good thing to do was make a little, low budget, shot on video thing in the backyard, in my apartment, using all friends, all acquaintances, and try to put something together that was sleazy, exploitative, marketable, and be able to hand a copy of the movie over to someone as I gave them the script. "Listen, here's a script I wrote that I would like to see possibly produced and here's a little video demo thing that I've done to give you some idea of what I think the tone should be like, so whenever you read this thing you'll understand where it's coming from in terms of the tone." And in many ways that turned out to be just a disaster because it was a feature length thing that was filled with all this nudity and blood and whatnot, and I had wanted it to be the most sleazy, exploitative thing ever during the writing stage, but now people were looking at it and going, "Oh, no, no, this has some serendipity to it, it's slow moving, it's got this gravitas or something." I'm like, "It's two chicks in a shower, dude! I'm glad you like it. Oh, and there's a gun fuck and everything!"

What struck me most about the film is how rich it is thematically. I didn't think of it as an exploitation film at all!

(laughs) I appreciate you saying that. That's unfortunately what happened! I wrote it very quickly and we shot it very quickly. It's one of those things—no time to think, no money at all. When Frank saw it he said the funniest thing to me, it was something I hadn't even thought of. He said, "What's really smart about *Shatter Dead* was that since you had no effects budget for zombie makeup, you just made them intelligent and saved all that money." And I was like,

Glenn Hetrick wraps Crawford James's head with plaster to create the mold on which latex facial appliances for *Sixteen Tongues* (1999) will be created. Photograph courtesy Scooter McCrae.

"Yeaaaah. Yeah, Frank. That's it." But you're right, on a certain level, as a writer, in your own mind, even if you don't come to it consciously, unconsciously there's always going to be some way of connecting everything; some kind of subtext. After the rush of doing it I took a look at it, too, and I was like, "Oh, shit, yeah, there's something thematic going on here."

Both of your films have strong images. Do you find yourself writing toward those images, or for characters, or plot, or themes?

Images always come first, when you ask the question that way. It always starts with me sitting around drinking, doing the dishes or reading, waiting for a train. *Shatter Dead* and *Tongues* both were children born of — I don't want to say *ennui*, I don't bore easily — but they were children of distraction, I guess. They were just happy accidents, you just never know where ideas are going to come from, or where inspiration's going to come from. When I sit down to write, though, I never think about images. So the image inspires the idea, and then when I sit down to write a script, I write specifically from a character perspective. "Okay, I'm going to start this character off in a room and see what happens and see where it goes from here."

I like to improvise that way, too.
I always say if you sit down to write something and you know the ending, you can stop. It's just not going to be very interesting, I think. I know technically you really are supposed to work that way, but that's never interesting. You can have a hint of the ending: "I think I kind of want to go in this direction." But if I'm sitting there knowing the final image, I can't even write anymore. I need to explore an idea, a space in that way. What usually inspired me to sit down and write in the first place is not what inspires me once I actually begin the writing process.

Do you use templates and paradigms?
Not at all. They're extremely useful if what you are trying to put together is a sellable script, either for Hollywood or in general. If that's what you want to do then these are fantastic books and fantastic programs. But if you're trying to do something that reflects your own personality, you know, I don't think people climb into bed with instructions on how to fuck; you kind of find your way around it, what you like about it and what turns you on, and I think that if you're doing personal art, where it's either — ah, I hate that word, sorry — whether it's a drawing, or taking pictures, or making movies, if you're following the manual, you've taken away 75 percent of what you should've been working with in the first place to get to the point where you have something that's personal.

The opening scene of Shatter Dead, with the angel having sex with a woman, has an almost lyrical quality to it, with the light shining through the feathered wings, which is a pretty stark contrast to the grimy, depressing look of the rest of the film.
That's interesting because that bit wasn't even in the script. The beauty of *Shatter Dead* being such a loose project was that there were no angels in the original script, it was one of those things where as I was going along I was kind of like, "Okay, God is the villain, I need angels or something. What the hell are they up to? Are they on strike? Are they helping him? Has the entire ethereal plane gone off in its own direction or something?" So that was something that kind of evolved naturally in the storytelling. My friend Wendy at one point

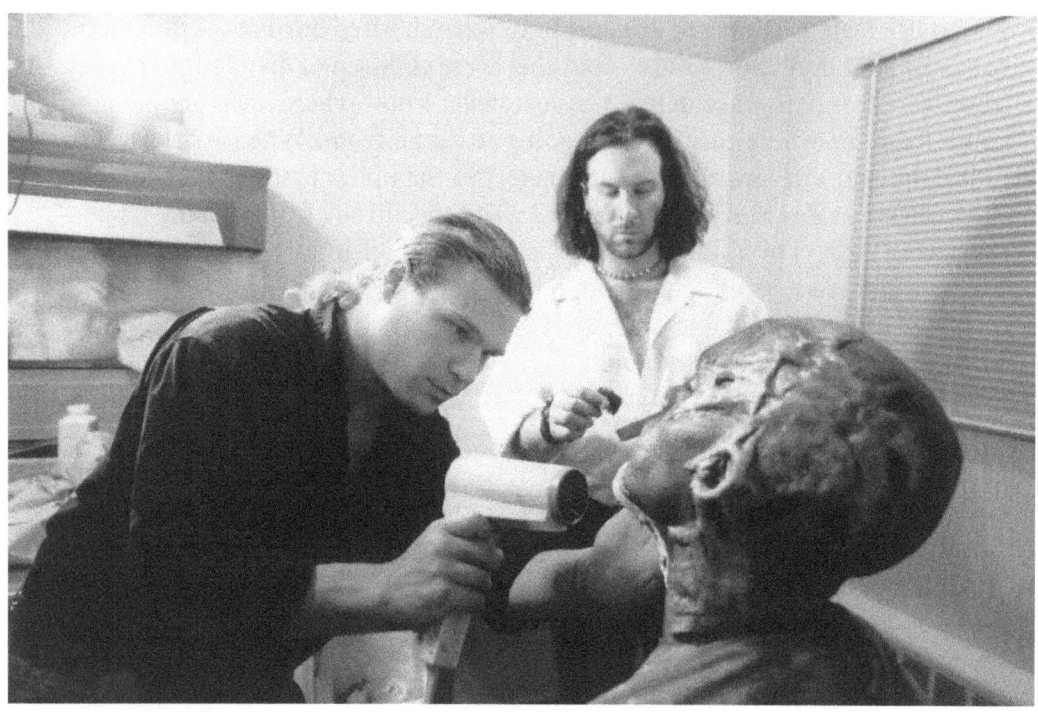

Glenn Hetrick watched Paul Sutt blow dry the finished make-up on Crawford James for *Sixteen Tongues* (1999). Photograph courtesy Scooter McCrae.

talked about going to a Butthole Surfers concert. When I asked her how it was she said, "It was amazing, it was fantastic, it was like being raped by angels." And I thought, "Whew, that's nice." So that was a major inspiration for that opening. And coincidentally that is my friend Wendy who is taking it from the angel. I said, "Honey, you're the one who gave me this idea, I want you to be in this scene. It's just perfect."

And yet if the DVD case hadn't stated so definitively that this sexual act is what causes the dead to rise, I never would have figured it out.

That's okay. I wrote that box copy, or at least that part of it. It was one of those things where I had been getting so much flack I was like, "You know what? Fuck it. Once and for all, let me just write it down." Trust me, when we were shooting it I don't think I knew what we were shooting. It was just, "This is such a great image, I really want to see it: a hermaphroditic angel opening up a movie fucking a woman. This is perfect, it's everything I ever wanted to see in a movie."

The film has a very deliberate pace. I think that's an accurate term, because it seems to be intentionally slow.

Yes, it is.

Tina Krause and Maria Pedersen have bedroom eyes in *Sixteen Tongues* (1999). Photograph courtesy Scooter McCrae.

But if you re-edited it to give it a faster pace it would lose much of what's special about it.

I'm glad you say that, thank you. It wasn't just trying to eat running time, you know? When we were shooting it I gave my poor cameraman a very hard time at certain points. It's funny, when I look back at it, the things you remember thinking to yourself, "No, we must stick with this or we must stick with that." And throughout I kept saying, "I always want to be at eye level with people (with the exception of maybe two or three shots). I don't want to be looking up or down at people or trying to find weird angles. I want the lighting to look natural—almost flat. And I want it to look like a made for TV movie, like an *After School Special*, almost. I want a style-less style; I want there to be no artistic commentary intruding, so that it feels almost like we kind of got here, plopped down the camera, and this is what happened. Not quite documentary, in that sense, but I wanted there to be an absence of any stylistic pretensions whatsoever.

My favorite two scenes are the shower scene, which is really drawn out and plays with our expectations, and the scene near the end when Stark strips down for her boyfriend. They're very well directed and do demonstrate a style.

In the case of the shower scene it was just a matter of, "How do I convey all this information in the right order?" That was a scripting thing. I remem-

Scooter directs Jenny Chase as Ginny Chin-Chin in *Sixteen Tongues* (1999). Photograph courtesy Scooter McCrae.

ber saying to the videographer, Matt, "Fuck it. Every movie we watch has a shower scene, but I'm going to write the best shower scene ever, except for *Psycho* (of course!). I'm going to write an exploitation scene like nobody's ever seen, I'm going to put two girls into the shower and they're going to stand there and talk and all this is going to happen." It was actually the very first scene I wrote.

"And one of them is going to be holding a gun."
Yeah, and one's going to be holding a gun, because I've never seen that either. It was just, "How far can we go with this?" When you've got a budget of a couple of hundred bucks, it's like, "How can I save money?" It goes back to Godard: to make a movie, what do you need? A girl, a camera, and a gun. And in this case it's a girl, a camera, a gun, and a shower — I added a little bit of water to Godard.

It was a brave decision on Stark's part to play that scene near the end the way she did. She's just got that glare on her face, with so much going on behind those eyes.
Oh, thanks, I'll have to tell her that because I've gotten a lot of flack for her performance. One of the extras on the *Shatter Dead* DVD is this self-indulgent half hour supplement filled with bloopers and people fucking around, and

15. Scooter McCrae

Scooter cradles a *Sixteen Tongues* prop (1999). Photograph courtesy Scooter McCrae.

I remember going through the footage and I was like, "I really want people to see that for all the flack I get — "Her performance is cold, she's not acting, she's not this, she's not that" — that's totally a performance. Stark's a total goofball, she loves to laugh. I remember putting in all that footage and going, "Fuck you, you're going to tell me that's not a performance? Here's what she's really like. See her screwing around on set and making jokes? That's her. If you don't like her performance, don't slam her, slam me. I'm the guy who directed her and said, 'Give me more Eastwood. Give me more cold. Give me more this. Scowl more.'" I wanted that from her. And part of it was — there's some pretension about to creep in — the idea that she's the character you're supposed to identify with. But really, as things are going along, you're kind of going, "Gee, these homeless zombies are really not so bad after all, and why am I rooting for her again? Is she really the one I should be identifying with?" That's the kind of thing I'm really interested in. And a similar thing happens in *Sixteen Tongues*. I think in movies, the first character you meet, it's like when you're born: you

Promotional sheet for UK screening of *Sixteen Tongues* (1999). Photograph courtesy Scooter McCrae.

remember your Mom's face, it's the first face you see, so there's an inherent trust. I always feel like the first face you show, you can get away with fucking with the audience, especially in *Tongues*: "Hey, here's the first guy we see, I guess he's the main character. Oh, no—he orally rapes and kills someone in the first scene." You still feel a little like, "Okay, this is the guy I'm with. You keep coming back to this guy, you keep showing me him, so there must be something I'm missing." There's something wonderfully manipulative about doing that.

You shot* Shatter Dead *in 10 days, on weekends?
    Yeah, I don't even think they were consecutive weekends, they were over a two month period.

I guess the advantage to shooting that way is you have time to take a breather and plan things out and don't get caught up in that whole whirlwind of, "Oh, my God, we've got to finish everything in three days!"
    That is a major advantage. And you're right, when you're on set and time is ticking, you have to make great decisions under pressure but the problem is,

every decision you make is under pressure and not every one is going to be great — or even correct.

How about shooting the next one in 20 days instead of 10?
You know what? I don't think I need 20...

Ten is a nice round number?
Sometimes the speed factor is great.

Let's be honest, though—if one of your days is 36 hours long, it's the equivalent of three shooting days!
(laughs) I actually adore working in exhaustion. The problem of course is that not everyone else around you likes that. But what's nice about it is you can tell an actor, "Go take a nap for a couple of hours, we don't need you, okay, relax." As an experiment, I would love to have a rotating crew, where one crew would come in and maybe do 12 hours, take a 12 hour break, and then come back, so that I could work 36 hours. I would like to do that maybe every now and then. But I love the whirlwind, I love the exhaustion, I'm a bit of a workaholic once shooting begins.

What did you do with Shatter Dead when you finished it?
I didn't really know what to do with it because I didn't know what was out there. Somewhere along the way I saw an issue of *Film Threat* and I saw what was going on in there, you know, like, "Oh, God, people do this?" And I had a screening at an art gallery, and Michael Gingold from *Fangoria* magazine came to the screening. Bless him, man, he's a total die hard, and he will go to watch anything in New York, to see who's up and coming with this stuff. We've become best friends ever since he saw *Shatter Dead*. I write for *Fangoria* every now and then, we hang out, we have mutual friends, we talk all the time. And Mike was like, "Oh, you've got to send it to this guy J.R. Bookwalter, you should really try to get it distributed."

And I think when I sent it to J.R. I got a little note back from him saying, "Oh, yeah, it's good, but you might want to make some changes here and there, do this and do that to it." I appreciated him taking the time to tell me this and I thanked him and said, "Well, you know, frankly it's done. There's no changes for me to make at this point. I just don't have the time or the energy, or more importantly, the money." I just wanted to see it over with. "You know, if you know someone who might want to distribute it, because Mike is recommending that, then let me know." And he got right back to me and said, "I'll take it as is."

I sent it to the New York Underground Film Festival because it was local and it was cheap, and they accepted it, which was great. And the Chicago Underground Film Festival took it as well, which was also great. That's where I met

Leif Jonker. He's a magnificent personality, a great guy, and *Darkness* is just so entertaining. And then it went to the Fanta-festival in Rome, which I don't even think exists anymore, and it actually won the award for Best Independent Film that year.

The opening of Sixteen Tongues *is literally so dark that I almost couldn't tell what was going on.*

Absolutely. I remember shooting it, going, "If I can see something through the viewfinder we're taking the light back. You know, pull it down a bit." The level of illumination — I've never worked with such low light levels as on this thing. When we shot it we pumped the camera gain up to 18 dB, so we pumped the gain up as high as it would go on that Sony VX-1000 camcorder, and then basically put a clamp lamp with a 200 Watt bulb, bounced it off a wall, put some diffusion on it maybe, or a gel, and I'd look through the viewfinder and say, "Okay, we're lit. Let's go."

And this was shot on Mini–DV, whereas Shatter Dead *was shot on—?*

Betacam SP. It was the only format I would shoot on. It's funny, when you look back on these decisions. I remember at the time going, "Look, the entire budget is basically going toward renting equipment to shoot it and then eventually edit it." After seeing what some of these camcorder movies looked like by the time they reached market on VHS, I was like, "No, no, no. It's a dead giveaway that it's amateur." At least if we shot on Betacam or Betacam SP, and it was in focus, we had chance of someone mistaking it for something professional, or at least a soap opera gone insane. I remember my breath was taken away when I saw Mini–DV, a three-chip camera, the VX-1000, which we shot *Tongues* on. Seeing the quality of the imagery was mind blowing.

Sixteen Tongues *is a science fiction film, but I would argue it's much more frightening and nightmarish than* Shatter Dead, *which is almost an anti-horror film more than it is a horror film.*

That's actually a great description, I should put that on there. I would agree with the assessment entirely that *Shatter Dead* is an anti-horror film, which is why it's completely bright. I like that whole Hammer esthetic, "Let the monsters come out in daylight," which we had to do; there's only one little night scene, it's very brief. But other than that it's by the light of day. It's a new millennium now, so science is the scariest thing of all. We've come to embrace serial killers and give them back stories, and totally negate any fright value to the human mind. Everything has to be explained now. That's why they do remakes of movies and give everyone back stories or tell you why things happen. And the beauty of science and why science fiction is now proving to be far more scary than your masked killer in a horror film, who had a lousy childhood or was cheated by a lover, and that's why he picked up the axe and started killing people... You can't explain science — you have to be real smart to understand science, and most of us, 99.3 percent of us, don't understand the higher sciences, so we're stuck wondering in fear and awe what's going on behind closed doors (or even in-between the atoms), what new inventions are going to come along that will end up killing people, or extending life in ways that shouldn't be extended, all sorts of terrible moral quandries that never had to be faced before in the history of humankind.

Your leads in Sixteen Tongues **were an African American man and two Asian women. Because you had such a small cast, you were able to achieve, through casting, what Ridley Scott did by surrounding Harrison Ford with huge crowds of racially intermixed extras in** Blade Runner.

I got lucky too. I love these actors. I'm so happy with them. Even when they go over the top, even when they go below the bottom, they were absolutely fearless and I'm so happy about that. Especially Crawford James, our African American guy —

He was brave, no question about it.
Well he was second choice for the role, and I say this much to my shame, because really he should never have been second choice. The problem with the first guy was the opening scene where the person is orally raped by him. He said, "Listen, I want it made clear that's a woman, not a man, in the opening scene." And I said, "No, no, no. You read the script. I don't want it to ever be clear if that's a man or a woman, that's the point." And he said, "Well, I've got friends. If they see this I'll never hear the end of it..." And I was like, "Thank you very much, this is where we part ways. I can't work with someone who's got these kinds of fears and problems, it's not what we're about." And Crawford was just fearless, he was wonderful. He was married and religious and a spiritual man, which made it to me even more impressive what he did for us and what he let us do to him. I have so much respect for that.

I'm somewhat surprised by the reaction the movie's gotten. It had nowhere near the impact that *Shatter Dead* had, in terms of the number of people who have seen it, or commented on it, or looked at any of that. Of course, every director is wrong about what his favorite movie is, they're never right. But in the end I prefer *Sixteen Tongues* to *Shatter Dead*. Not that I hate *Shatter Dead*, but I have warm place in my heart for *Tongues*, insane, fucked up thing that it is.

When you sent me the screeners you warned me they were pornographic and I thought, "Oh, that's just an extreme comment." And watching Shatter Dead, **I didn't think it was pornographic at all, I thought the nudity was kind of avant garde, at least with the angel. I guess** Sixteen Tongues **really is pornographic, but it's not designed to titillate.**

There are those who would argue pornography isn't designed to titillate in the first place. It's so gynecological that it takes a certain mindset to be titillated by pornography. Is it really a movie? It's just a masturbation aid. Like music, it's an art that occurs in time. And one can say that pornography is a masturbation aid that occurs in time, it's own time as opposed to your time, although the magic fast forward button makes that an argument for another night.

It's hard to imagine Sixteen Tongues **working as a masturbation aid; I can't picture anyone saying, "I want to go do that!"**
(laughs) For God's sake, man, I hope you're right! There's all kinds, but I would not want to meet anyone and shake their hand, at least not without a glove, if all they could tell me was, "Your film is my favorite masturbation aid."

Regardless of budget, do you intend to continue on this path?
It's funny you should say that, because I always think to myself, "The next thing for me to do is completely re-invent myself and pull a David Lynch and do a G-rated film like *The Straight Story* just to really confuse people." It is unfortunate because there simply is no G-rated film in my heart, and not because there is anything wrong with G-rated films, it is simply not the way that my mind works. I guess I think it's cool that there can be violence and nakedness and they can intertwine and become confused — that to me is what it's all about to some extent. I sometimes feel most relaxed and comfortable when a movie is making me uncomfortable. I love that feeling.

I have one project that Alex (Kuciw, producer of *Sixteen Tongues*) would like very much for me to do and I would like to do as well if I can get it straight, which currently has the working title *The Shadow Children*, which is a much friendlier little project, my idea of maybe a Jean Rollin project, where there's nudity in it but the nudity is intentionally beside the point and it's a love story. To some extent I would consider both *Tongues* and *Shatter Dead* to be love stories, but I mean maybe something more conventional as a love story that would have a lot of skin in it but isn't trying to be exploitative, but saying nakedness can be a very integral and wonderful part of love. .

And then the $200,000 project that I'm trying to see through to fruition is called *The Sad Ballad of Sister Cyborg*, which is a direct descendent of *Sixteen Tongues* except it is the polar opposite: it's a sci-fi western thing that takes place probably in the same future that *Tongues* does, but out in the middle of the New Mexico desert. It's all wide open vistas and landscapes, with people running around with their various body modifications and cyborg enhancements. In the end, it's really a noir. If all these disparate interests come together for me, it is remarkably commercial in many ways, in terms of having a beginning, a middle, and an end, and even a "sting in the tail" and a resolution and all these very traditional narrative things. I wrote it extremely fast and it's I think my best script. But having had people take a look at it at this point, they go, "This is fantastic, this is great — but it's rated X." And I look at them and I go, "Rated X? Have you seen my other stuff? By my standards this is PG-13 at best." And they go, "Ho, ho, ho, no it's not!" So apparently I have absolutely no clue as to what good taste and ratings are in movies. I have no idea.

The most recent development as concerns my next project is that my distributor, Ron Bonk at Sub-Rosa, came to me in November 2007 and said he could get some money together for a *Shatter Dead II* project. Well of course, at first I was dubious about the idea of revisiting that story, but after walking around and thinking about it for a day or two I had a real brainstorm. I realized that doing a direct sequel with any of the characters continuing onwards in it didn't have any appeal to me, but what stopped me dead in my tracks (no pun intended) was the idea of being able to address some of the more delicate political and ideological issues that we've been confronting since 9/11 and America's retaliatory invasion of Iraq. I touched a bit on the idea of zombies as a kind of terrorist group in the original *Shatter Dead* in one scene where a bunch of them attack a house full of people. What I want to do now is take that to the next level; deal with zombie terrorism, the government reaction to it with Abu-Ghraib-ish facilities where they are torturing zombies for information and how zombies and our own homegrown fundamentalist religious zealots actually find common ground in dangerous ways. It screams commercial, doesn't it? The current title is *Shatter Dead: Death and Taxes*, and I hope that's what we go with.

What screenwriting program do use?

I don't, I just type into Word. I'm on a Mac. Someone gave me a copy of Final Draft and I started using it a little bit and I just hated it. I really like typing in my own margins and spacing things myself. But you're talking about someone who spent years on an IBM Selectric. Now I love working on a word processor, I really do. I guess eventually I will probably move to Final Draft, but not anytime soon.

What would you like to see different from people making no budget horror films these days?

I sometimes think that, based on the way you asked the question, the worst punishment that a lousy filmmaker should be subjected to is to be forced to watch their own movie over and over and over again, until they learn something from it. I feel like a lot of people making some low budget — even big budget, I'll take it to all filmmakers, really —

We're addressing the ones there's still hope for...

(laughs) Just learn from your mistakes, and the best way to learn from your mistakes is just watch the final product and be honest enough to figure out what the hell's wrong with it. And watch it with a stranger, someone who doesn't know you. It's worth the money to pay a stranger to watch something of your own with you, and watch their reactions, and talk to them after, and actually learn something from it. Because I think a lot of people don't. I see a lot of movies shot on video, or low budget stuff, because Mike from *Fangoria* knows that I'm the most patient viewer with this kind of material, just as he is. So every now and then he comes over here, and he brings a stack of seven or eight movies from fledgling moviemakers who would like to be covered by *Fangoria*. But some of this stuff is just so dreadfully bad; it's people who must think," Oh, just making sure we have 90 minutes of something strung together makes it a feature, makes it a movie." Or trying to make sure they're making something that's like what everyone else is making, because if everyone else is making it, it must be, if not good, then acceptable. And removing yourself from a standard of excellence that comes from within yourself and trying to make something that's as good as a commoditized product, the thought of it is just so soul killing, and so horrifying, that I don't know what anyone would have left to do or say in a movie anymore at that point, because you've squeezed everything that is you out of the equation.

If you don't have a story to tell, then shut the fuck up, because that's what it's all about. If you're trying to tell a story you think people want to hear, that's nothing. If you're trying to tell a story that everyone else is telling, what's the point? It's already out there. You've got to have something that is unique and is different and is you, and that's the story you tell—horror, sci-fi, love story, I don't care what it is—and if you don't have that, just please, do yourself a favor, do me a favor—go do something else. My time is valuable, isn't yours?

16

Directing

You cannot learn how to direct a movie by reading a book. You learn to direct by acting, by editing, and by *directing*. Direct short films. Act in them. Edit them. See where you're making mistakes. Avoid those mistakes when you shoot your feature. Make new mistakes and learn from those. Directing is about learning as much as it is about anything else. Work for free on a low budget horror film —*one* low budget horror film — and learn how a set is run.

There are ways a director can cover his ass. The first is to shoot plenty of coverage of a scene. If you're a micro-budget filmmaker, digital video is cheap, so shoot as many angles and takes as you can. On my 16m features, we only shot one or two takes, On *I Was a Teenage Zombie*, John Michaels actually shot his close ups by having the actors go through all their dialogue in a scene, without receiving cues from the other actors in the scene, and without them reacting to those other actors' lines. This is no way to inspire a performance.

Frank Capra used to shoot a scene straight through as a wide shot. Then he'd move his camera closer and shoot the scene straight through again. And then he'd move the camera still closer. And so on. Some directors are known as "four corner" directors because they shoot every scene from all four corners in a room. This is a little extreme — and very time consuming and costly. But you should get proper coverage, which is at minimum a master shot of two characters and one close up of each, plus maybe a medium shot of each. Doing so enables you to control the rhythm of a scene during editing, and to delete embarrassing moments or unnecessary lines of dialogue. In other words, if you shoot an entire scene from one angle — as I've done did more than once — you are stuck with every second of dead space in the scene. You cannot alter the scene. You cannot quicken the scene. You cannot improve the scene. You can only marry the scene or cut the scene.

These days, there is no excuse for having a static film, unless that is your creative intention, and it's nearly impossible to generate suspense without moving the camera. Because digital video cameras are so compact, every micro-budget filmmaker is free to make handheld moves. And a simple internet search will turn up plans for a homemade dolly with skateboard wheels that run over PVC pipe; you can build this from scratch for a couple of hundred

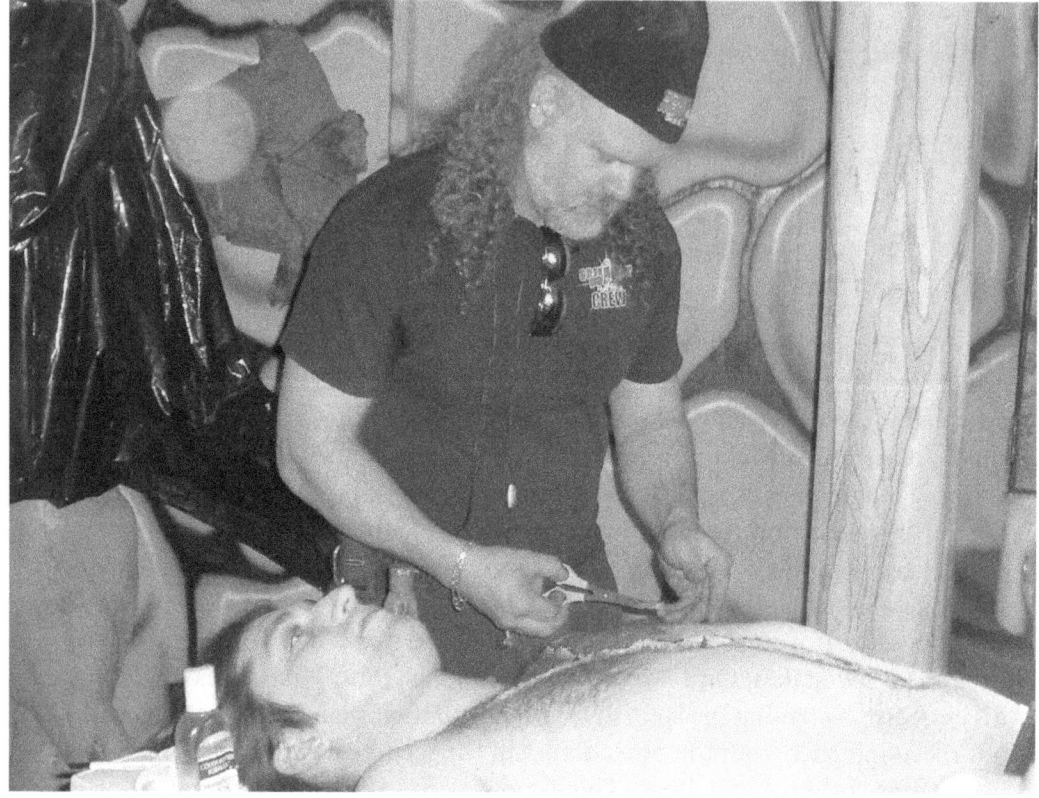

Special effects artist David Gray uses wax to create a Y-incision on Ryan O'Connell for *Gruesome* (2007). Photograph courtesy Jason Mager.

dollars. Do you know how much production value 10 feet of PVC pipe can add to your film?

A Steadicam is another way to add mobility to your production. Jimmy Muro shot much of *Street Trash* with a Steadicam, and he did some shots for *Slime City* and *Brain Damage* as well before heading out to Hollywood. A decent steadicam operator is not cheap, so if you can schedule as many shots as possible for none day of shooting, you can add some real sparks to your film without depleting your budget. Just make sure you see your steadicam operator's reel before you hire him; operating a Steadicam is not easy, and I once worked with a guy who's framing was so inadequate that I couldn't use any of his shots, which means we wasted much of our production day. And remember: Steadicams require a *lot* of setup time.

Of course, these are matters of technical direction, and directing a feature also means directing actors. I love working with actors, but I'm not what is known as an "actor's director"—I do not know the various acting methods, and I lack the skills of a maestro who can inspire an actor to dig deep into their subconscious and recall a childhood trauma which will reduce them to tears. My directing style is more collegial: I allow my cast to offer dialogue sugges-

"Nobody moves, nobody gets hurt!" Director of Photography John Rosnell shoots *Undying Love* (1992) while director Lamberson moves.

tions during rehearsal, but prefer that they not do so when we are shooting; it is just possible that an actor will change a line which has no consequence within a scene, but may create a contradiction in a subsequent scene. Even if you've written the screenplay yourself, it may be hard to remember every story thread in the moment that an actor makes a suggestion. I encourage actors to interpret their characters as they like, and I give them a certain amount of freedom to experiment with line deliveries. I'm no Sidney Lumet, but I'm no Ed Wood, Jr., either. I believe Larry Fessenden and Scooter McCrae are "actors' directors"— they realize that their performers are true collaborators who are instrumental in breathing life into the material on the printed page

On a cabin in the woods movie that I worked on, the director kneeled on the ground while his actors performed a scene in which two couples hiking through the woods cracked jokes. The next time we see them, they're pitching tents. One of the actresses said, "Shouldn't we be carrying backpacks or something? Where do our tents come from in the next scene?" The director barked, "Will you just *act*?" This wasn't my idea of good directing.

Good communication is essential on any shoot, and the director must communicate better than anyone else. If a director can't articulate what his vision is, and can't inspire his cast to embody that vision, he has no one to blame but himself if the performances fall short. A director sets the tone for a film,

Dan O'Loughery and Erin Brown (aka "Misty Mundae") at Buffalo's House of Horrors for *Gruesome* (2007). Photograph courtesy Jason Mager.

so it's essential that the director establish an atmosphere that's conducive to creativity and collaboration. No one wants to work for someone who yells at his cast or crew and creates friction on the set. If you project a professional demeanor, so will the people around you.

I do have some common sense recommendations. Eat well. Try to sleep well. Delegate to others whenever possible — few people have as much energy as Scooter McCrae or J.R. Bookwalter, and you can't do everything yourself. At the start of each shooting day, set aside a few minutes to read — not skim — the screenplay pages you plan to shoot. Discuss the setups you have in mind with your DP — *and with your AD*, so he can answer questions from cast and crew as he encounters them. Remember, your AD is there to run interference for you so that you can concentrate on creative decisions.

Block each scene with your actors, so the technical heads can determine what factors they need to consider while setting up, then dispatch your cast to wardrobe, hair and make-up. Aim for getting your first shot as early as possible, to get the day off to a productive start. I like to shoot for an hour after set call, but that rarely, if ever, happens. 90 minutes is more common, and two hours is not unusual. Have your AD record when that first shot occurs, so everyone is cognizant that you're striving to stay on schedule and "make your day."

Stay cool under pressure. People are looking to you for leadership. Don't blow up in front of people when something goes wrong. Instead, ask your department heads or closest collaborators how you think the situation should be resolved. If you're experiencing conflict with someone on your team, discuss the matter with them off set, away from others. Finally, lead by example. "Do unto others as you would have them do unto you" is a great motto to live by on film shoots. You want to bring out the best in your people, but you should also allow them to bring out the best in you.

17

James Lorinz

ACTING SCARED

Like Robert Sabin and me, James Lorinz worked for the Cinema 5 movie theatre chain in New York City. We worked at different locations, but occasionally I would see him at premieres which required additional staff. I'd also see him at SVA, where he was in the class ahead of mine. I never would have guessed that the guy walking around and doing impressions of Abbott and Costello and The Three Stooges would star in two of the biggest cult films of the 1980s, *Street Trash* and *Frankenhooker*, or that he would direct the brilliant short *Swirlee*, starring a young David Caruso. Lorinz is a real NYC actor, and he's proven himself to be a talented filmmaker as well, committed to making a feature he's been developing for two and a half decades.

What made you decide to attend the School of Visual Arts?
I always wanted to be a filmmaker. I made movies when I was a kid, like 12 or 13. Me and a friend of mine, Victor Triola, used to take a little Super-8 and go around... I remember the first film we made together was called *Strange People in Astoria*. All we did was film weird people walking, and little skits and stuff. We filmed a lot of movies when we were really young. I remember being 15 and seeing *Taxi Driver*, and that changed everything. That made me want to be a filmmaker. We were real working class kids. Our big movie was called *Easy Money*, and it was about these two construction workers who find a briefcase full of heroin and they don't know what to do with it. Of course, my grades weren't so good. I applied to NYU and UCLA, but, uh ... well, SVA came through...

I remember seeing Easy Money *at some SVA festival. I had no idea you'd made that in high school. The next time I saw you on screen was at the Ziegfeld, for the invitational screening of* Street Trash. *What did you do between graduating SVA and doing the film?*
Well, I didn't graduate...

Neither did I. Neither did Jim Muro. SVA's most interesting students never graduate!

I didn't graduate because I lost interest. There was a teacher at SVA named Bob Brady, who taught a class called Acting in Film, and everyone wanted to take it because as a filmmaker you have to know how to work with actors. That was the whole idea behind that class. He had a big impact on me pursuing an acting career. I was already at the point where I was failing editing. Back then they were still using Steenbecks. I was like, "Arrrgh!" cutting this freaking stuff, how to thread a camera inside a bag, and reading the light meter. This is what the focus was on and I was really lost, because I wound up being the guy in front of the camera, you know? Everybody had a job. I couldn't do anything.

Bob Brady treated everybody with respect no matter how good or bad they were. And he taught a real interesting class. He tried to get me into the American Academy of Dramatic Arts, but I'd already wasted my loans on SVA. It was funny because they were willing to help me out, they were going to give me a thousand bucks or whatever, but I couldn't do it. So I quit school, I took an acting class, and I stared doing theatre, like Off-off-off Broadway: all these great plays at the American Theatre of Actors, with a guy named James Jennings. And I studied with him for a while. He put me in the plays there and I got to do everything. They were such unpublicized, true artists. I got to do a lot of different things, and along the way, I stayed in touch with Roy Frumkes.

Roy called me one day and he said, "Look, one of my students is making a film, I know you're trying to be an actor, I want to help you out." He was just being a decent guy. He said, "Look, I have one line for you if you're willing to play a doorman in this movie called *Street Trash*." And I said, "Gee, thanks, that's great." I went down to the set and I had this one line, and I really worked on it. I made up my own bit of business, where I had a bottle of booze and I took a shot — I was trying to milk it as much as I could. And I got to meet Tony Darrow, and while we were waiting to shoot the scene we were fucking around. You know, "Hey come here, you little son of a bitch — sniff my fart!" I guess Jim Muro, the director, and Roy, were like, "Hey, this is pretty funny, why don't we write it into the movie?" So we shot this stuff and it was great; we ended up improvising this whole scene. And that was it. I was like, "Great, I hope they don't cut it out, I've got this great scene in this little movie." But then they called me like a month later. They said, "Listen, it went so well we want to write another scene for you guys." So they wrote another scene and we did the same thing and fucked around a little. Another two weeks went by and they said, "We want to write another scene."

What was your initial reaction to the finished film?

Well, you gotta understand something; I really didn't know what the movie was about. The premiere was at Lincoln Center. This guy David Whitten was in charge of the promotion of the film. Everybody's in tuxedos, and there's a crowd outside, they don't know what's going on. And all of the sudden he has the whole cast show up in a garbage truck, fresh with the garbage from that day or whatever, it was horrible. Me, Mike Lackey, all the main characters in the movie. It was really funny. That's the first time I saw the movie in its entirety, with everybody else. It was really something.

What did you say to Roy?

I tried to hit him but we got separated in the crowd. He thought I was trying to high-five him, I think.

Did you think, "Oh, yeah, my career is taking off now!" or did you think, "I'm not putting this thing on my resume"?

I didn't even think about a resume. I wanted to be a serious actor, I wasn't thinking about being a star. I was never embarrassed by it, I was just shocked; I really felt that something was happening, I was being taken for a ride. That movie helped me get an agent and a manager. I remember these reviews started coming out. *The New York Times* reviewed the movie. They didn't care for it, obviously. In the bottom line they mentioned me and this guy Tony Darrow as a plus in the movie. I was like, "Wow, that's pretty good." And then I remember *Playboy* came out with a review that specifically mentioned me and Tony Darrow. I was like, "What did I do?" The movie had a lot to bring attention to it, but obviously something I did must have stuck out, because we're not main characters; we were sort of a bridge through the film, which I thought was perfect, because it needed some laughs. It needed something like that. I mean, after the severed penis scene and all that, you need a little relaxation, you know?

Roy told me you auditioned for Scorsese for Goodfellas. **Can you describe what that was like?**

Well I got an agent from the movie, and I got auditions, and I got a call: "Martin Scorsese wants to meet with you. He saw you in *Street Trash*." So I go there and I meet him and I'm really nervous. We're talking, and I remember he corrected me saying, "I really like Joe *Peski*." He went (whispers), "Pesci, Pesci, Pesci." I remember talking with him for like half an hour, about, remember that movie *The Incredible Mr. Limpet*?

One of my favorites.

One of his favorites, too! And one of my favorites. Don Knotts reminds me a little bit of Joe Pesci. We're talking and talking, and I feel like, "What's going on here?" He didn't ask me to read anything. I'm sitting there for half an hour, in Martin Scorsese's office, and I'm talking about—

Nick Duran (Tony Darrow, right) and goons menace "Doorman" (James Lorinz) in *Street Trash* (1987). Photograph by Karen Ogle, courtesy Roy Frumkes.

Crusty and Ladyfish.

Yeah! So finally he goes, "Look, I just want to let you know, we're having everybody read the same part, but it's already been cast. It's going to Joe, he's an old friend of mine." So we read the scene and he goes, "I don't know what to do with you." And I took this in a good way: he goes, "I could give you a part as a waiter or one line here, but I don't think that would be right." So then I'm about to leave and he goes, "Well, wait, come here." I say, "Yes?" "What are you doing today?" I said, "Nothing." He goes, "Would you mind staying and being a reader for the other actors?" I said, "Sure"—and that was the best experience ever. I got to hang out and see all these guys like Vincent D'Onofrio come in and read, and they were just as nervous as I was. It was really good to see that, because I felt like, "You know what? It's the same for everybody." You're going up to meet the Master. But I was relaxed, because I was just there reading for two hours, reading the same scenes over and over. Jennifer Grey was there. It was mind boggling. Suddenly you're in an office with people you've seen in movies and they're trying to get a job, so it's a different dynamic. And it was funny because then he called me and offered me a part, and I said to my agent, "Well, what part?" And he said, "Well, he doesn't know. You're going to be part of the Lufthansa heist." I guess maybe he thought I would improvise and would be a good addition to whatever was going on. But

A boy and his drill: Lorinz as Jeffrey in *Frankenhooker* (1990). Photograph by Eric Maché, courtesy of Unearthed Films

I couldn't do it because I was doing *Frankenhooker*, the only time in my life I had two jobs at once.

How did Frank approach you about playing Jeffrey in Frankenhooker?

He got my home number somehow and he said, "My name is Frank Henenlotter, and I'm going to be making a movie called *Frankenhooker*, and I'd like you to play a part in it. I'm still working on getting the money and putting it together, but I just wanted to let you know." I literally had no idea who he was. I went, "Yeah, okay. Whatever." I didn't know about *Basket Case*. A year passed, and I still had to audition for the movie. It wasn't like, "Hey, we're giving you the part." I remember going to some casting call, and meeting a casting director and being put on tape, and then getting an interview with him. I remember he offered me the part, and I must have been nuts, but I said, "Are you *sure*? You want *me*? There's a guy with a drill in his head! I don't understand what you're doing." He goes, "Nah, nah, you'll be great, you'll be good."

Did you ever find out if they held that casting call because Shapiro-Glickenhaus required them to?

I don't know, maybe. Maybe he was trying to get around them.

Frank is shrewd in the way he gets what he wants while keeping the appearance that he's going through "proper" channels.

You have to do that even while you're dealing with these little schmuck companies like Shapiro-Glickenhaus. All this bullshit, come on. They act like they're Warner Brothers or something. Give him the money and let him make the movie. They're just going to ruin it if they get involved.

Were you encouraged to improvise on that film?

Well, I was and I wasn't. It's funny because, I don't know, for some reason I think this guy Henenlotter hates my guts. I don't know why, but — I think I know why. I started improvising on the movie. I don't think he liked that. But at the same time, I had the guys from Shapiro Glickenhaus coming to me, "Oh, it's terrific, keep doing what you're doing."

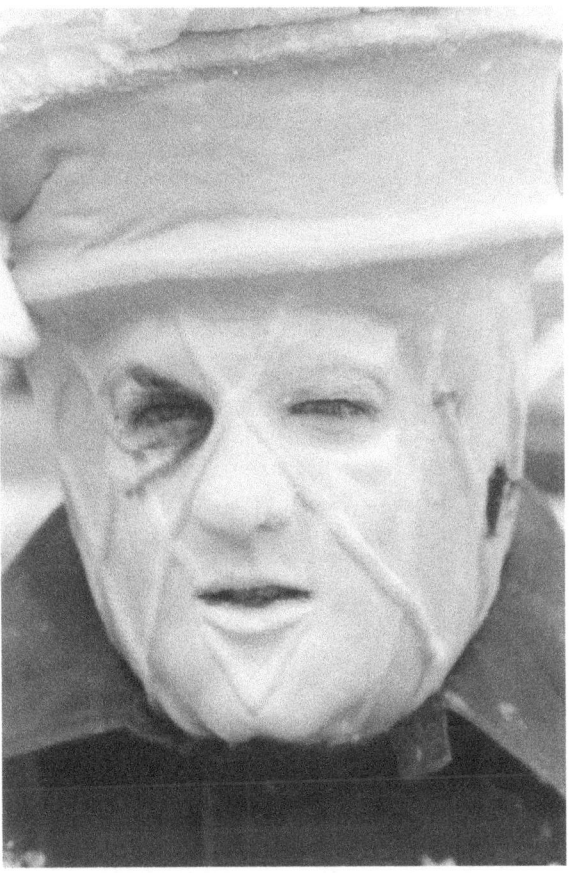

James Lorinz as *Swirlee* (2000), in the short film version of his proposed feature, makeup by Kelly Gleason. Photograph courtesy Roy Frumkes.

And of course, in the back of my mind, I'm thinking, "Who are these guys?" So I'm trying to figure out, like, "What should I do here?" I thought what I did helped the movie. I don't think that's the movie Frank wanted to make. I think he wanted the movie to be much darker, and I think because I was doing this blabbering, you know, because I felt that's what I should do, and the producers liked it and I guess the rushes looked good... I think it helped the film. I mean, think of the whole concept of it screamed for some kind of outside voice. At least that's what my publicist said to say.

You got all sorts of feedback for Street Trash. **Did you get any for** Frankenhooker?

Oh, yeah. I had a much bigger role. It's funny, I watched it a couple of years ago. It's not a bad film. For the money he had to spend, all of it is on the screen. Nobody made any money. He didn't, obviously. If he did, I'll sue.

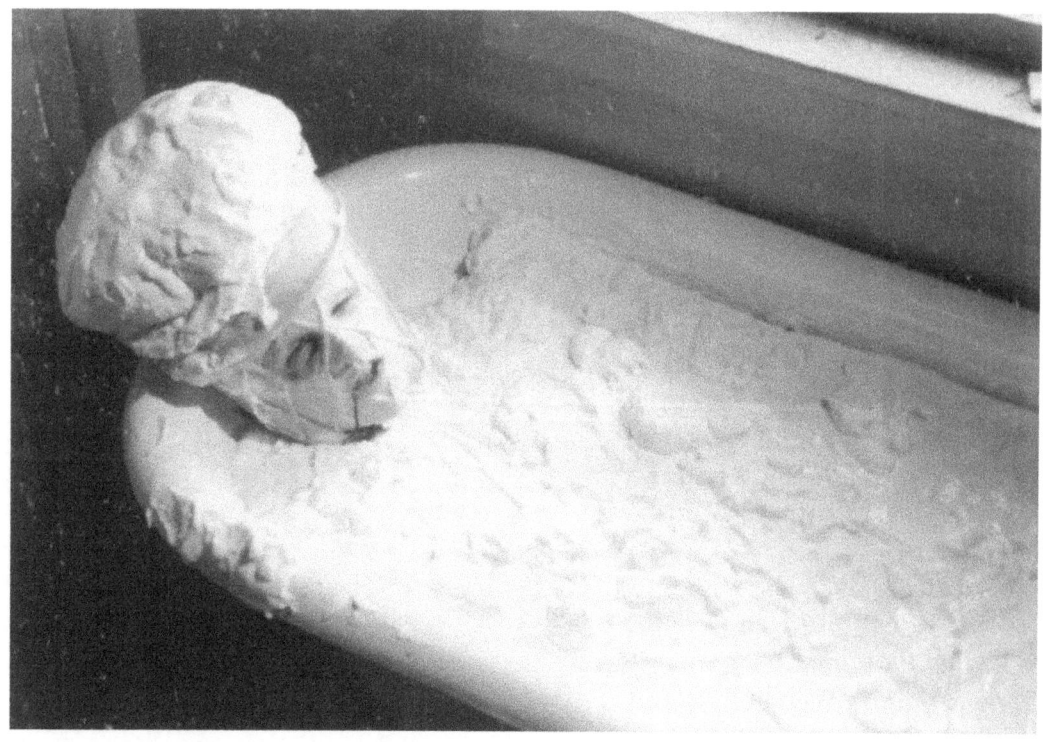

In a scene that helped doom Lorinz's dream project, *Swirlee* attempts suicide in a hot bath. From the short film (2000). Photograph courtesy Roy Frumkes.

You've acted in a boatload of movies and TV shows, and I'm not going to name them all, but I have to acknowledge that you were in one of my favorite films from that period, King of New York, directed by Abel Ferrara.

I remember Abel told me I was the first person hired on that movie. All I did was talk to him and say a few of my non sequiturs. I ended up playing a cop. I actually ended up having a lot of scenes, but they were all cut out because my improvising didn't work on that film. I was doing *Frankenhooker* shit.

You played the clean cut member of the cop squad.

There was this whole wedding scene that was chopped down to like nothing. I mean it was like the wedding scene from *The Deer Hunter*. They chopped it down because they wanted to fit in 12 more gun battles, because that's what sells and that's what he was really interested in. I'm grateful to have been involved, I'm in the movie a little bit, it was great working with him. It's like he's got a guardian angel — somebody else is working with him. But also, that movie was a big highway robbery, because nobody ever got any residuals or got paid, it was terrible. That movie's shown everywhere on TV. Somehow they got around SAG and made it as a foreign production, like with a Limited Liability Company. There's nobody to go to to collect.

You starred in two of the biggest cult horror films of the 1980s, both of them extremely over the top and tasteless. How did you parlay those into a regular role on a CBS sitcom?

I didn't. I think if they had seen them I never would have gotten onto that show. (laughs) None of them came out yet. I was auditioning. I was a real actor for a couple of years, going out and meeting with directors, going to CBS and NBC. I had no idea what I was doing. I went to some audition and I guess it went well and they called me back, and that went well, and they called me back again, and that went well, and then they told me, "Okay, they want you to fly out to Los Angeles and audition again for the network." And I got the part. It happened so easy. The minute I started to go after it, it all fell apart. The minute I said, "Hey, maybe I'll try to do this for real," everybody ran.

It was one of those shows set in New York City but taped in La-La Land?

No, no, it was supposed to be a fictional city. The name of the show was *City*.

I saw an episode. It was supposed to be Valerie Harper's comeback.

Yeah. What a great experience that was, because I got a little taste of what that life was like.

And you played the security guard?

I was the security guard.

I remember you standing there.

As the show went on, they kept writing more and more for me on the set. If it had gotten picked up I probably would be in a different place now, not talking to you from a rooming house.

Thirteen episodes, right?

Thirteen episodes. Made some dough. But had I stayed there, I might have gone on to something else. I came back to make *Swirlee*. I still had that in me: "I'm a filmmaker. I want to make this movie, and I'll use my own money. Fuck everybody." That was the biggest mistake I ever made! Never use your own money. That's what all they told me. "No, I want to invest in my own future."

Were you out there long enough to go Hollywood?

No, not really. I was out there for six months, I guess. Another friend was doing a movie that he wanted me to be in called *Me and the Mob*, and I said, "Okay, I'll come back." But I wanted to make this film.

***Let's jump back to the origins of* Swirlee.**

This was a long time ago. I remember always waiting for Mr. Softy to come down the block, and the truck would come and you'd see his cartoon face and you'd think, "What if this guy was alive? What would it be like?" Then when I was at SVA I tried to write a script about a guy made out of ice cream, but it was real crude.

Did you play the character then?

No, no. I just directed. It was one of the students. That really never got anywhere. But I always wanted to make it, and then I had the opportunity. I had some money and I hooked up with Roy.

What state was the story in?

I had a 12-page script. It was very rough. See, the whole idea was, I wanted to create a character you would believe in a drama, and not take as a joke. Like, after the first 10 minutes, "Oh, yeah, yeah, he's an ice cream cone. But wait a minute, the guy's crying. Oh, wait a minute, he's cursing. What *is* this?" And then draw them into the themes that you want to deal with. And I think people can experience it better that way. So I brought in Rocco Simonelli, and Rocco wrote a real clean draft of it.

Of the feature script?

No, he just rewrote the short at this point, and added some elements, and then we shot it. Roy put together a nice budget. I paid everyone on the shoot — that was the best thing I ever did, it was so easy — I paid the grips, I paid the cameraman — a cameraman gets two grand a week — I paid everybody. I wanted a professional film. They did a good job, a really good job. The makeup cost like five grand. Kelly Gleason did it. Now she's like a superstar; she's a female Stan Winston.

What was it like working with Mike Lackey on the storyboards?

Let me tell you something: I hate to say this, but he saved my ass with those storyboards, because that's how I directed the movie, meaning I never directed anything and the script went out the window. As a director, you have to think visually. All I had left were his storyboards. And I was like, "Okay, I gotta do this, I gotta get this shot, I gotta get that shot and then I'm done." That's how important fucking storyboards are. Forget the script; let the actors take care of that. Know what you're shooting and what you need to have so you can put together the movie. I'm sure he'll charge me extra for that now.

How did you end up spending on the short?

Altogether, not only with the production, but like flying back and forth and all that, about twenty grand. I didn't have a lot of cash; I had, like,

30 grand, what I'd saved from the sitcom, and slowly it started dwindling away...

But the first company I took it to — it's funny, they had flown me and Patty Mullen out to Las Vegas for one of these video store conventions, to promote *Frankenhooker*. I had just finished the rough cut of *Swirlee* and I brought it with me. So we went out and we were shaking hands and taking pictures with all these goofballs from video stores and all this stuff. And when there was a break I put *Swirlee* on in the Shapiro-Glickenhaus booth, you know, just to watch it? And people would come around, "What's this? What's going on?" So they made me take it off: "Ah, you can't show that here." I said, "Okay."

So I took it off, went back to New York, and I got a meeting with Jim Glickenhaus. He saw the footage. He goes, "Look," — I'm tellin' ya, this is word for word — "I love it. I love the idea, I love what you did." He goes, "You can write, produce, and star in it. I'm gonna take care of the music. We're gonna do it for $750,000. Get started on the script. I'll cut you a check for $10,000 as good faith money." It's called a memo deal; it puts down the basics. Okay, great. Meanwhile, Rocco had already written the whole script. I'm not gonna tell them that...

What was your arrangement with Rocco? Was he just writing on spec?

Rocco was writing on spec, yeah. He kind of took off with it. Most of that script is his; the characters stayed true and everything, but he just loved the idea. He did a great job.

So here's the deal: we know — me and you know — that if somebody's going to give you 10 cents, they're going to make your movie, because they don't have money to throw around. All I wanted was that check for $10,000 upfront, because I knew if I got that check we were going to make the movie. Jim Glickenhaus was out of the picture; he was making this movie called *McBain*, he left town. And now everything was in the hands, literally, of the people — kids — who were on the set of *Frankenhooker* delivering coffee and making sandwiches. I'm in the room with these guys and they all have their legal pads out, because they're the staff of Shapiro-Glickenhaus. And I brought Rocco with me to this meeting. "Well, we don't care for this suicide scene. It's just too depressing. If we could just..." Rocco was really burning, because he knows he wrote the whole script; I'm trying to play an act. It didn't go well, let's just say (laughs). They didn't like the script.

We made a mistake, I think; we gave them the whole script to read before they gave us the money, and they turned us down. They didn't like the adult themes in it, they didn't like the suicide. They wanted to make a kids' movie, like *The Ice Cream Man Hero*. Now, this is the first company I ever took it to; I didn't give a shit. I was like, "Fuck you. Ha-ha! I've got a million places to go with this." If I could only do it all over again I would have just said to them, "Yes, yes, we'll do that, yes" — and then just did what I wanted to do. Because that's what Henenlotter did, you know what I'm saying? They probably said,

"Oh, you can't have a drill in his head." "You're absolutely right." But he did it anyway! And that's the whole trick to getting your movie made on somebody else's money. But they were stupid, because I think they could have made a lot of money with my movie. I showed them how they could distribute it: it's a gangster movie; it's a horror film; it's a comedy; it's this; there's a nude lady; worldwide you could sell this! They were like, "Well, it's just too weird..." So I said, "Can I speak to Jim Glickenhaus?" "He's out of the country." And that was that.

And you never tried to get hold of him when he came back?

Because part of me was like, "Hey, listen. You know what? You don't want to do it? Fuck you, I gotta lot of other places to go." And I did. I went everywhere, and everybody saw it, and everybody wanted to meet me, but nobody made the movie, you know? Now I know what to do. I've been in the car business for 10 years. Now I know how to sell the movie...

Why didn't you send Roy to these meetings?

Roy was out of the picture; I hired Roy to produce the short. In the beginning, Roy did a script breakdown. Roy did the budget for me. His sources weren't interested either. Roy is a master at raising private money. He went to all the *Street Trash* people, and they were all like, "Oh, this is ridiculous." They didn't understand what it was.

They understood Street Trash but not Swirlee?

I guess so! So I went around to all the companies, turned down, turned down, turned down, turned down, turned down, turned down, turned down... Then it got to the point where a couple of years went by. Then, of course, my good friend David Caruso became a big star. And then that complicated things, because at some point we had Chris Gore involved, from *Film Threat*, and he said, "Look, let's do this: I'm creating video games. I have a budget of $2 million to create a video game. Let's make a video game and a movie." I said, "That sounds like a good idea." In other words, one will compliment the other. But now I'm joined with someone that's a big star. And that's different. Now a different element comes into the film.

So when did you decide to put it away?

Well, I never put it away. I'm trying to make it right now.

Did there a come a point when you said, "I have to go back to acting to support my family"?

No, there came a point when I couldn't get any jobs acting and I became a car salesman to support my family, because I had a wife and a kid and we were out in L.A., which is this desperate town; it's terrible. So we came back to New York.

You acted again in The Sweet Life **for Roy and Rocco.**

I did *The Sweet Life*, and that was great. It was a good job and they hired me as soon as I came back.

You got to play a sensitive romantic lead, different than what you're typically known for.

Exactly. I got to play something closer to *Easy Money*. And then that was it. Then I had to go to work. My wife and I were separated when we first came back. We had a lot of problems in L.A. It was not a good town. It's not a good town to be in if you're struggling. I'd rather be in New York, I think.

I think a lot of New Yorkers have trouble adjusting to L.A.

It's lonely and it's brutal, but if you're making it, it's the most beautiful place in the world. I mean, you'd never want to come back to New York if you're doing okay. I still want to go back there, I just can't afford to right now.

I heard there were 1,000 people lined up to meet you guys when you did the Street Trash **reunion in Ohio.**

There were a lot, and it's funny because we were selling our autographs. I was like, "Oh, God"—it was really uncomfortable. Now, I'll do every show if I can make a living at it. It was funny because I felt weird taking money from people, so I'd spend like 10 minutes with them: "Oh, how's everything going?" And while I was there they let me show *Swirlee*. So I told everybody that I met, "You gotta come to the screening." And it was packed; it was perfect. I got to see it in a room full of people and they all reacted to it, and that's the best feeling. I realized, "You know what? This is what it's all about"—for people to see it and enjoy it.

When Roy and I screened Street Trash **at a theatre I managed in Buffalo a lot of people asked about you. There are people out there wondering when you're going to do something again.**

I'm going to do one last thing here with *Swirlee*. I started writing a script for it that I want to actually make. Because I think that at this point, to try to make a movie, you have to do it yourself. You can't rely on anyone else; you have to figure out how to do it all by yourself. Obviously, I'm going to need some help from some people, but I have locations in mind and I rewrote the whole thing. It's a lot different, but I think it might work: Swirlee's a killer now, he's a murderer.

Is he a killer throughout the film, or does he go bad at some point?

He's a killer by accident; he's like Frankenstein. He wants the warmth, he wants a family, he wants connection. And it's great because I'm dealing with all kinds of themes like voyeurism. There's a lot of provocative sexual scenes.

Is Roy involved at this point?

Well, yeah. It's funny, we sat down we had lunch a couple of months ago. I said, "Roy, I want to do something. I think we're wasting our time, we need to be guerrillas again and just shoot something. It has to be horrible and terrible, and technically it doesn't have to be as clean." And Roy was like, "Yes, I agree." Roy had a short film that he had written about two cops, so we kind of combined the two movies. I got about halfway through the script, and then of course depression set in, and here we go again.

Will you still play Swirlee?

I would like to. I mean, if it's going to be mine I may as well. But there are a lot more characters in it now, there's a lot more feeling; it's not as one-note, like it was before. It's very dark; I'd like to make a horror film.

How much of the material that was in the short film is going to appear in the feature script that you're writing now?

Because I'm on a budget, I want to use some of the footage that we already shot as a flashback. That way I can kind of explain what happened and who he was and what was going on, and still salvage what I've done (laughs).

You stuck to your creative guns regarding what you wanted that film to be, but you've said you should have taken the money when they came knocking at your door. How do you feel about that now, if you wind up with a better film because you waited all this time?

I don't think it will be a better film. I should have taken the money and made it. Can you make the print look like a tear drop fell and the ink is running?

18

Post Production

Post production entails all of the steps involved in finishing a movie: picture editing, sound editing, sound effects editing, adding optical/computer generated effects, cell animation or stop motion, color correcting — everything that is required to transform your unedited film into a completed feature. Inexperienced filmmakers usually underestimate the time and money required for this phase of the process.

Editing

In the 20th century, editors literally cut and spliced processed film — called a work print — and then a negative cutter matched those cuts on the film's negative, from which release prints were made. I cut *Slime City* and *Undying Love* on a Steenbeck, a flatbed editing system which I rented and stationed on my front porch. Today, editors work at computerized editing bays, such as an Avid, and filmmakers can cut their movies at their homes, on Final Cut Pro, Media 100, or several other programs. All you need is memory space. Because we shot *Naked Fear* on Hi 8 video, editing on a flatbed wasn't a possibility, and I've never learned computerized editing. So Marc Makowski enlisted Phil Gallo — who scored the music for *Mother's Day* and *The Redeemer* — to edit the film for us. I sat in on all of the sessions, and collaborated on the process, but Phil pushed all the buttons and did a much better job than I ever could have on my own. His contributions were enormous, and in many ways, he saved the film *A director can learn as much about directing by editing his own work as he can from any other step in the process.*

Whereas I had edited *Slime City* and *Undying Love* in a very literal, linear — and predictable — fashion, Phil taught me to overlap dialogue, to hold on shots I was in love with for much shorter periods of time, and to cut for performance over technical considerations. A slightly shaky shot with an actor's best delivery is more effective than a perfect shot with a shaky performance. *Naked Fear* is a performance-driven film — and features the best acting in any of my films, largely because the inexpensive cost of video enabled us to do multiple takes.

Stop motion animation and other special effects are executed in post production. This Spinosaurus model was created by Brett Piper for an unproduced feature, *Dinosaur Kid*. Photograph courtesy Brett Piper.

The Hard Truth

As Phil digitized our footage, it became apparent that our sound was a disaster. For *Naked Fear*, I enlisted the services of a cameraman whose name I discovered on a bulletin board at a cheap rental house. This was in 1995, and Mini-DV had not yet become the rage. Filmmakers knew much less about shooting on video than they do today; J.R. Bookwalter and Scooter McCrae were truly pioneers in terms of what they achieved with their video features. This person did not represent himself as a DP; he was just a guy who had bought a camera, which he was looking to pay off and learn to use. He knew little about lighting and nothing about sound. Not only did I buy into the lie put forth by manufacturers that Hi 8 was a good Pro-sumer format, but I bought into the fallacy that a good shock microphone mounted on the camera could replace a sound recordist, a mixer, and a boom mic. The end result was that our footage — which was quite "noisy," meaning it had the video equivalent of unwanted film grain — was riddled with dropouts and our sound was almost inaudible. Today, most filmmakers know to frequently playback audio, but we didn't; we saw on the camera's indicators that we were getting sound, and some-

The cell animation laid over the Brain in Brett Piper's *Shock-O-Rama* (2005) is another special effect achieved in post production. © POP Cinema, L.L.C.

one always wore headphones, so we thought we were set. The first cut of the film also came in at 64 minutes, too—far too short.

So Phil and I undertook the laborious, pain staking process of dubbing the entire movie. We had to work around the schedules of our actors, and around Phil's freelance work schedule. Peggy Crown, our lead actress, departed for Europe, so I asked Mary Huner to dub her lines. Ironically, I had written the role for Mary, but she had just joined SAG and was afraid of stepping on her union's toes. Peggy gave a wonderful performance, as did Robert and Tommy, and it's a shame she didn't get to do her dubbing. But Mary did a wonderful job of preserving the performance, and it's nice that she participated in some way. In the middle of this process, Phil raised money to direct his first feature, the Super 16 crime drama *West New York*, starring various cast members from *The Sopranos*. *West New York* had a $150,000 budget, which eventually grew to $200,000. Phil and his partners, Donna Miller and Steve Bretschneider, had a lot riding on this project, so *Naked Fear* understandably took a back seat—for two years!

By the time Phil was ready to get back to my film, I had decided to shoot 10 minutes worth of additional scenes to pad out the running time. This led to a major departure from the screenplay, which was set entirely in two apartments to convey the claustrophobic nature of Camden's (Robert Sabin) agoraphobia, the fear of open spaces. For the most part, the additional scenes depicted murders which had previously occurred off screen, and a back story for Tommy Sweeney's character, Randy Carver. I shot the new scenes myself,

20th Anniversary *Slime City Soundtrack CD*, score by Robert Tomaro. Artwork courtesy Eric Maché.

and discovered that while I'm no director of photography, I'm a decent cameraman; the new scenes are the most fluid in the film. One problem I encountered on these pickup scenes is that people's appearances changed over the course of three years. Tommy needed a fake ponytail to match his previous scenes. I wanted Robert's character to open a copy of *Helter Skelter* and discover photos of Randy with the burglar he kills 20 minutes into the film; that relationship had not existed until the re-shoots. When Robert showed arrived from California for the shoot, I discovered he had gone bald, and what little hair he had was gray! I got around this by the framing the camera extremely tight on his face…

All in all, it took me four years to finish this little $7,000 movie, and by the time we started screening it at various venues around Manhattan, Mini-DV had made the scene and I knew it would be hard to find distribution for my Hi 8 movie. The film was well received at its screenings, and Mike Raso at E.I. Cinema liked it, but no one wanted to release it, despite solid acting, some decent gore, and, for the first time in one of my films, nudity. So it sat on my shelf. In 2003, when Mike decided to release *Slime City* on DVD, I convinced him to include *Naked Fear* as an extra on the disc. In essence, I gave the movie away for free, but at least it was distributed, and people saw it and liked it. Just because you *can* edit your own movie doesn't mean you *should*. Editors are unsung heroes in the film business, and directors who don't edit their work know that the editor has just as much impact on a finished film as they do.

Sound Editing

I didn't stick around SVA long enough to learn sound editing. I finished the picture edit on *Slime City* but brought in Kevin Bunce to do the sound editing and serve as post production supervisor. Kevin separated all of he sound elements onto different tracks, and created the cue sheets for our sound mix. Back then, soundtracks were mixes in studios, at a cost of hundreds of dollars an hour. Now sound is mixed in an editor's computer, whether a film has been shot on film or in a digital format.

On *Undying Love*, I hired an old SVA classmate as my sound editor. He committed a major error: whenever a song was playing on the soundtrack, and a character entered a different room, he cut the magnetic stock for that song so it would be easier for the sound mixer to change the levels on the song. This is not how it was done. I took over the sound editing chores—and proceeded to botch the dialogue tracks. Without proper ambient tracks, there is an audible hiss whenever my actors stop speaking.

Sound Effects

I've recorded most of the sound effects in my films because when I've entrusted anyone else to record them for me, I've been unhappy with the results. I've discovered that food stuffs—twisting a full head of lettuce, snapping a carrot, squishing macaroni—make excellent sound effects for horror films. And now, with home editing software, it is a simple task to slow those sounds down or speed them up, giving them an otherworldly or supernatural quality.

As fun as recording sound effects can be, I loathe editing them. Try staying focused when you have to edit a lot of footsteps. This slow, tedious work can take as long—or longer—than picture editing. But it's necessary. I've seen microbudget films that lack even the most basic sound effects. This amateurism is noticeable and distracting.

The Score

Music plays a very important role in the success of a movie. John Carpenter's *Halloween* was deemed a failure when its studio executives viewed it without music. Then they saw it with John Carpenter's distinctive score and they knew they had a hit. Can you imagine *Friday the 13th* without Harry Manfredini's score? You only have to watch the remake of *The Omen* to recognize how important Jerry Goldsmith's score was to the original version, directed by Richard Donner.

I hired Robert Tomaro to score *Slime City* after being impressed by a demo tape he made. The score cost me $1,800 — about $1600 more than I'd hoped to spend — but it was a quality score with instruments besides a synthesizer, and it added a lot to the film's overall quality. In 2008, to celebrate the film's 20th anniversary, Rob re-Mastered the original recordings and we released the soundtrack on CD. It was one more way for me to promote the movie.

On *Undying Love*, I got the $200 synthesizer score I wanted for *Slime City*, and it turned out fine. Mauro J. De Trizio and Danny Sciarra created the background score and contributed not one, but two different songs called *Undying Love* (which makes it all the more mystifying that E.I. Cinema released the film on VHS as *New York Vampire*), and Nelson Wakefield's band at that time, Street Child, allowed us to use some of their heavy metal material. On *Naked Fear*, Nelson and Stephen Buckley created several themes for me for free; unfortunately, due to all the dubbing, we needed wall to wall music or we'd have spent another year recording and editing 100 times more sound effects than we already had. We got permission from two different bands to use their existing songs, and persuaded a rapper, The Mugger Mega Bugged, to record an original song for us.

"Mars" from Dead House Music has composed scores for *Prison of the Psychotic Damned* and *Lovecraft: Fear of the Unknown*. "The primary obstacle with smaller budget films tends to be time," he offers. "Most independent films go way past their production schedules, and this impact their post schedule as well. So, what usually happens is that I end up having materials handed to me later than agreed upon, which means I have to hustle my ass off to get them done in order to maintain my schedule on the next project I have lined up. I pride myself on getting my work done ahead of schedule if at all possible. The other reoccurring dilemma I face is that most inexperienced filmmakers don't know to budget for two vital elements of their film that both happen near the end of the process: music and promotion. If I meet with a filmmaker who doesn't have advance money allocated for promotion after their film is done, that's a pretty big red flag. Invariably they haven't allocated a reasonable budget for music and are scrambling to get something on the cheap at the last minute."

And the Rest

There's more involved in post production than just finishing your film; you also need to prepare it for eventual distribution, or at least exhibition of some kind. Cut a trailer before you take all that memory-consuming footage off your hard drive; while you're at it, cut a five-minute demo and a 10-minute demo; if you're lucky enough to have a distributor interested in taking your film to a film market like the AFM (American Film Market), these can come in handy. While doing that, you may as well cut together some behind the scenes footage to be included on your DVD; I personally never watch the extras on new micro-budget horror films, but it's better to have something than not have it.

Did you ignore my advice and neglect to hire or assign a set photographer? Then now is the time to grab images from the film itself. These "frame grabs" are inadequate for real marketing purposes, but they're better than nothing. This may also be the best time to record a commentary track. I find commentaries more entertaining when some time has passed and the filmmakers have gained enough distance to laugh at their mistakes, but it's probably better to have a full package when you approach a distributor.

19

Brett Piper

Renaissance Man

Brett Piper is a filmmaker who can do just about anything on a film set, and often has. He's written, directed, produced, shot, and edited several micro-budget features and created special effects for them including stop motion animation. He used his skill set as POP Cinema's in-house filmmaker and post production supervisor, which enabled him to fashion *Screaming Dead*, *Bite Me!*, *Shock-O-Rama*, and *Bacterium* for the company. His films show a love for fun special effects like stop motion animation and man-in-suit monsters, often eschewed by young filmmakers weaned on weightless CGI. By staying outside the Hollywood studio system, he's enjoyed autonomy over his films, even while working as a salaried employee.

One of the reasons the DVD market is so glutted right now is because everything has gotten so inexpensive, equipment-wise and product-wise.

That is true. I hear this all the time: "Oh, well anyone can make a movie now." It's almost like saying, "Anybody with a typewriter could be Hemingway." It's not true. One of the things I hear from people making their first movie is, "The cameras are so sensitive now you don't need to light." These are people who don't know the difference between lighting and illumination. They're not the same thing.

Were you ever tempted to move out to L.A.?

No. When I was a kid that's what I thought you had to do. But as soon as I realized you didn't have to do that — this was a time when I was reading articles about Romero making *Night of the Living Dead* outside Pittsburgh — I never thought about it again.

What about film school?

I didn't graduate from high school. If I'd gone to film school, I wouldn't have had to run around and buy my camera in a second hand store and stuff like that; there would have been some kind of equipment available to me. The first time I edited a movie on the Italian equivalent of a Steenbeck I'd never seen one before. I rented the thing and I had to sit down and teach myself how to use it.

Have you taught yourself everything you know?
Entirely. When I sat down with the editing machine I had read everything I could find about it. It wasn't like it was equipment from Mars that I had no way of relating to; I knew roughly how it worked and what buttons to push but there's still that leap between theory and practice that you have to make.

What were your various jobs outside of filmmaking and what was your filmmaking outlet?
I come from a real blue collar background: my family had a construction company and I worked for them when I got out of school, which was very helpful in making cheap movies because it taught me all the practical nuts and bolts things to do; obvious things like building sets, and even less obvious things like, "This is a job. We're not here to screw around." So that was very useful. And then after that I just took any job I could get to bring a little money in and support myself while trying to get a movie made.

Was your goal as an adult always to make movies?
Yes, from the time really that I got out of school.

Did you bother at all with short films?
No, I wanted to make features all along.

That was my attitude as well.
What I would make that was equivalent to a short film was a scene from a feature to get it off the ground. I was never dumb enough to go out and shoot a trailer; that's something you constantly hear about people trying, but you never hear of it working. In some cases they spend as much on the trailer as they could getting the feature started. One guy who did that constantly was Jim Danforth. He would go out and spend $100,000, $200,000 to put a reel together to try to raise financing and I kept thinking, "Jim, make the movie. Stop dicking around. You own the equipment. Just take that money and go out and make a movie."

What I like most about your films for POP Cinema is the stop motion animation.
I don't think I've ever done a movie that didn't have any stop motion animation in it. The first feature I made was something called *Mysterious Planet*, which is a rip-off of *Mysterious Island*, only in outer space. It was a home movie,

like *Equinox*, but not quite as polished. And it was much cheaper. The actual cost of making it on film was $5,000.

Who released it?
   The broker was a guy named Tom Moore, who had a company called Reel Movies International down in Texas. He handled it, and it was just a matter of timing because it came out at the beginning of the video boom when you could sell any piece of crap before the big studios realized there was money to be made in home video, and so people were desperate for product. I think we ended up making about $50,000 on that thing. And by the time we paid the actors, who worked for deferred salaries — by the way, I'm proud to say that any of the actors who's ever worked deferred on my movies has ultimately gotten paid — the total cost was 10 grand, so that's a pretty good profit margin.

Did you initiate Raiders of the Living Dead?
   It was a finished movie that I sold to Sam Sherman. What he essentially did was take my movie, which is available, I believe, uncut, on one of the DVDs, and used it as stock footage; he built his movie around it. That's why it has two directors, me and Sam, listed on it. He took some of the same actors that I had used and he brought them down to New Jersey and that tied everything together. He invented the whole subplot with the kid and his grandfather, and making a laser weapon out of a laser disc player, scratching the emulsion on the film to get the laser effect, which I would never have done.

What was your reaction when you found out what Sherman was doing to it?
   I didn't care. Hemingway or someone, when they asked what it was like to sell a book to Hollywood, said, "Well, you go to the California state line, and you make them throw you your money first, then you throw them the book and forget you ever did the deal." And this was the same thing. You sell a person a movie and it's their movie, and they can do whatever they want with it. I didn't bitch when Troma changed the name of *Dark Fortress* to *Nymphoid Barbarian in Dinosaur Hell*; in fact, I thought it was funny.

I'm going to lump these next three, which you wrote and directed, together: **Drainiac!,** **Psyclops** *and* **Arachnia.**
   You're missing two movies in there...

I also have **Gorilla Warfare: Battle of the Apes** *—*
   I don't know anything about that! Is that a Polonia Brothers movie?

You're credited with doing miniatures.
   When I was moving from New Hampshire I had all these leftover props and I was going to throw them in a dumpster. And I thought, "You know

Brett Piper operates the full puppet Lake Critter from *Mysterious Planet* (1982). Photograph courtesy Brett Piper.

what? The Polonia boys might use these." I packed them all in a box and shipped them to Pennsylvania. And ever since then movies come out with my name in the credits for special effects, creature design, or something. But it's all junk out of a box. After *Raiders of the Living Dead* I did something called *Battle for the Lost Planet*, which was sort of a science fiction epic, again, shot on film for $60,000.

And what was the story with that Battle?

It was sort of the third in a series that I did with the same people who financed my first movie. It was through an investment broker in New Hampshire. Basically, he got his buddies together and had them all put up a little money. This was the most expensive, but I had such huge problems making it that except for being bigger in scope it was not an improvement on the previous movie. It was sold to a company, Cinevest, owned by a guy named Art Schweitzer in New York. In those days, you could do an outright sale with a movie like this. You can't do that anymore. That's how we made money: we'd make a movie for $60,000 and in this case, sell it for $90,000. We made $30,000 profit. And then they wanted me to do another one for them but they shot down all my ideas because basically they wanted more of the same, so I wrote a sequel which I did under the title *Mutant War*, and which Art Schweitzer

Zombie from *Raiders of the Living Dead* (1986). Photograph courtesy Brett Piper.

released as *Mutant Men Want Pretty Women*. It came out the same year as *Pretty Woman* with Julia Roberts, so naturally they squeezed *Pretty Woman* into the title. I guess it makes sense: if you've got a Julia Roberts romantic comedy and a cheap movie about an invasion from outer space, of course the same people are going to want to pay to see it if you put the same words in the title.

So you kind of bounced around from executive producer to executive producer?

I never had a real producer on a movie until I got to E.I. I was always the producer. But what would frequently happen was there was someone controlling the money who thought he was the producer, and they really contributed nothing except signing the checks and more often than not getting in the way and screwing things up. When the guy who calls himself your producer gets you thrown out of your main location on the first day of shooting, it's a hassle.

On They Bite, *were you the first guy to direct Ron Jeremy in a horror film?*

I cast him in a short, one of the segments of what was to be the original *Shock-O-Rama* 15 years ago. Ron Jeremy showed up for one day to play a bartender, at his own expense, because he was desperate to get out of porn movies

Swamp monster from *Nymphoid Barbarian in Dinosaur Hell* (1991). Photograph courtesy Brett Piper.

and do straight roles. And then he ended up being in *They Bite* also, but I didn't cast him. I didn't object to casting him. He's a pretty good actor, but he's a handful.

I laughed when I saw that Trapped: Buried Alive **was a TV movie and that Gabrielle Carteris from** Beverly Hills 90210 **was the star. How did you get hooked up with that?**

I knew the people at Edgewood and I had done a little bit of miniature work for them. They were the same people I wrote *Moving Targets* for. I was hired officially as Second Unit assistant cameraman but I was really there to do miniature effects. But the people who financed the movie didn't want any miniature effects, they wanted everything CGI, so they kind of kept it a secret that I was there doing miniatures. And the miniatures, to be perfectly frank, are the only effects that look good in the movie. The CGI is awful.

Somewhere amidst all these films we really do get to Drainiac!, Psyclops **and** Arachnia, **which you really did write and direct...**

Yes, I did. *Drainiac!* was kind of interesting. I was sitting down trying to figure out how cheap I could make a halfway decent movie shot on film. I just happened to be talking about this with a guy I'd gone to high school with and I said, "Yeah, if I had about 10 grand I could shoot this thing" and he said, "Okay, I'm in." And I said, "What do you mean you're in?" He said, "I'll give you the 10 grand." And that's how that got financed. And we shot it for a little over 10 grand because we rented a camera that was no good and had to call everyone back for an extra weekend to re-shoot stuff.

What was the shooting schedule before re-shoots?

It was supposed to be five days but it ended up being seven. And the funny thing is it was a totally amateur cast, more so than usual because a lot of them were high school kids who had never done anything. At the end of like the third day they kept coming up to me and saying, "When are we going to be done with this? It's been three days already!" But they were good, they worked hard. One of the unintentional benefits of working with people that inexperienced was they'd simply take off for lunch. They'd say, "Hey, are you going to be busy? Can we take off for half an hour?" I'd say, "Sure," and they'd go buy their own lunch at McDonald's and they'd come back. I even said to them the first time they did that, "Bring me back the receipt" and they said, "Yeah, yeah," and didn't bother.

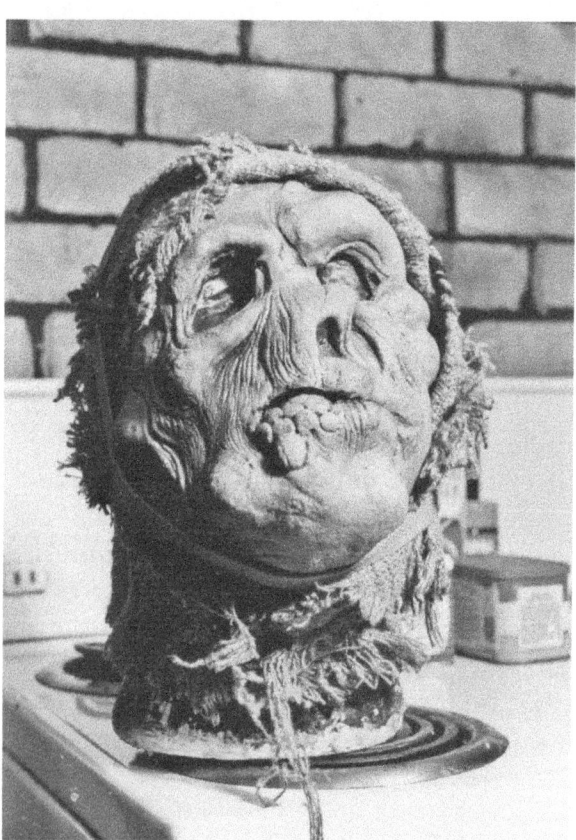

Finished clay sculpt for mutant mask in *Mutant War*, aka *Mutant Men Want Pretty Women* (1992). Photograph courtesy Brett Piper.

And what were these shooting schedules and budgets like?

Psyclops was supposed to be eight days, and I think it was $12,000, and it went to 15 for exactly the same reason as *Drainiac!:* we rented a camera with a bad lens. I mean, the shooting was fast, and unlike shooting on video you don't know if there's a flaw with a camera until you get your film back and you're halfway done. We had shot the first four days when I started getting footage back and realized that there was a problem with the camera and everything was out of focus in certain shots. We stopped shooting for two or three days while I did some tests and figured out a way to get around it. I found out that by never shooting with my aperture more than f.4, and focusing about a foot behind everyone's head, everything was fine. But we had the same problem in that we had to basically call everyone back for a few days and re-shoot. I went to my actors and said, "You know, I've got X amount of dollars left and that's earmarked to pay you guys when we're done. But if I do that I can't finish the movie. I'm leaving it up to you: I'll pay you and then I'll find some way of finishing the movie, or we'll just finish the movie and I'll pay you later." And they said, "Don't be such an asshole. Pay us later." And that was that.

Fish monster from *They Bite* (1996). Photograph courtesy Brett Piper.

Were all three of these movies released?

Yeah. *Drainiac!* was handled by a company out in California called American Film Partners. I have no idea how it did, really; they stopped giving me statements and returning my phone calls, which is a depressingly common thing in this business. Distributors simply stop bothering with you. They're releasing your movie and they just brush you aside and you get no information, and as I said, I sued the people over *Psyclops* and *Arachnia* and I still got no real information

Does this lead us into the E.I. Cinema/POP Cinema era?

Pretty much. I left Vermont after finishing *Arachnia*, although the studio claims I never finished it. The actual fact is I not only finished what I was contracted to do but basically threw in about six months work for free. And then Mike Raso tracked me down and called me up. I was staying with some friends back in New Hampshire and he said, "You want to make a movie for us?" and I said, "Yeah, sure," and it all just fell together in a matter of weeks.

So your initial contact with him was to write and direct Screaming Dead?

Well, we had spoken off and on a number of times. At one point he wanted to distribute *Drainiac!* but by that time someone else was handling it, which was unfortunate because if Mike had distributed it we would have made money off of it. I had just finished writing *Screaming Dead* when he called me, and he said, "Got anything ready to shoot?" and I said, "Got one right here." And he said, "Is there a part for Misty in it?" And I said, "Yeah, there is." He said, "Good, come on down, we'll talk." And that was that. It was amazing, the first time I met him. You know how this usually goes, you come down and talk, that means that you have lunch and you chat, and then a week later they say, "Let's have another meeting," and you have another lunch and you chat. I went down to E.I. and everybody from the company and myself sat around a big conference table and hammered out a deal, and wrote it out on a legal pad, and it was a done deal in like an hour and a half. And I thought, "My God, these guys mean business." It was originally a one-shot deal, and what happened was the movie was about finished and they were pretty pleased with it and they said, "Why don't we sign a deal for a couple more?" And that became *Bite Me!* and *Shock-O-Rama*, and then by the time *Shock-O-Rama* was done, I was an employee, basically. Instead of working for a flat fee as an independent contractor they just hired me. I did *Bacterium* for them and I worked on two or three other movies while I was there.

Was Screaming Dead ***Erin Brown's first non-softcore movie?***

I think it was. I remember one day we were almost finished, and as she was leaving one day she turned to me and she said, "When's this thing going to come out?" And I said, "Oh, I don't know when it will come out, but I'll be finished in about a month." And she said, "Good, I want to be able to tell my friends I finally made a real movie." So she saw it that way. Another actress on the movie said that "It's basically just like everything else I've ever done for E.I. I still have to take my clothes off." And I said, "Well, if that's the only thing you're looking at, then, yeah, I guess it's the same, isn't it?"

What was your budget on Screaming Dead?

We had a budget to start with of $35,000 for *Screaming Dead*, and it went substantially over that. But at the time E.I. was doing very well, so when it started to look like it was going over budget, the first thing they told me was, "Don't worry about it, that's not your problem." Which is something people like to say but which is never true, because when you're making the movie, everything that affects the finances ultimately affects you. You either have to cut back on days or cut back on people, it always comes back to you. But in this case it didn't, because as I said, they were doing pretty well at the time, so they just kept expanding the budget, they just kept throwing more money into it. It was still cheap; it was not a $100,000 movie.

What was the format on that one?

We shot that with the Panasonic 24p.

Is that what all the ones you shot for them were?

No. *Screaming Dead* and *Bite Me!* were, *Shock-O-Rama* was shot in Super 16, film, and then *Bacterium* was shot with the Sony Hi Def camera. It was a nice camera, I've got to say. I was very pleased to be shooting with that thing. The look you can get on screen for the money you're spending is pretty remarkable.

Do you remember what the Screaming Dead *shooting schedule was?*

Two weeks. I think we did a day of pickups, and obviously I did a lot of inserts afterwards, which I shot by myself.

How long did it take for them to release it?

Oh, Gosh. I think it came out later that year, but I don't remember what the street date was.

And they were happy enough with that—

Oh, they were delighted. Although Mike Raso didn't even know what the movie was about until he saw it. He didn't read the script. He never does.

Was he equally hands off on the screenplay for Bite Me!?

The original idea was Mike's. He said, "Let's do a movie about some place infested with killer bugs." The strip joint idea came from an actress who ended up not being in the movie.

I was so happy to see stop motion in a low budget film.

The funny thing that people don't understand about stop motion is it's a very inexpensive medium. It's time consuming, but when you look at a movie like this, you're the only person who's there and there's no crew.

What are the drawbacks of shooting stop motion on digital video instead of film?

We don't have the software to do it on video. Not to do it right; we have no frame grabbers or anything. So what I have to do is videotape the entire process. So if it takes me two hours to animate a cut, that tape is running for two hours. And then I go back and pull the frames I need on the Avid. That's laborious and not a whole lot of fun. It works fine.

I think that of most of these, that's the one that knows the POP Cinema audience the best and delivers all of the elements in a fun way.

And that was completely intentional; that was by design. And yet, the audience never really found the movie. It gets good reviews, it gets bad reviews. But the thing I've found with my movies—and this may sound a little egotistical, but I've found this to be true—is that the people who really like my movies are the people who really know about movies, and the people who don't like them are sort of average amateurs who think they know about movies; so they tear them apart for reasons that they actually don't understand, whereas people who understand movies and like movies and understand what it takes to make a movie like this appreciate the things.

Misty said something very perceptive once. We were having lunch before shooting *Shock-O-Rama*. She said, "You know, if people understood what goes into making even a bad movie, maybe they'd shut up." And the only thing I disagree with is they still wouldn't shut up. She's right. When people look at a movie and they complain about the acting, they don't realize those were the best people you could get. If they could only see the people you turned down they'd have a better sense of perspective.

It was obvious to me that Shock-O-Rama **was conceived as an anthology film. Was there a marketing decision behind trying to make people think it's one feature even though it's really three shorts?**

That's exactly what happened. I had finished shooting it and had started editing when they came to me and said, "You know, we don't want this to be an anthology." I said, "But it is." They said, "Yeah, but can we disguise that?" and that's how that came about.

You shot that on 16m film, and it's filled with effects.

Yeah, I'm very happy with that. I would have to say it's the closest to my idea of a good movie of all of the movies I've done.

How do you find time to do makeup appliances, like the brain creature, when you were directing?

"The brain" did part of his own makeup. The guy who played the brain, Mike Thomas, is actually a well established makeup man. He's worked on *Saturday Night Live* and a lot of other things. So he's been doing it for a long time and what I asked—not that he isn't a good actor, because he is; he played the studio head in that too, so he played two parts—I had him play the brain primarily because I knew he had a life mask I could borrow. So I borrowed the life mask and the brain was built around that, so it already fit him, and all he had to do was basically glue it on, which he did himself. It was easier for him to do than it would have been for me. And then I touched it up, I just blended it in. So the whole process for me took 10 minutes. And then it took a lot of time in post because it was easier for me to go back and hide the seams in post than to keep touching up his makeup while we were trying to shoot. The real rule of thumb on a movie like this, with this kind of money, this kind of crew and schedule is, anything you can push back to post, you do, because you're going to have more breathing space there. So I would go through and, with the primitive technology I had at my disposal, clean up the seams in his close ups and stuff like that in post.

When they asked you to come on board and work in house, what did they want you to do for them?

The idea was basically for me to make more movies for them, with the understanding that if they had other movies they wanted me to work on I'd try to find time. To give Mike a lot of credit, even though he was paying me a salary, whenever he had me work on another movie he would always offer me more. He'd say, "We'll give you an extra $500 to do this." And I'd say, "Mike, that's not necessary. You're paying me. My time is my time, I don't care what I work on." But actually it worked out well when I worked on a Polonia brothers movie, *Splatter Beach*. Mike sent me out there to be the DP and I said, "You know, they don't have enough help. They don't have enough people. Take the $500 you were going to give me and hire somebody else too, you'll have an extra hand on the movie." So that's what they did.

Where was Splatter Beach *filmed*?

It was filmed near Lake Erie. They rented a very nice location, but I was only there for two and a half days. It was a slightly disconcerting experience because the Polonoias are identical twins. They split the shoot basically into two units. In the three days that I shot there, they got six days worth of shooting done. They had two cameras, but they wouldn't have had two sound people if I hadn't suggested hiring another person to Mike. So they had two cameras, they shot one themselves and I was supposed to be the DP with the other, and they had two sound people. This was weird enough in itself, but as I said, they're identical twins, so after a day or so you actually get the impression that it's one person in two places at once. And if it wasn't for the fact that Mark — I think it's Mark, maybe it was John — *one* of them had grown a little beard!— I probably couldn't have told them apart. It was the strangest experience.

Justin discusses Skin Crawl *earlier in this book. Years ago, when the Tarantino films were big, I wondered if so-called "spatial editing" would work in a horror film. Did you recognize right away that* Skin Crawl *had the material you needed to do this?*

Yeah, because that was the problem. Originally the movie had a perfectly straight, linear plot. When Brian did the rough cut, the first cut, it just went A, B, C, D, E, F, G ... from start to finish. And what I did was to cut all the slow parts out; Justin loves dialogue. This was an E.C. comics' story, and that was part of the problem because an E.C. comics story might run four or five pages, not enough for a feature film. What he had done was take four or five pages worth of material and padded it to 70 minutes, mostly with dialogue. And by the time I went through and cut all the padding out, the movie was literally less than 30 minutes long. It wasn't that long to start with, a little over an hour. So I cut maybe 55 percent of the movie out. I looked at it and said, "My God, how am I going to make this feature length?" The thing that came to me, obviously, was to simply keep retelling the same story from different angles. That way I got to use the same material over and over again and hopefully it wouldn't be boring. So it was a technical thing, "How do I stretch 30 minutes worth of material to feature length?" and that's what happened.

I don't know what the film would have been like otherwise—the acting is good and the direction is solid—but I think it's a fine film.

I think Justin did a really good job, he just tends to be verbose. The funny thing is, I edited most of it while he was on vacation, at Mike's urging. I kept saying, "I need to go over this with Justin," and Mike couldn't understand why. I'd say, "Because it's Justin's movie," and Mike would say, "No, it's mine." "No, Mike, you paid for it, but it's Justin's movie. I'm a director too, I have to respect that." They sort of pushed me into editing it without Justin and I said, "Fine, I'll do a first cut but I'll sit down with Justin." When Justin finally saw it we got into—I won't call them arguments, because no one ever lost their temper—but long discussions. He kept trying to pressure me to put things back in, and I just kept resisting. There was one scene where I cut from basically someone setting up a reaction shot of Julian getting screwed up the ass, and I cut directly from the setup to a hilarious close up, I thought, of Julian's face, and I cut out probably three pages of dialogue that went in between there. And I said, "Justin, here's how you do it: setup, payoff; setup, payoff; you don't need all this stuff in the middle.

Justin had a very mixed reaction. He liked what I had done with it but he hated the fact that I had taken so much of his material out. He actually had to sneak in behind Mike's back to work with me on it because Mike didn't want him involved with it at all. Mike's attitude was sort of like they worked at 20th Century Fox in 1940: once the director's done, he doesn't touch the movie, which goes on to the editor. That's just not a good way to work. And Justin wound up being immensely helpful because I couldn't make heads or tails out of the way that Brian labeled the original footage, so all I knew was what I could see in his first cut. I didn't even know if there were alternate takes available, unused scenes, or anything. And Justin did, he had them all in his head. If he hadn't been there, it wouldn't be anywhere near as good a movie, just from an editorial standpoint, because I wouldn't have known about all this missing material.

What was your title when you were in house at E.I.?

My checks called me an editor. I don't know why. I was there to make movies. The plan was to make three movies this year, and then it got cut down to two, then it got caught down to none.

What led to your departure?

It wasn't my decision. That was E.I.'s decision. Ostensibly it's very simple: the market's bad and there's no money coming in. I went in to discuss what my next movie was going to be because, as I said, they had cut the slate down from three to two, but I was still supposed to do two movies. I went in to discuss that in Mike's office and he said, "We can only pay you for another three weeks." And that was it. That was the discussion. It had nothing to do with me striking out on my own.

The first thing to go is the production value...

Yes, very true. I know they're still planning on doing more of these $3,000 or $4,000 movies.

What are your favorite aspects of filmmaking?

I like the actual hands on stuff best. Writing used to be fun but now it's turned into a chore. What I seem to enjoy best is building the creatures, props, and the weird stuff that the movie needs. That's the most satisfying. And that's probably the last thing people would think. "Don't you like directing?" I hate directing. With very rare exceptions, I think directing is a huge pain in the ass.

I've always loved effects of any kind, at least until CGI became so prevalent that even amateurs could use it in their low budget films.

90 percent of the fun of watching monster movies when I was young was wondering how they pulled off the effects, and that's completely gone because there's only one acceptable way for anybody to do effects now and that's CGI. You have to do it that way. That's what's so frustrating about this business: if you don't do it the way everybody else is doing it you're doing it wrong. It's taking all the fun out of it.

Independent filmmakers can still attempt these so-called "antiquated methods."

This is also the only medium that considers itself an art form that uses words like "antiquated." You don't hear people talking about "antiquated music," or "antiquated paintings." We call them "classics" sometimes, but they're not antiquated because we just keep adding new techniques to the old ones. But in the movie business, new techniques push the old ones out.

We've got younger and younger studio executives dealing with younger and younger filmmakers who have less and less familiarity with the older, tried and true ways of doing things, and everything's got to be "cutting edge."

Yes, and they don't know what "cutting edge" means or what it is, but that's a phrase they like. But that's the other problem, which is this entire industry is run by people who don't actually care about the movies. The movie business isn't run by movie fans, it's run by money fans and marketing people. When you try to get these movies into the video stores you have to deal with people who brag that they don't actually watch the movies; they want to see your artwork or they want to know who's in it, but they don't watch the movies and they're proud of that. You know, a long time ago, this was probably back in the 1930s, some writer was talking to a producer and he got pissed off and said, "You are the asbestos curtain between the audience and entertainment." I think that's a great line because now that's all we've got: all of these robots between the filmmaker and the audience, and they've got nothing to do with movies.

20

Distribution

Congratulations, you've finished your first movie.
Now what?
When you finished shooting your film, you thought you were almost done. During post production, you realized how much work remained to do. Now that you've completed post production, the battle may *still* be only half over.

And it's cold out there, Jack and Jill.

Don't expect people to knock down your door for a chance to see your film; you have to knock down theirs just to get them to look at it. The market for low budget horror films—particularly for micro-budget horror films shot on various digital video formats—is glutted with product. There is more out there than the distributors who are willing to release these films can handle. Your chances of landing a distributor are greatly improved if: 1. you shot your feature on film; 2. you have "names" in your cast; or 3. your film is exceptionally good. If you couldn't afford to shoot on film, and you lacked the foresight to take advantage of the SAG Ultra Low Budget Agreement to get at least one name into your film, you can till beat the odds in this harsh environment if you've actually made a good movie. Cream rises to the top, even in this unforgiving economy.

Theatrical Exhibition

The market for releasing low budget horror films made by unknown filmmakers theatrically no longer exists. Of course, there are extremely rare exceptions: an indie horror film shot on Mini-DV may follow in the footsteps of *The Blair Witch Project* and *Open Water* and do so well at a non-horror film festival that a distributor will pick it up for a theatrical run. But that is *extremely* unlikely. *Blair Witch* may have made over $150 million around the world, but *Open Water* made only $ 6 million domestically. That's a big difference, especially when you figure in the expenses incurred by marketing a theatrical release. The first *After Dark Horrorfest: 8 Films to Die For* did quite well its first year, but when people realized this national mini-film festival was a ploy to market DVDs of the various titles, lightning failed to strike twice despite an enormous marketing budget. Anchor Bay, owned by Starz, has been trying to compete with Lion's Gate on a theatrical level, but so far their runs (number of theatres) have not been significant, and the releases still seem geared toward selling DVDs. The chances of your film receiving a theatrical release are almost nonexistent.

Self Distribution — Theatrical

Of course, you can always self distribute your film. Tom Laughlin did this with *Trial of Billy Jack* and Larry Fessenden did it with *Habit.* There are two methods of self distribution: in the first, you convince a theatre to show your film for a percentage; this will probably be for a 65/35 split in the theatre's favor. To pull this off, you'll either need a 35mm print of your film, or you'll have to find a theatre equipped with a 16m or digital projector. More and more theatres are installing digital equipment, but are they willing to give indie filmmakers a break? If they'll show your film, and if they go for a split, they may insist that you pay for newspaper advertising, which is expensive and may absorb your entire cut of the admissions. As with any other product, people are unlikely to spend money to see a film that hasn't been advertised by conventional means, unless you manage to generate a great deal of media buzz for it. Your goal is to get the exhibitor (theatre owner) to share in the advertising costs as well as the revenues.

Let's say you succeed in doing this at a theatre in your home town. Imagine how much harder it will be to pull off this same feat in a town where you have no connections. Now imagine doing that on a national level. Unless you're wealthy, you simply cannot afford to promote your film across the country. You can try a less ambitious release, going from college town to college town with one or two prints—but this will still be more expensive than most indie filmmakers can afford. Your best bet may be to play only as a midnight movie in your town, in which case the theatre owner may not insist on advertising, and you might actually make a few dollars to put into marketing your film for DVD.

Another option is called "four walling." This means that you pay the theatre owner a flat fee to rent the theatre and keep all of the proceeds. You can set the admission price and you can decide whether or not to advertise. Tom Laughlin made so much money from *Billy Jack* that he four walled *Trial of Billy Jack* across the country and turned a profit. But he attempted this again with *The Last Gunfighter* and *Billy Jack Goes to Washington* and lost every cent he had, because neither film delivered the elements his audience had come to expect from him. Laughlin was a marketing genius, but timing is everything.

I four-walled *Slime City* as a midnight movie at the Bleecker Street Cinemas in New York City for six weekends in 1988 and advertised in the *Village Voice.* The first weekend, we competed with Fred Olen Ray's *Hollywood Chainsaw Hookers,* starring Gunnar Hansen and Linnea Quigley, and we creamed

Camp Home Video box art for the first domestic VHS release of *Slime City* (1988).

them. In fact, we sold out the 80-seat house for four of the six weekends we played. As a filmmaker, I've had no greater experience than sitting in that run down independent theatre while people screamed and laughed and cheered during my movie. One night a guy walked in during the middle and I thought, "Wow, that guy paid full price to see the second half of my film!" But that's all ego. We broke even on our advertising, but we didn't turn a profit. *Variety* reviewed us just like any other theatrical film, and when Camp Home Video released the film on VHS one year later, they trumpeted our theatrical release. For me and my partners, the cost was worth the way the film was perceived.

Undying Love played as a midnight movie for five weekends at the Village East Cinemas, also on NYC. This time, we got the 65/35 split. We advertised in *The Voice* again, and I was excited about the opening because The Phantom of the Movies gave us two and a half stars in *The New York Daily News*. That may not sound like a ringing endorsement, but he gave most of the *Elm Street* sequels only two stars. His review told horror fans that my $35,000 movie was better than more popular horror films that cost millions. *Variety* also gave us a positive review, and when we arrived at the theatre opening night, the line stretched around the block. Imagine the word of mouth that a crowd that size could generate! Sadly, the theatre had recently been renovated, and something triggered the new sprinkler system, canceling our show. Another disaster preempted us the following night and we never recovered; we had those people based on the reviews and we lost them.

Because *Naked Fear* was shot on video, we played it at a community center in the Bronx, and at a lower East side venue called the Millenium, and at the Two Boots Den of Cin; it never took off. *Brain Damage* actually had a wide release within New York City: it played in Times Square and a few theatres in New Jersey, and I remember being stunned to see TV spots for it running in prime time. Those TV ads cost a *lot* of money. Ed Walloga and I attended a showing in Jersey, and there were only two other people in the theatre (to add insult to disappointment, the projectionist, anxious to get home, shut off the projector before our names appeared in the closing credits). When I managed the 86th Street East in Manhattan, I was excited when the owner booked *Basket Case 2* for a full week. I probably went into the auditorium every screening to watch the twisted ending, but the attendance was pitiful.

It is extremely difficult to play a film theatrically now without a major national release and a multi-million dollar marketing blitz. Just ask Troma Entertainment. They tried hard to release *Poultrygeist* territory by territory and had trouble finding theatres willing to show it.

International Sales

It cost us $35,000 — our projected total budget — to see *Slime City* through the rough cut stage. I screened our edit for a representative of Vestron Video, the largest independent video distributor in the world at that time, and the rep liked and recommended it. I had a single telephone conversation with an acquisitions person, who brought up an acquisition fee of $150,000 — the same figure that the Wall Street wizards had proposed financing the film for. $150,000 would have enabled to us to complete the film, pay back our investors, pay off our

Eric Maché's theatrical poster for *Undying Love* (1992).

deferments, and distribute some Net Profits. Who knows? It might have led to a career for me. We left off that the acquisitions person would get me a contract the following week. That weekend, after a string of theatrical fiascos, Vestron Pictures scored their first major hit with *Dirty Dancing*. On Monday, the president of the company decreed that they would no longer acquire low budget horror films. My deal evaporated before I even received the paperwork, and to this day I hold a grudge against Patrick Swayze.

With our resources dried up, Marc Makowski and I approached Alexander Beck, a foreign sales agent based in Times Square, whom we knew of because of an article on him that had appeared in *Fangoria*. Alex was famous for two things: importing *Godzilla* and buying *Friday the 13th* from Paramount when they thought it was a dud — and then selling it back tot hem for a million dollar profit when they realized they'd made a mistake. Alex was a friendly guy who had his ex-wife and his then current wife working for him in his office at the same time. When I told Frank Henenlotter I was going to see him, Frank said, "Take your own Vaseline and be prepared to bend over."

Alex liked what he saw ("It's no *Gone with the Wind*...") and advanced us $20,000 to complete the film. Our deal called for him to take a 25 percent fee off the top of any sales he made, and apply the balance toward the money we owed him. He also wanted credit as executive producer, and for us to pay him $200 for every film festival he attended, to defray his expenses. This is where Jerry Gold came into play. I did not want Alex to receive executive producer credit, or any credit; I feared that doing so would tie us to him forever, and I knew we'd want to walk away from him at some point. Marc didn't want to pay the $200 festival fee, speculating that he could make sales, not tell us, and we'd be paying him money out of *our* pockets. With a couple of phone calls, Jerry made certain we didn't have to worry about either of those concerns.

Alex didn't do a horrible job for us. He sold several countries — Japan for $10,000, Korea for $4,000, Taiwan for $4,000, Spain for $6,000, Brazil for $4,000, and the deal that finally set us free, Great Britain for $10,000. In the end, we finished our film, made $3,000, and took back our baby. To retrieve our materials, we drove out to his mansion in Scarsdale, since he had closed his Times Square office by then. That house, paid for on the backs of independent filmmakers, had a two-level basement with a full sized screening room. As we left, Alex said, "You're the only guys who ever took a picture back from me!" Over the years, I've met several filmmakers to whom he told the same thing.

One of the frustrating things about dealing with foreign sales agents is that they come back from film festivals with numerous deal memos signed by foreign buyers, and few of them ever amount to anything — or that's what they tell you. You have no way of knowing if they're ripping you off. All a foreign distributor has to do is re-title your film. In fact, you'll sleep better at night if you assume they are dishonest, and just hope that they're not *too* crooked. Always have a lawyer review any contract you're considering signing with one

Theatrical poster for *Naked Fear* (1999), emphasizing Tommy Sweeney's claustrophobic serial killer. Photograph courtesy Eric Maché.

of these guys, and, if possible, don't turn over any negatives, prints, or Masters to them. Provide them with all the screeners they need, and duplicate the other materials yourself as needed, out of your own pocket, to at least try to regulate who's getting them.

Home Video and DVD

Alex Beck wanted to control domestic distribution of *Slime City* as well, but on Jerry's advice we only gave him foreign rights. By the time we finished the film and had our midnight run, the market had become glutted with low budget horror films and companies willing to distribute them stopped paying advances. One company, United Home Video, offered us $25,000 for domestic home video, but Jerry said, "I'm putting this contract into a folder and saving it, so I can show it to people as an example of the biggest invitation to rape I've ever seen." We requested changes and never heard back from them.

Camp Home Video, which had released several Fred Olen Ray films, as well as *Gore-Met Zombie Chef from Hell*, offered us a $13,000 advance. As soon as we expressed interest, they tried to knock that down to $9,000, but I held firm. They paid us in three installments: one upon signing, another upon receiving our materials, and the final payment when the film was released. Our contract specified that they had to release the film within a year of signing, or we'd get the rights back, so they couldn't sit on the film and delay that final payment indefinitely. The contract stated the company would recoup the advance they paid us after selling 2500 units (store cost: $49.99; retail price: $59.99).

I was happy with Camp's marketing campaign. They designed snazzy box art and mailed full size movie posters to video stores around the country. Our very first statement showed they had sold 2500 units, so our next one should have put us into profit. But there was no next statement. I started calling Sal Richichi, the company's owner, and whenever he answered the phone he would pretend to be someone else and said "he" wasn't there. Registered letters were never answered. The phone was disconnected. Rumors circulated that he had gotten into trouble with the mob over pornography, and had gone on the lamb, into witness protection, or been whacked. For all I know, he's sitting in the same Wilshire Boulevard office right now with a different phone number.

Soon I started seeing the film advertised in horror magazines. What we eventually learned was that Camp home Video had closed shop owing money to several vendors, including the warehouse where its inventory was stored. To recoup their losses, the warehouse sold the inventory in bulk, at a discount, to any sub-distributor willing to take them. Our only statement showed that the initial press run was 5,000 units, which means another 2,500 units were sold for which we never saw a dime. Fortunately, we'd held onto our negative, one 16m print of the film, and one of the two one-inch Masters that we'd made, or the film would now be lost.

We filmed *Undying Love* in 1991 and played it as a midnight movie in 1992 (the fastest turnaround for any of my films). Due to drastic changes in the market, it then sat on the shelf for four years. No one would touch it until Eric Maché and Carl Morano showed it to Mike Raso at E.I. Cinema, who acquired the film for no advance. Mike changed the title to *Curse of the Vampire*, which I loathed, because he felt *Undying Love* sounded too much like a Meryl Streep movie. Then he changed it to *New York Vampire*, which I felt sounded at least a little less generic. They marketed it toward their audience — the horror T & A crowd — kept me in the loop, and, I felt, did the best they could with it in a very hostile market. We made about $2,000 once they recouped their expenses — on a film that cost $35,000. No one involved with repping the film — not Eric, not Carl, and not Mike — ever made a foreign sale, and I consider it a better film than *Slime City*. The film has yet to be released on DVD, and I know a lot more about marketing now than I did then.

I was pleased enough with the way E.I. treated *Undying Love* that I suggested to Mike that they re-release *Slime City*. My contract with Camp officially expired in 1996. In 1998, I screened a slightly re-edited version of the film — new titles, with some of the more embarrassing moments cut — as part of a 10th anniversary reunion with some of the cast and crew. E.I. released that version of the film, along with a mini-doc, *Making Slime*, in a slip-foil VHS case that opened up like a book. I was pleased with the presentation, but with DVD on the horizon, and at least 5,000 copies of the film in circulation, not to mention bootlegs, the release didn't exactly set the world on fire.

Which brings us to the 21st Century. In 2004, Mike invited me to supervise the transfer of the existing 16m print of *Slime City* to DVD. When we'd originally shot the film back in 1986, we'd hoped to blow it up to 35mm, so we deliberately left extra space at the top and bottom of each shot. The blowup never happened, and for years I was embarrassed but the composition of the shots. During the transfer, we letterboxed the film, so for the first time it appeared the way Peter and I had always intended. It was like seeing an entirely new movie.

I persuaded Mike to include my third film, *Naked Fear*, as an extra, essentially giving the movie away. But I believe I was smart to do this: no one else would ever have picked this film up, and POP Cinema has a habit of releasing their acquisitions as double features. Had I not thrown *Naked Fear* into the pot, they might have released *Slime City* with another film, and then what little money they paid me in royalties would have been split between myself and another filmmaker.

The DVD was released in 2005, under E.I.'s Shock-O-Rama Cinema label, and I screened it at several horror conventions, and sat at the Shock-O-Rama table several times with POP employees Paige Davis, Justin Wingenfeld, and Henrique Couto. The film received a lot of attention, which I attribute to a resurgent interest in 1980s horror films. Timing is everything, and for once it worked in my favor. I did dozens of interviews, and continue to do them, promoting the film. A new generation of horror fans thrives on the Internet, and the majority of new reviews were surprisingly affectionate and enthusiastic.

In the end, POP turned a profit, so I saw a few dollars: a little under $500 over a two year period. I've attended dozens of conventions to promote the film, and the amount of money I've made would cover maybe one of them.

When I asked Mike to release the film on DVD, it wasn't because I expected to get rich, or even make money on the film. It was because I wanted it to be available in the current dominant home entertainment format. As a producer of the film, it's my responsibility to keep it available so it can be discovered by new fans. And it's enjoyed an entire new life thanks to the DVD, so I'm grateful to POP Cinema for releasing and for doing such a good job promoting it. But the deck is always stacked against the filmmaker when a distributor doesn't pay an advance, and you should take a cold, hard look at the above figure, because thousands of copies of my film have been sold.

If a distributor acquires your micro-budget film, make sure the contract spells out when it will be released. If they give themselves a three-year window, don't sign the contract. You're not going to make any money on the project, so the only benefit you derive from such a release is satisfaction that people can see your product, and the possibility that having a film distributed may help you raise a larger budget next time, or get a paying gig as a director for hire.

Making a Buck

Your DVD distributor will allow you to purchase your movies "at cost." My deal with POP Cinema allows me to buy copies of *Slime City* for $6.00 each. Any distributor that produces thousands of copies of a DVD and charges the filmmaker $6.00 per unit is actually making money off that filmmaker. I discovered that the company was selling copies of my film that Best Buy had returned — "returns" — to e-bay sellers for $1.00 a piece as long as they ordered a minimum of 30 units. When I tried to buy copies for myself at that same cost, I was told that as a filmmaker, I needed to order *1,000* units! The next time I enter into a distribution agreement, I'll know to stipulate that I will never pay more than anyone else for my own movie, and that I must be notified anytime the distributor offers copies to someone at a lower price.

On-Line Distribution

We are fast approaching the day when distributors will deliver movie purchases and rentals to customers directly to their homes via the internet. Netflix has already taken the first step in that direction. This is the future: eventually movies will stream through internet connections to the large screen TVs in people's homes, making DVDs— Hi Definition and otherwise — as antiquated as DVDs made VHS and Beta tapes. This is a huge future market for independent filmmakers, but, as with any media, what remains to be seen is whether or not these internet distributors will spend money marketing microbudget product. Without audience awareness, micro fare will struggle just as much as it is in the current theatrical and home entertainment markets. It will be fascinating to see how this develops.

21

Stephen Biro

UNEARTHING FILMS

Stephen Biro is the president of Unearthed Films, a DVD distributor specializing in horror films. We met at the Halloween Horror Picture Show in Florida, then ran into each other again at Chiller Theatre in New Jersey, and at the HHPS again the following year. Finally, we wound up sitting side by side at Spooky Empire's Screamfest, another Florida con — and my table was completely obscured by a *Frankenhooker* display he had set up. This is a cutthroat business! Through Unearthed, Stephen distributes a nice variety of cult, foreign and indie horror films, and because he is a screenwriter himself, he understands the needs and expectations of filmmakers.

How was Unearthed Films formed?
Unearthed Films started with me, two VCRs, and a couple of underground bootleg tapes. I used to sell copies of anime and gore films without copyrights through a comic book store I used to own. I was doing really well with it; the comic book business started slowing down and the underground movie industry started picking up. I knew video traders in the underground all over the world, so I was doing a lot of trading to get my customers at the comic book store cool stuff to watch. I gravitated toward the horror and gore because that's what I love, what I collected for years. I've been a gorehound since I was 13. My business partner in the comic book store screwed me over, so I took the computer, whatever VCRs we had, and all the underground bootlegs, and I went home and learned the internet and started a website called *Video Mayhem in Florida*. I became one of the big underground video collectors. I did a phenomenal amount of business, and this was back in the videotape days. As videos moved into DVDs, I thought, "I can't keep doing this forever." I was making a decent living at it, but things started coming out, and getting re-released, and movies from allover the world started getting releases here in the states. So I opened up an underground cult video store called Video Mayhem in Ybor City, specifically for anime, kung fu, horror, and sexploitation.

And then this guy named Paul White got in contact with me and told me. "Hey, I have the rights to those *Guinea Pig* movies. Take them down. And then I called him. We started talking and he offered me the rights to the *Guinea Pig* films for $80,000. I said, "There's no way I could do that with the money I have. How about you give me the movies and we'll split it 50/50 and start a new company?" And he laughed at me and hung up. 30 days later he calls back: "Okay, Steve, I realize that you know everything about the horror genre. How about I sell you the *Guinea Pig* movies for $10,000 and we split the money 50/50?" And I'm like, "No, I can't do that. The manufacturing, and the marketing, and the advertising... How about you give them to me and we split it 50/50?" He starts laughing. "Oh, I can't do that!" He hangs up. 30 days later he calls back. "Okay, so if we start this company, we're going to split it 50/50 and move on from there?" I'm like, "Yeah, I know what I'm doing. I know what movies are good and what we could do." That was the birth of Unearthed Films.

What the hell is this Guinea Pig *movie?*

The Guinea Pig movies were a series of underground, fake snuff films out of Japan. When they were making the bootleg circuit, Chas. Balun made a party tape for somebody in Hollywood, and Charlie Sheen saw one and he thought it was a real snuff film. It's basically just a samurai dismembering a chick for an hour, so the effects are gruesome. The FBI realized it was fake, but they'd already created a stir, because this was before the internet, back in like '88. *20/20* did an expose on it and just made a big hoopla because everybody thought it was real. So I realized that if we released the *Guinea Pig* films, a total of eight movies, we'd make a name for ourselves. And then we slowly started releasing some really good genre product, like *Junk*, and it just started snowballing.

How many titles do you release a year?

One to two a month, so 12 to 20 a year.

How many conventions do you attend?

I used to do quite a number of conventions, but the cost — airfare, shipping, electricity, hotel, food — tends to eat up the money you make. So now I tend to only do local conventions.

What ratio of units do you sell through your website and at conventions vs. through distributors and sub-distributors?

I sell about 500 copies of the titles to consumers and to the indie DVD cult guys, like Exploited Cinema, Diabolik DVD, HK Flicks. Through the distributors that we use we sell anywhere from 5,000 to 30,000, which is great; that's what we need to stay alive. Doing it ourselves, yes the money comes straight to us, but it's not worth it.

What usually turns you off to a film someone has submitted to you?

They've got five minutes. I put in that movie, and if in five minutes I don't have something phenomenal, then I know that movie's going to suck. It's the same way with a script: if a script doesn't grab you within the first 5 to 10 pages, then what's going to grab you at all? "Oh, but there's a great twist 80 pages into it." Um, it doesn't work that way.

What if the beginning is slow but they have a kick ass trailer?

The problem with that is I don't see any kick ass trailers. Ever. I've seen so many suck movies I still wouldn't release even if they had phenomenal trailers. If people put their money out, and they sit there for an hour and a half and go, "This sucks," then it looks bad on us.

When you pick a film up, what delivery materials do you need and what delivery materials are usually lacking?

A lot of indie filmmakers now are shooting on Mini–DV, and they spit it out on a DVD-R and send it to me, which is acceptable to watch. After I've watched a film, and I like it, materials should be on a Digi-Beta, a Beta SP, or, at the least, a DV cam tape, because that has high resolution and it's better for the authoring process. I'm also getting uncompressed files on hard drives, and that works out great because there's no degradation in the signal. I've had people who have shot on Mini–DV, put it on the computer, edited it, compressed it, and shot it back out on a Mini–DV tape, double compressing it — no, that's *triple* compressing it. When we author it, we compress it again and it starts looking like crap. So if you're going to shoot on Mini–DV and do all of your post and extras and fine tuning on the computer, when you contact a distributor or DVD company like us, offer it to them uncompressed on a hard drive. That way we can compress it correctly and it will look beautiful.

What do you prefer as far as supplements?

The way I look at it, the extras don't sell DVDs. Unless the film is phenomenal, and I can sell 10,000 to 20,000 copies of it, people aren't really going to want to hear a commentary from the boom man. They're not going to want to hear four different commentaries from people they don't care about. The only reason that anybody would is if they're trying to make a movie themselves. So the extras can be bare bones or filled with so much stuff you won't even bother watching them.

What do you need as far as stills and artwork?

Other than the original artwork, I do need quite a lot of stills from the movie; high quality stills, so we can make some kind of DVD cover. Sometimes we just get the movie, maybe some extras here and there, but nothing for the DVD cover, so we have to have an artist paint, or draw, or adobe Photoshop a

Frankenhooker (1990) box art. Photograph courtesy Unearthed Films.

cover. You want to have some really good, high quality stills from the set, from the scenes, while you're shooting the stuff. Because if a DVD cover sucks, sales are going to hurt.

If you can have a separate music and effects track for foreign sales, God bless you, good job; most indie guys don't. Not every film is going to get dubbed as far as Germany and Japan or whatnot, but if they think it's a good enough movie they'll have it dubbed so they do need separate dialogue, music and effects tracks. If not, the film will just have to be subtitled.

When you acquire a film how many years do you try to lock up the rights for?

I generally try to lock it up for seven years. Ten if I can, five at the least. Nothing shorter than that because then it's a waste of my time and your time. And if any company ever says, "We just want it for two years," do *not* do it. That's a fly buy night company that just wants to release your film, get the initial release sales, and then bail. Once it comes back to you in two years, you're going to be like, "Hey, we want to sell this." And everybody is going to go, "Well, it was just released. The market's flooded with your product at three dollars each, so I'm not going to touch your film." And then you're stuck anyway for that five-to-seven years.

How much time generally passes between the acquisition of a film and its release?

For us it's about a year. By the time the contracts are signed, the materials have been sent, money is paid, and we do the authoring, menu design, DVD cover... We can whip one out in about three or four months, but when people come to us with their movie, we're sitting with 10 or 12 movies in front of us. So it takes a good half a year to a year.

What is the process of announcing a film to the horror and DVD markets?

It's usually immediate. I have the producer or director announce it for us and then we do a follow up. We're a DVD company; we're here for us and the filmmaker. But we want you to promote and push yourself as much as you can from when the film is picked up to the day it's released, and after, because it's your career that's important. It's you who are trying to get people to say, "Wow, this film is great — here's some money, make us something." Because the way the industry is right now, most indie filmmakers are not making any money.

What happens between the period when you announce a film's street date and when the film actually comes out?

When we announce the street date we usually have the finished DVD artwork, one-sheets, and advertising materials all set. It takes a good three months from the announcement to the release date. You have two months to build it

Frankenhooker (Patty Mullen) returns to her Times Square roots (1990). Photograph by Eric Maché, courtesy Unearthed Films.

up and that's when DVD distributors send out the one-sheets to all the stores, individual buyers, and magazines, and get the stone rolling down the hill. We send out to over 4,000 independent video stores and retailers. That's quite a lot; with other distributors, it's only 300 or 400. The distributor that we're with now does a lot of brick and mortar stores, music stores and so on. Nobody really does that anymore. But the whole marketing scheme of it gets a little tight. We have to have the advertising ready for the magazines for that month when it's released, any web work, any reviews ready to go. Personally, I like to have the reviews start hitting after the release date. Usually the reviews will start showing upon the web before the release date because the filmmakers are desperate, they're trying to make names for themselves, so they send out screeners. Our screeners start hitting a week after the release date. It's already been reviewed on-line, but it gets another push because it's still a little bit buzz-worthy. You have two months after the release date to continue pushing the film before it drops into obscurity.

How many screeners do you typically send out?

Anywhere from 50 to 300. We've been cutting down a little bit because it seems like every horror fan out there has his own website or podcast or MySpace page. If I continue to send screeners to all the horror fans with their own little web page or something, I'll just be sending out free stuff and I won't sell a single thing. So we've gotten a little bit choosier with who we send to, usually just the Big Boys.

Is stuff shot on film still easier to sell than digital video films?

Oh, God, yes. DV films are popping up out of the woodwork because all anyone needs is a nice Mac, a DV camera, and some downloaded software. Everyone and his mother is making a film. A cult enthusiast will forgive a boom mic, they will forgive bad acting, they will forgive a lot as long as there is enough boobs, blood, and gore. If you don't have much boobs, blood and gore in it, they will not bother to watch a Mini–DV movie. Keep that in mind. If you're going to do a little indie movie with a bunch of your friends in your garage, you've got to have more boobs, blood, and gore than you can shake a stick at; otherwise, the horror fans will not bother. You can think that you have the most phenomenal story on the face of the earth, but Mini–DV shows like a bad heart attack in a 400-pound guy at McDonald's. Don't do it unless you really know what you're doing: use lighting, move that camera around. The beauty of Mini-DV is you can have as many cuts as you want in it instead of letting that camera sit there. When I get movies where the editing is bad, camera is bad, it's usually a Mini–DV movie. If you're going to pay for film, whether it be Super 16, 16m, or even 8mm, you're going to take your time. You're going to light correctly and work correctly because you're paying for it. People don't really pay for Mini–DV: they just slap in a cassette tape, shoot something, throw it up on their computer, and spit it out.

Frankenhooker (Patty Mullen) is the creation of Frank Henenlotter, the man behind *Basket Case* and *Brain Damage*. Photograph by Eric Maché, courtesy Unearthed Films.

How hard is it to sell a Mini–DV feature that's been properly shot, and has the elements you mentioned, overseas?

If it has the boobs, blood, and gore, it's usually an easy sell. If it doesn't — if the filmmaker is trying to be suspenseful, usually most filmmakers can't pull it off. If you have a gore-tastic movie, a sale to Japan is very easy; a sale to Germany is very easy.

What's the shortest and longest running time you like?

72 minutes is the shortest for a feature length film. Any shorter and the buyers don't want to look at it for overseas. A lot of people try to put 10 short films on a DVD, but they're just blowing smoke. I think we're the only company that's actually released short films and sold over 10,000 units, but that's because the films were historical in the cult genre. There were the *Guinea Pig* films, which were 60 minutes. *Aftermath* was 30 minutes; the sequel to it, *Genesis*, was 30 minutes; and the first film in the trilogy was 10 minutes, so it equaled 70 minutes, but everybody just bought it for *Aftermath*, and that was shot on 35mm.

And anthology films as well, right?

Anthologies, short little trilogies, anything like that, are just horrible.

Do you have a minimum press run?

Our minimum press run is about 2,000. So far our maximum has been 35,000. 2,000 units barely makes up for the pressing, authoring, artwork, etc. If I release a film that sells only 2,000 units, then I did something really bad: I picked the wrong movie.

In a case like Frankenhooker, *where the film already has a reputation, how aggressively do you have to go after the rights, and then how closely do you work with the filmmakers in creating the extras? Because obviously in a case like that, the fans do want extras.*

We did have to run after Frank Henenlotter. We had to search for that film, we had to get into like this bidding war over it. Luckily for us, we're good friends with the other guy, so the bidding war didn't really last. We put a lot of care into *Frankenhooker*, quite a bit of money. Something like that definitely deserves the full DVD treatment.

I thought there weren't any prints of it around anymore...

We managed to find one print, and we did the telecine from that, and had Frank do the commentary from the telecine work. For other materials, we had to get everyone who worked on it to cough up stuff they were not supposed to have. It was a closed set; Frank refused to allow anyone to have a camera. But a couple of people did sneak some shots. I even had to get permission from

Frank to show one picture with him in it (laughs). Somebody snuck a video camera onto that set, and we found out about it and hit the person up. He said, "I can't give it to you unless I get an okay from Frank." Luckily for us Frank was a great guy and he allowed everything that we came across to go onto the disk.

What's the mini and the maxi that you're likely to spend marketing a title?

It varies. The minimum might be two grand, which is like one advertisement in one mag, with banner exchanges and this and that. I think our most expensive marketing was for *Rock and Rule*: we had stickers that we were giving out at the San Diego ComiCon, we had release parties, we did film festivals with it, we did full page and double page ads in some of the magazines. And actually, when it came down to it, it wasn't worth it. We sold over 30,000 copies, but the distribution game can be very vicious and we were totally ripped off. So no matter what we did with that title, we didn't see a dime except for our own sales. *Rock and Rule* was a $10 million movie that was buried for its theatrical release and was only shown on HBO and Cinemax for like five years back in the eighties, so it had a huge cult following. So it was a huge film that deserved all the marketing and promotion that we did, and if we had seen the money it would have been worth it.

But cult horror movies are a different story. It's not often that you get something that deserves a full page ad in every horror magazine across the country, and in the world, unless you're one of the Big Boys. If you don't generate the sales to match the marketing it's not going to work. I've known plenty of people who have released films, and they marketed the hell out of them, and they ended up losing everybody money. I've seen companies go out of business because they put their horse behind the buggy. Marketing is a tricky thing; I think we've got it down to a science.

How frequently do filmmakers receive financial statements from you?

Usually it's quarterly for the first year and twice a year after that. If a film does well, we send out a check. If a film does terrible, we just send out a royalty report that just says, "Horrible." It varies on the film. If you make a crap film, DVD sales are not going to be good. If you make an OK film, hopefully at the end of a year or two years you'll see some money. If you make a phenomenal film, you'll make plenty of money, especially with the international sales. When you make something that's crap or is just okay, you really don't get the international sales. If you make something good, you'll get the international markets, and that's extra money that you'll take to the bank.

How have you weathered this current glut with Best Buy and some of these other major retail chains no longer carrying indie product?

The industry is in massive turmoil. DVD companies are going under left and right. Retailers are no longer stocking the indie product hat they used to, and they made a lot of money on them. It's much easier for them to get a better discount from Warner Brothers, to get an extra two dollars per disk and stock 20 copies of *The Matrix* and 20 copies of *The Shining* than take two or three copies of *Guinea Pig* or *Frankenhooker*, even though there are customers that want these films and will go into Best Buy looking for them. Ever since Best Buy knocked out all the independent DVD and video retailers, they turned their back on what made them big, which has really hurt the industry. And the glut is insane. There's too much competition. I have a list of 50 to 100 films that I know horror fans would love to see, but for me to release a film that will sell 2,000 or 3,000 copies, it's really not worth it. There's some things I'll take a chance on, but if the whole idea is to keep Unearthed going, and I make a couple of bad decisions regarding movies, we could go under faster than you can snap your fingers.

I remember how excited you were when My Space started catching on. Are you able to tell if it's helped your sales?

Not at all (laughs). My Space is great for the one night stand, the potential hookup, telling people what kind of eggs you ate for breakfast. It's basically an ego-driven, wannabe star-studded, "look at me" phenomenon. For companies that are excited because they have 10,000 "friends"—it doesn't matter. My Space is a waste of time now. It's good if you're a porno chick, but that's about it.

You send out a newsletter, right?

Yeah, we have a newsletter. Its membership stays around 1,000 people. But these are real people; it goes to their e-mail address. So that's okay. I have like another 1,500 people that we send it to, reviewers and retailers and so on, so we really have about 2,500. And my current distributor, which is TLA, sends out to about 10,000 people, mostly buyers and sellers and retailers. So when we send something out it reaches about 15,000 people. When there are 50 to 60 cult films coming out every month, where do they put their hard earned money, you know? That is the hardest thing. And with everybody talking about downloading, and Video on Demand, and PSP, and iPods, and ITV, and with so much product available, it's not looking good because everybody's already drifting away because there's so much in life. It's going to be rough for everybody. Judging from the state of the industry now, it's going to be interesting to see who survives. Hopefully we will.

22

Promotion

You should start promoting your film even while it's in preproduction. Start a list of contacts at horror magazines and websites and local media. Learn how to draft press releases and send out updates at key moments in your film's evolution: announce the film will be made; if you cast a semi-known genre figure; when production has started; when the film has wrapped shooting; when you'll have your premiere; what film festivals accept your film; and, hopefully, when you have a DVD release date. Start a website, a My Space page with the film's title, and a blog, and post your press releases on these as well. I agree with Stephen Biro that My Space does not help with sales, but it may help create familiarity with your project, and that can help later on.

A press release filled with hyperbole is a sure indication of an amateur at work, and no one in the media will take you seriously. If you're shooting a $15,000 feature on digital video, don't promote it as a major event in the year you expect it to be released (which is often not when a film really is released). Just present the facts you wish to state, and a quote or two, and leave it to the venue publishing/posting your release to "color" it if they wish. By creating awareness of your project, you may make it easier for yourself to find a willing distributor once your film is finished.

It's a good idea to start a monthly newsletter with updates and links to any press you've received. Make this newsletter available to people through your website, My Space page, and blog. One thing I strongly caution you *not* to do: if a friend or industry professional sends you a mass e-mail, and the other recipients' e-mail addresses are visible, don't copy and paste them into some kind of master list of your own. People resent when they are deluged with unwanted updates on projects they have know interest in and you create bad will towards your project.

Premieres

I recommend holding a premiere for your film in your home town if that's possible. It's a great way to show your friends, family, and neighbors what you've devoted the last year of your life to, and to develop community interest and support. Do your best to get local media there; it's a human interest story even if the outlet doesn't like horror. This is also a way to raise a little capital that you may need on your quest for distribution. In Buffalo, my friend Greg Sterlace makes quirky character comedies (*Sweet Jesus, Failure*) for under $1,000. He invites everyone he know to the premiere and charges admission, then shows his films on a local show which pays him $200 for broadcast rights. Between these two events, he recoups his investment and moves on to his next project.

But I also recommend holding a premiere in New York City or Los Angeles, because that's where the film distributors are based. If you plan your premiere far enough in advance and promote it well enough, you might create some buzz for your film — and some interest from distributors. If a rep is unable to attend, they will most likely ask you to send them a screener, and your screener will probably receive

Robert Sabin reads *Fangoria* over T.J. Merrick's corpse at the Bronx location of *Slime City*. (1988). Photograph courtesy J. Scott Coulter.

greater attention than it would have otherwise. At the very least, you can invite the *Fangoria* crew and some NYC filmmakers to the premiere and a party afterward. I've had some miserable experiences with premieres.

We premiered *Slime City* at the Waverly Twin theatre, where *Basket Case* ran as a midnight show for two years and *I Was a Teenage Zombie* ran for six weeks. The theatre brought in a 16m projector, but the projectionist was too lazy to move the heavy 35mm projector out of the way because this was just one showing, so he aimed the 16m projector around the larger one. The result was that one half of the screen was out of focus at all times. The projectionist would correct the side that was out of focus, and then the other side turned blurry. It was literally one of the worst nights of my life, and because of this incident, we booked our midnight run at another theatre, the Bleecker Street Cinemas.

Eric Maché's artwork for *Undying Love* (1992) before E.I. Cinema changed its title to *New York Vampire* (1998).

We premiered *Undying Love* at the Village East Cinemas, where our midnight run was already booked to follow. This time, we held a technical screening in the morning, to make sure everything was okay. And it was—until halfway through the movie, when the projector plug fused into the wall socket, creating a 45-minute delay, during which we lost half our audience. This was especially disheartening because the audience was really enjoying the movie. You should always hold a technical screening before such an important event—and even that won't guarantee you a fool proof premiere.

Film Festivals

Devi Snively discussed film festivals earlier in this book. Horror film festivals didn't really exist when I did *Slime City* and *Undying Love*, and Fantasia (which I would love to attend someday), in Montreal, Canada, was probably still in its infancy when we finally finished *Naked Fear*. I screened the *Slime City* DVD at several horror conventions and film festivals, but never really explored the festival circuit until I made *Gruesome*, the short film/extended music video created to promote my novel *Johnny Gruesome* and the rock CD based on it. Overall, I didn't find the experience terribly productive: I submitted the film to 16 domestic horror film festivals and four overseas ones, at a cost of $500.00. I was accepted into four of them, and was invited to screen at two others; I was rejected by maybe half, and never heard back from the others. At the festivals I attended, I observed poor attendance, *no* industry people, and generally poor organization. Film festivals may be a fun way to show your film to a small crowd of enthusiastic horror fans—and audience reaction is extremely important—but I don't find them to be a cost effective way of promoting your career.

One of the two on-line comics I produced for my *Johnny Gruesome* website won "Best Comic Book" at the 2007 New York City Horror Film Festival, but when I arranged for Roy Frumkes to accept the award on my behalf, the festival director forgot about the category and never called him to the stage, completely wasting his time. Not only that, but I had to contact the festival several times to find out if I'd won because they didn't notify me on their own. If you want to enter your film into these festivals so you can network with other aspiring filmmakers, go ahead. Who knows, maybe you'll make a contact that will come in handy in the future; I met both Devi and Stephen Biro at the Halloween Horror Picture Show—now called Halloweenpalooza—a small indie horror festival run by Rick Danford, whom I later hired to write for *Fear Zone*.

If you've directed a horror feature and you believe in it, you might be better off submitting it to a more mainstream festival which devotes one day or night to genre fare; they tend to be better run, and industry people may take them more seriously. Remember, *Blair Witch* and *Open Water* caused a stir at Sundance, not at some niche horror film festival with 1,000 My Space friends. Rob Tomaro and I launched the *Slime City* soundtrack CD at the Beloit Inter-

Lobby card style promotional still for Brett Piper's *Shock-O-Rama*, starring Erin Brown ("Misty Mundae"). © POP Cinema, L.L.C.

national Film Festival, which presented two 20th anniversary screenings of the film. BIFF isn't a horror event, but a mainstream-indie-international film festival, and they treated me better than any horror event ever has: they flew me, Robert Sabin, and Mary Huner out there and put us up in a hotel — and even asked us to stay for the whole four days! It was a wonderful experience and a great way to celebrate the friendships that grew out of the production.

Horror Conventions

If horror film festivals are about getting your work seen and networking with other filmmakers, then getting a vendor's table or booth at a horror convention is about promoting yourself and your work, connecting with fans, making contacts, and, hopefully, selling DVDs and merchandise related to your film. Horror cons can be great, or they can be extremely costly wastes of time. I strongly suggest you attend specific cons before buying a table package. Tables can cost anywhere from $200 to $600 for a weekend, and if you add in hotel, food, and transportation expenses, there is no way you'll break even on your expenses, let alone turn a profit. I tend to only attend cons that list me as a guest and at least give me a free table, and more and more often I insist on a hotel room as well—which is why I'm attending fewer cons. You have to decide how important attending such an event is to your overall marketing strategy.

Some of the better cons I've attended are Rue Morgue's Festival of Fear in Toronto, which is part of Fan Expo Canada, which draws 40,000 to 50,000 fans annually (not just horror fans—there are also SF, comic book, and anime fans, as well as autograph hounds); Chiller Theatre Expo in New Jersey; and Fangoria's Weekend of Horrors. Fangoria stages their events all over the country, and some are busier than others, depending on the guest list. Horrorfind Weekend in Baltimore was busy the first time I attended it, but was slow the second. Rock & Shock in Worcester, MA was a well attended event, but I did few transactions there because attendees seemed to be saving their money for the music events at night. I've heard wonderful things about Cinema Wasteland in Ohio, but I have yet to attend it because they won't feature me as a guest and gift me a table; at this point in my life, I'd rather stay home and write than haul my family to a show that may not pay for itself. Dragon*Con and ComiCon are two major cons that I have yet to attend.

I've had some wonderful experiences at cons, and you just have to shrug off the bad ones. *Slime City* has developed a legion of fans since it was released on DVD, and I'm always surprised by how many people who are the same age now as I was when I made the film bring me beat up VHS copies to sign or ask me to take a photo with them.

What depresses me about horror conventions is when I see first time filmmakers trying to sell DVDs of their product, which no one has ever heard of, and which doesn't have a distributor behind it. They set up monitors on their tables and show their movie over and over, hoping someone—*anyone*—will buy their movie. I think their time and money would be better spent exploring other avenues of promotion. Then again, some smaller cons, like Halloweenpalooza, specifically cater to fans of these micro-budget films, which is why you need to research which shows best serve your needs. When you buy a table and book a hotel for a con, you've invested in the entire weekend.

The Internet

Your film should have its own website and its own My Space page. As I've already noted, neither of these may result in direct sales of your film, but both can generate product awareness. More important, these sites enable interested parties to contact you. When I launched SlimeGuy.com, I was lucky to get 200 hits a month; now I get between 200 and 500 a day. I've had people who worked on my films get in touch with me through the site long after we'd lost touch with each other, and if I've benefited from My Space in any way it's this: I receive e-mails from fans of my films all over the world every week; people in England, Ireland, France and Spain, who remember *Slime City* from its original foreign sales in 1989 and 1990; people who claim it was the first gore film they ever saw, and who tell me what an impact it had on them; people who bought my books because they read a positive review of them somewhere on-line. It's good for your ego to hear that you somehow touched someone else's life — even if only for 75 minutes — and it's advantageous to build a data base of people who already know your work.

We live in an age of video streaming and downloads. You can find the trailer for any upcoming feature film on-line, so why not the trailer for your production? My Space, You Tube and many other sites in addition to your own can help you spread the word. Just don't get carried away, or you may find yourself spending an inordinate amount of time at these venues, in which case the rewards are ultimately limited. There are also countless websites devoted to horror that conduct text based interview with filmmakers, podcast interviews and reviews, and even video features. Promote yourself as well as your films.

You can sell your work on-line; all you need is a website and a Paypal account. I've never self published a novel and I've never self distributed a film, but I do self distribute the *Gruesome* rock CD, the *Slime City* Soundtrack CD, and the Johnny Gruesome Death Mask, through Slimeguy.com and Johnny-Gruesome.com. I also sell autographed copies of the *Slime City* DVD, which I purchased at discount from POP Cinema. I sell as many of these items on-line as I would at a convention, without the expense. Every time I ship something, I include promotional materials for the other products, and I have seen return customers. I believe these sales also have a positive impact on sales made by my publishers and distributors.

Print Magazines

Getting press in a print magazine — especially one distributed at newsstands — is a tough nut to crack. Because publishers sell more copies of their magazines when they feature heavily promoted films on their covers, it is harder for independent films to get space in those publications. *Fangoria* generally covers films that already have distribution, and give indie films only minimal article space in its pages. However, *Fangoria* has two different review sections, and both regularly cover indie and cult films. The website also pays a lot more attention to smaller films than the print version does, and it has devoted generous space to my projects. *Rue Morgue* covers all aspects of horror entertainment in culture, and are more likely to cover films that actually reflect or impact that culture. However, they devote more coverage to new films screened at film festivals than any other horror magazine out there. *Fangoria* has its own weekly radio show, available to Sirius satellite subscribers and hosted by Dee Snyder and Debbie Rochon. *Rue Morgue Radio* is a weekly podcast which covers all aspects of the genre, with an emphasis on music and sound bites.

There are several smaller magazines, like *The Hacker's Source* and *Ultra Violent*, which are devoted to more independent and obscure films. However, both of these quality magazines are published bi-annually, which means they're of little promotional value to the films that need their support most. We live in the age of the Internet, and you're better off concentrating on websites like *Fear Zone*, *Creature Corner*, *House of Horrors*, *Dread Central*, *Rogue Cinema* and *Horror Yearbook*. The list goes on and on, and grows daily.

Afterlife

Stephen Biro states he has about two months after a film is released to maximize a its return before it "fades into obscurity." This hasn't been my experience; POP Cinema continued to take out full page ads in *Rue Morgue* featuring *Slime City* among 10 or so titles over a year after its initial release. Stephen's comment also reflects the distributor's position, which should *not* be the filmmaker's position. 2008 marked the 20th anniversary of *Slime City's* theatrical run — but 2009 marks the 20th anniversary of its national video release. By producing and self-distributing the soundtrack, I've called attention to the film all over again. If I'm able to get *Slime City Massacre* off the ground, the whole cycle will start over. Again, I'm working with a film that already has a following, so I have a leg up on other micro-budget filmmakers in this regard. But every filmmaker has the ability to generate attention for his film *if his film is good*.

You cannot anticipate trends or fads; what's hot when you start a film may not, and probably will not, be hot by the time you've completed it and a distributor has released it. All you can do is stay true to your vision and make the best damned movie possible. If you persevere, and your film is good, the possibility of getting it seen is much greater, and the possibility of the film enjoying a long life will dramatically increase.

23

Paige Kay Davis

MARKETING MAYHEM

Paige Kay Davis started working at POP Cinema shortly before the company geared up to release *Slime City* on DVD and quickly became my main contact at the company. She pointed me to film festivals and conventions where I might screen the film, and helped me arrange various interviews. She also set up various promotional contests and was never stingy on sending out screeners to interested horror journalists. You won't always find someone this helpful at distribution companies; yours isn't the only film on their release schedule, and there isn't always someone available to hold your hand and walk you through the process. Obviously, such a relationship can be extremely advantageous.

Paige grew up the daughter of a military man, and as an army brat, lived on military bases in Hawaii and Germany. At college she studied Radio, Film and Television, and Political Science, before obtaining her Bachelor of Arts in English and Literature. Among other professions, she toiled as a nightclub manager and as a corporate sales rep responsible for half of Texas before making a name for herself as Vice President of Sales and Marketing at POP Cinema. She's built a solid reputation in a short period of time, and I've learned a great deal about DVD distribution and promotion from her.

How did you come to be hired at POP Cinema?

I met Michael Raso in Los Angeles, and I had spoken with him on the phone a couple of times, and I asked him to invest in a business I was thinking of starting. And through these conversations he learned that I knew a lot about sales and marketing.

Did you replace someone, or was this a new position created because they were expanding?

Because the company was expanding, and the volume output was increasing, and they'd begun to really focus on horror once again, or were intending to expand the number of in-house productions for horror. I think they just realized they needed some extra people on board with a brain and some experience.

What were your initial responsibilities?

My areas of responsibility were primarily acting as liaison with press, coordinating the events—all of the out of town events; it was the first year that the company decided to have a presence at some of the larger events, such as Comic-Con. So one of the first things I managed since coming on board was our table at Comic Con. I'm sure you're aware that there are hundreds of thousands of attendees. Three years ago I believe it was 100,000, up from 80,000 the previous year. It was almost literally that quick, I was out here moving in, settling in, and boom, I'm coordinating with shipping and order fulfillment operations, the shipping of inventory, off to San Diego to Comic Con, making my hotel reservations, coordinating the company talent, three of the stars of the Seduction Cinema label: Julian Welles and Andrea Davis and Gloria-Anne Gilbert. It was an experience, five days of *insanity* in San Diego, with promotional materials, and talent, and food to be coordinated, and money to be taken in, and change to be given, and receipts to be made, and inventory to be taken, and setting up and breaking down. Sort of a trial by fire, but it was successful.

What was it like familiarizing yourself not only with the product, but with the whole subculture the product is targeted at?

It was definitely a new experience for me. The product itself was something I'd never been familiar with, the culture itself was something I wasn't really familiar with, the incredible fan base and popularity of lower budget, independent, horror genre filmmaking was all very unfamiliar to me. But I feel very strongly, and I've felt this about every job that I've had, that you cannot accurately and ethically sell and represent your company and your product if you don't know what they are. So I dove right in: I watched everything possible, I familiarized myself with what wasn't possible. With a rather large library, which POP has, obviously watching each and every film in its entirety was just not going to happen. I checked out five minutes of things here and there, spoke to people, read a considerable amount, but made a concerted effort to really familiarize myself with the product. Whether it is a small event, like a more casual, really kind of micro-cinema con to a ComiCon, it's your duty, it is the profession, sales and marketing, to know your product and to be outgoing and to represent your company professionally, and I made that my goal. I thank you, because you've always made it clear to me that you've thought I was successful with that, and I appreciate that.

Your title now is Vice President of Sales and Marketing. What was it when you started?

Apparently we couldn't decide on a title. I think I've had two or three business titles. Communications Director was a blanket title we used at one point because we were going back and forth on whether we were going to hire an outside publicist, so I was handling a lot of the publicity for the company, etcetera, and then that all sort of fell under a marketing banner. But Marketing Director and Communications Director were two titles that sort of came and went. Initially I had been involved to a minor extent with production. I produced the DVD ancillary feature, the extra feature, on the *Prison-a-Go-Go* release, *Shock-a-Go-Go*, and then I helped out here and there on the sets, and that's not something I do as much anymore now that I'm focused on sales. At the time we had an executive here by the name of Michael Weiss. His title was Business Affairs. Michael had a degree in law, so he was sort of in-house legal counsel as well as being heavily involved in sales across all markets. So, international sales, digital media sales, physical product sales. When Michael left, it seemed very logical for me to assume, because of my background, his areas of responsibility in regards to sales, with some minor changes, and for us to again have an outside legal counsel.

You're attending fewer conventions than you did when you first started.
Since assuming the position as primary company representative and liaison with third party distribution partners, the vast majority of my time is taken up in those communications, specifically regarding how the sales force for the third party distributor presents our products to which retailers; initial orders, making sure that they're realistic given the changes in the market as opposed to excessive — we're the ones who are going to get tons of returns; ensuring that our titles aren't shown to a Wal Mart, which is not a good match for them, and again, there's a returns issue; flying out to meetings; giving presentations to the sales force and executives of our third party distributor. So that takes up an incredible amount of time. I generate the sales forecast by title based on not only how comparable products are performing in the market but also what our needs are in regards to revenue as a company, our bottom line. Focusing on that, being involved with the sales department materials, either creating them entirely or working with other individuals who create them — and by creating them I mean the content; I'm not the graphics. That takes an incredible amount of time and that's where I need to focus, and have needed to focus since I assumed these other areas of responsibility and the new title. That really cuts into my ability to attend conventions, and travel for conventions and PR purposes. So subsequently, I've brought people on board, and I'm now going through that process again. I'm currently reviewing applications and looking for an executive assistant to help in the marketing department, i.e., my assistant.

I read ad copy for a book similar to this one which stated there has never been a better time to be looking for distribution for a low budget horror film...

I strongly disagree and I will have that conversation with this individual any day. Absolutely not, absolutely not. Again, being relatively new to this industry, though not to sales and marketing, I just plunged in. I made sure I learned as much as I could about this industry, so I feel I can competently talk about the video boom of the 1980s, event hough I wasn't involved in the video boom of the later part of the 80s and the early part of the 90s, when one could still see the occasional really great low budget film in a theatre—a theatre like the Pioneer and a film like yours, *Slime City*. New technology and new formats always reinvigorate, to a certain extent, the industry. So right after the video boom everybody could finally make their own movie without having to go into debt for 30 years, and be worried about paying back hundreds of thousands of dollars to investors, etc., made it so much easier and there was this great amount of aspiring filmmakers, and much product in the market, and mom and pop chains, and consumers really had a variety; they had a lot of choice. People involved in the industry from a more financial perspective—and trust me, as I'm sure you can attest, Greg, it's all great to be an artiste and want to make your film, but everyone wants to make some money when the day is done. You don't want to be in debt and have to struggle for your vision and be trying to climb out of that debt for the next 20 years of your life. So following that huge boom, you had, of course, DVD, and all of these films are now available on DVD, and DVD introduces—which is just brilliant—and I'm leaving out Laser here for the sake of brevity—the whole concept of extras: commentaries, and interviews, ancillary features, which has become so common place that reviewers review the package as much as the film. Many times a reviewer will play a commentary, or a feature, or a "making of," or here's where they explain how they rolled that car they did this stop motion, etc., and they add another star to their review, even if they didn't like the film that much. It's really interesting how the format sort of dictates the medium and how that has changed.

Nothing exists in a vacuum, so this is going to be very much oversimplifying, but when chains—you know, the beginnings of the Wal Marts and all that—became more and more dominant and prices began to fall, and people became increasingly comfortable with purchasing over the Internet—not terrified that someone was going to be stealing their credit card number—these and a variety of other events conspired to create this incredibly competitive retailer market and prices started dropping on the product. You know what we used to be able to charge or spend on a VHS or a DVD, and now one walks into a Wal Mart you see a Hollywood blockbuster from only a few years ago in a five dollar bin. All of these things working together have drastically changed the market. It is a fact that in 2007 there was 40 percent more horror product in the market than there was in 2005. It's a fact that the major Hollywood studios over the past few years just dove into DVD premiere product. With the Weinsteins' ingenuity, with Lion's Gate really cornering the horror market and snapping up everything from theatrical to micro-budget products that a few

Key art for *Shock-O-Rama*, released by Shock-O-Rama Cinema (2005). © POP Cinema, L.L.C.

years ago would have been sent to us to look at, if not to pick up, and some of them we actually might not have picked up, which Lion's Gate took. Things have changed so very, very drastically, and we all know that the Mom and Pop video stores are practically a thing of the past. Because of the competition with the dot-coms, the brick and mortar retailers have been closing their doors, going out of business, declaring bankruptcy. It's really very depressing. Having said that, there's more product in the market now than there ever has been in the history of this industry.

Why do people make horror films? Because they love the genre, and as an aspiring filmmaker, what can you get away with using a small budget? A horror film. Historically, you have a better chance that it's going to catch on, that it's going to achieve a market share, some revenue, some notoriety, some buzz going that you just aren't as likely to have with an indie comedy with a no-name cast. And the fans of horror are so passionate. When horror began its recent boom five years ago, and all the sudden the genre began to get really strong again, and all the fans were so avid and rabid and enthusiastic, and everybody was excited because all of the sudden horror is king, well that only set into motion a series of events, so, "Oh, God, horror's big!" Now even more people are going to be creating it. The end result is that we have an incredible glut in the market right now.

There's literally more product out there than there ever has been. Within the genre, you're looking at more and more competition. Because the buyers at the brick and mortar retail chain have to be so concerned about their bottom line because they have all of this overhead, they're not a dot-com; they don't have one warehouse and shipping directly to the consumer or maybe a sub-warehouse. You know they're carrying a lot more expenses and have to generate a lot more revenue, and how can they do that when the dot-coms are selling for a miniscule profit margin? So all of these things conspired so that for the independent filmmaker, it's incredibly challenging now. It is almost impossible to get your product into Best Buy over the past year. The mini-majors are having problems getting their product into Best Buy. If it doesn't do theatrical; if it doesn't have a major television campaign; it's become so very difficult and challenging.

The way to combat that, in my opinion, is nothing new or novel whatsoever. It's tried and true, and there's no magic formula, but the best way to meet and try to exceed these challenges and differentiate your product from everybody else's—it's common sense and industry standards from way, way back when: don't just put your product out there; *press release, press release, press release*. Get as much press going as possible. Send out as many press releases as possible. Before you even create the thing, find an angle or a hook that differentiates it from everybody else's film. Use every avenue possible—*grass roots, grass roots, grass roots*—whether it's conventions, submit it to every film festival under the sun. Don't be naïve and don't give yourself an incredibly short

Paige K. Davis at the POP Cinema table at the Rock and Shock convention in Worcester, Massachusetts. Photograph courtesy Henrique Couto.

time frame to see results; you've got to work this stuff. *Network, network, network*. Go to film festivals, go to events, make contacts, and just get the word out there. Because the days of the independent film company — taking it for granted that they have an output deal, so to speak — they're over. They're really over. And when I say independent, of course I'm not speaking about a Lion's Gate or an Anchor Bay. The mini-majors are so powerful now that I lump them in with the majors. It's the Charles Band of yesteryear, the POP Cinemas of today, the Tromas, etc. I don't think there's ever been a more challenging time. And that doesn't mean that one can't succeed. It just means that you have to work very hard and be very smart.

How many titles does POP typically release, under all of the various imprints?

The combined library is well over 150 titles. We will be releasing a minimum of 24 titles annually. We are looking for a certain amount of revenue to keep the company in profit and those financial goals could require a number of releases. We don't break it down to a formula such as "We will release eight Seduction Cinema films because we know we can count on X amount of revenue." The retro product does what the retro product does, and they're not as strong of performers as the contemporary product, which might be surprising. With the exception of *Inga* and a few other widely recognized retro titles, the retro product is very much "slow and steady wins the race," it goes in like catalogue and it keeps performing like catalogue. The contemporary product, whether it's a horror or an erotica, that's what we're looking to for some higher numbers and higher revenue. But we do divide it up between the labels, we release a few more of the erotic titles, it's not that much of a disparity, it's like one or two titles, but things are not set in stone. I can plan out for an entire year, and then the best laid plans come to nothing because you might have a problem with the post production on something, you might pick up something else, you might decide, "Oh, wait a minute, we need to release this right now" because rental criteria, if we want a shot at one of the top rentailers, it needs to be a new production, and by "new" I mean within the last two years. They're pretty savvy out there, especially when they're looking for a reason not to take your product. All sorts of things like that can cause you to revise your release schedule.

Take me through the basic process of marketing a micro-budget film that you've acquired, once the release date's been set.

The process is announcing the release either via a specific press release or a newsletter. Quarterly we release a POP Cinema newsletter. Upon occasion releases will be announced initially in that: "We're announcing our fall titles." Depending exactly on where in the year the release falls, it will be announced initially through a press release. Things have changed. We are now announcing nearly as much on My Space as we are with the traditional written press release sent out in an e-mail blast, un-mailed. But we're doing a combination of both. We will work with scheduling events. I will specifically look at if we have a release that will street soon after or right around the date of the event it is far more likely that I will finalize plans for the event even if I'm not sure how we will fit it into our schedule. We organize — either I or someone in my department, depending on staffing — on-line giveaways with top performing

Tony Timpone, *Fangoria*'s Editor-in-Chief, and Erin Brown ("Misty Mundae") at the Fangoria Weekend of Horrors in Chicago. © POP Cinema, L.L.C.

horror sites such as *Bloody Disgusting*, *Horror Review* and *Rue Morgue's* website, to name a few. *Fangoria*, of course, is always ideal, not always successful; I can't blame them, *Fangoria* is in huge demand. They do an excellent job of giving us a fair share of what time they have. We will, upon occasion, coordinate with a retailer, schedule in-store events — we did this for the release of *Bite*

Me! in Manhattan. We brought in the cast and an actor dressed up in the costume that John Fadelli wore in the film, which was a lot of fun. Unfortunately, those are a little less available nowadays for retailers. So one of the things I'm doing is trying to look outside the box, as opposed to doing an event with X,Y,Z; doing more mom and pop events. I think that's a great area to focus on moving forward, they're very, very appreciative, and that's the type of place that's gotten unusual product now moving forward. So the small chains and the Mom and Pops. Consumer advertising for our titles as well, leading up to the street date, and then frequently creating posters and other print media that we bring to the conventions and disseminate there as well.

What are some of your favorite campaigns that you've created?
  I thoroughly enjoyed *Skin Crawl* . I felt the key art was a great marriage with an eye toward that very trendy Lion's Gate horror look without being a disservice to the film itself. I liked the fact that we chose not to sell it with a perhaps clichéd chick-ass zombie with a low cut bodice on the cover. I don't mean so much clichéd for POP but just sort of across the board. We scheduled Justin on Fangoria Radio to do an interview, which I understand was very successful. I got a lot of satisfaction out of that. I had a lot of compliments. We had a lot of unbiased positive feedback from people who had no idea I was involved with regards to the look of the piece. That's a very specific aspect of marketing, but I thoroughly enjoyed that.

Other than publicity stills, what are some of the other materials you wish you saw more of when you acquire films?
  Oh, that's such a great question, and we have to stress: *photographic materials, photographic materials, photographic materials.* It's crazy how important that is and how neglected that is. Although we're not adverse to creating features or adding additional bonus material, it would be wonderful if the product arrived with the commentary already in place; if the product arrived with a "behind the scenes" already in place. If the director and the producer thought to—and trust me, I know how very difficult that can be — really focus on creating as much supplemental material as possible while they're filming, really capturing the enthusiasm and the challenges as opposed to going back after the fact and trying to recreate kind of thing. Though a commentary after the fact can be a lot of fun.

Do you develop business relationships with the filmmakers behind your acquisitions, or are they not always involved with some of the marketing?
  To a limited degree. And I'm not being PC, that's simply the reality. I do interact directly. Different filmmakers have different requests in different agreements. Some people aren't that interested in being a part of the process of marketing the film and others are very, very interested in being a part of that process,

from the key art to the event promotions to in-store to screenings. So it really varies, and a lot of that depends on an individual director and their understanding, and obviously we try to have this conversation either before or while the film's being acquired so that there's no misunderstanding or confusion after the fact.

24

Justin Channell

NEW BLOOD

Justin Channell is an excellent example of today's micro-budget filmmakers, and what can be accomplished with extremely little money. He shot his first feature, *Raising the Stakes*, while still attending high school. His second feature, the zombie comedy *Die and Let Live*— shot the summer before he started college — was released on DVD by Heretic Films. He's already achieved more than filmmakers twice his age, and he's no rich kid playing with toys that Mommy and Daddy bought him — he used his wiles to make his films with almost nothing. Almost innately, he understands how important marketing is to a film.

What was your first camera?
My first camera was the one we shot *Raising the Stakes* on, which was a Canon Optura 20, a Mini–DV camera. Before that we shot on Digital 8, so I've never worked in the analogue video format. I always wanted to make movies. When I met my friend Josh Lively, we found we were into the same horror movies, and he also wanted to make films. And then he introduced me to Zane Crosby, and Zane was into horror movies as well, and he wanted to be a make-up artist. He ended up getting a job at the local costume shop, where he learned make up and stuff like that.

What was the genesis of Raising the Stakes?
I was 16. A year before that I had wanted to do a serious horror anthology, and we started shooting one short, but nobody wanted to take it seriously and I realized that maybe trying to do something serious at that point wasn't a good idea. So I wrote *Raising the Stakes* as a comedy. The main reason I wanted to jump into a feature was because my friends were graduating the next year. They were all going off to college and this was most likely going to be the last thing we were ever going to do together, so we might as well do something people would remember and not just a bunch of short films. That ended up not

being true at all; we all still see each other on a regular basis. I never really wrote a second draft of the script, I just kind of went through it and revised little bits, which was a big, big mistake. I went on a school trip to Disney World, and I did not want any Disney souvenirs, so I got all of this money to go on this trip and didn't spend a dime of it. I'd saved up a little money on my own, and had $110 altogether, and that's what we used as the production budget. To get my camera, I told my parents that I needed to get a new computer, and I was just going to get the parts myself because it would be cheaper. My parents don't really know anything about technology and I told them I needed $1300 out of my savings. So they gave me this money, and the computer showed up with a video camera and a shotgun mike kind of tucked away with it.

What editing program did you use?

Vegas Video for Windows. I've never found a thing I could not do in Vegas. That's my personal recommendation, though I do have to say, since Sony bought the company that created it, it's not as good as it used to be. Sony's kind of tinkered with it a little too much. It seems to crash a lot more, but it's still a good program.

How old were you when you shot Raising the Stakes?

I was still 16, a junior. I wrote the script over Christmas break and we shot it in that summer. By the time we were done I had turned 17, though. We spent seven months on it. One thing I enjoy about these long shoots is, even though there are some horrible continuity errors, it leaves you so much room. If something doesn't work out, you can re-shoot it or figure out what needs to be done. But we've come to the conclusion we don't ever want to do one again because it's too straining on us.

How did Lloyd Kaufman's cameo come about?

I'd always wanted to see *Cannibal! The Musical* because I was such a big *South Park* fan. When I finally found it I discovered it was released through Troma and I got the DVD — it was the first DVD I ever bought, I didn't even own a DVD player. I was going through the extras and that's when I started renting this stuff. I first rented *The Toxic Avenger* and *Class of Nuke 'Em High*, and I absolutely loved them, and that's because Troma had that real "Let's make a movie!" attitude. Online, there were really no Troma sites that had all the information I was looking for so I decided to start my own. I had a guest book on there and one day I checked it and there's a message from Lloyd Kaufman saying, "Hey, get a hold of us." I got a hold of him and Troma ended up hosting the site. And through that I ended up getting interviews with a whole bunch of people. I got screenwriting advice from James Gunn; he told me what software to use. I had a long chat with Buddy Giovinazzo, who did *Combat Shock*.

I got to talk to a lot of indie filmmakers I really admired and made several contacts. I was pretty much doing P.R. for Troma on my own accord with their blessing. Of course, I like to be really honest with the fans, and Lloyd loves to give me shit for that. The reason Lloyd's in the movie is because he was coming to Pittsburgh at that time. We had a newscaster part and I said, "We could get Lloyd to do that," because Lloyd will do a cameo for anybody pretty much.

So you went to Pittsburgh to shoot the cameo?

Yeah, my Mom drove us. I first met Lloyd at a signing at Incredibly Strange Video. My Mom really wasn't familiar with Troma. We're standing on line and she's starting to notice the trailers playing on the TV and there's this look on her face of, "Oh, my God, what is my son getting into?" I remember the guy who I worked under for the website told me, "Okay, when you meet Lloyd, ask him for free stuff." So I did, and Lloyd kind of laughed and said something like, "Oh, well I could give you some free fellatio, I have very sweet lips." And I don't think my mother knew what the word fellatio meant because she mentioned something about it, and I was like, "I don't know, Mom, I think it's some French word." The second time we met Lloyd, for the cameo, she was less worried. She was like, "Okay, once you get to know him a little bit I kind of understand." Because I was such a big fan, that was pretty cool that Lloyd did the cameo. Before that it was like, "Oh, this kid's making a movie." But then after Lloyd was in it all the sudden there was some sort of prestige, like a whole bunch of people were really impressed. "Oh, wow, you got Lloyd Kaufman?"

It was an astute decision for a 16-year-old to make.

I told someone at Horrorfind that I had met Conrad Brooks at another convention, where I talked him down on the price of a signed copy of *Plan 9 from Outer Space* on VHS from $20 to $10. This other person said, "You know, he's not too far away from you. You should try to get Conrad involved in your movie." So I sent Conrad a letter, and he replied to it and we started talking on the phone, and it looked like he was going to do it. As things proceeded it started looking like a bad idea, mainly because he would call me every Sunday. I'm not kidding, every Sunday the exact same conversation: "So, where are you from? Fairmont? Is that near Morgantown? You know who lived in Morgantown? *Don Knotts!*" We were like, "Now, would you like us to come to your place, or would you prefer to come to Fairmont?" and he goes, "Well, I don't know, I could come there if you could give me a ride." I was like, "Ooh, I don't drive. This isn't going to work out." So we decided to drop Conrad.

You couldn't get your mom to schlep Conrad around?

Can you imagine that, if someone's Mom showed up in a mini-van? "Now, Conrad, you sit in the middle…"

Key art for Justin Channell's zombie comedy *Die and Let Live* (2008). Courtesy Justin Channell.

Zombies attack the pizza delivery man in *Die and Let Live* (2008). Courtesy Justin Channell.

Once you finished editing Raising the Stakes, what was your plan for it?

Our plan was just to get in video stores, which obviously didn't happen. I sent it to reviewers, distributors, a couple of festivals. We submitted to the West Virginia International Film Festival because they have a student competition. We got first place in the high school category. But the $150 prize money was nice ... we broke even from one screening.

How did you meet Henrique Couto, who distributed the film for you through Freak Productions?

I met him at Horrorfind, where I recognized him from the B-Independent board. After we showed the film to him he was pretty much like, "Listen, you guys are probably not going to find distribution. I would like to distribute it for you guys."

What did he do as your distributor?

He authored the disc, which looks great. He burned all the discs, because he has the disc printer which allows you to print right on the disc. I know a lot about homemade CDs and DVDs, and I knew I did not want anything made

Justin Channell directs zombie action for *Die and Let Live* (2008). Courtesy Justin Channell.

with one of those label stampers. I hate those, because they ruin discs within, like, two months. The sticker starts to come off the disc and it actually peels some of the metal off with it. I didn't want that happening, so we ended up giving it to him because he knows a lot about micro-budget DVD-R distribution. There was no contract between us. He was basically, "I'm going to make the DVD, you're going to get 50 free copies, and get others at wholesale," which was maybe $1.25 a copy. "If you ever get distribution we can cut the deal off."

What was his cut?

It was his website. He took over all on-line sales. We got our 50 free copies that we could sell. Whatever we sold, we kept all of our profit because we obviously paid him for the cost of replicating. His cut was basically, "I can sell this at cons and everything, and obviously I have to make back my money. After that we'll split everything fifty-fifty." There was never anything substantial that came out of that and I had no problem with that, because he did authoring and printing — I did the graphics, but all I did was I sent him the materials. I designed the menus and then he animated them. My brother and I designed the cover art.

Ws it your senior year of high school when you this deal up?

Yeah. We ended up making about $400 or $500. We ended up getting two of our reviewers to throw in money, so we got another $500, and that's where the budget for *Die and Let Live* came from: DVD sales and people that were generous enough to give us a couple of hundred bucks.

What was your goal for the second film?

One was, "We've got to get more lights." We had one light; we were shooting on the street with streetlights, going, "This will look all right. I can clean this up"—and then you can't. The idea was to use not too many locations, and to use all locations that we were able to light or had enough available light that to shoot and look decent. Adding gore was a major goal. And to open it in a way that wasn't so dry—an attention getting opening. There would be no IWC (Idiots with Cameras) Films if it wasn't for Zane's mom. After *Raising the Stakes,* she bought us the Panasonic DVX 100-A. That helped us to make a movie that's watchable as far as image quality goes. I spent about $200 and bought a bunch of used sound equipment. It didn't survive the whole shoot, actually. We ended up having to use on-camera mikes for the last couple of shoots.

Henrique Couto as a slacker zombie in *Die and Let Live* (2008). Courtesy Justin Channell.

You made really canny use of the songs, too.

For *Raising the Stakes* we used all local songs, except for Mike Park, from Asian Man Records, who let us use a little music. But when *Die and Let Live* rolled around, I realized there were a lot of indie bands we liked that we could easily get music from.

What was your budget on* Die and Let Live*?
One grand.

And what was your strategy for finding distribution this time out?
POP Cinema wanted a first look and they turned it down. From there we were just like, "Let's just see where we can go." We used every connection we had, we pulled contacts from everywhere. "At this point, let's just go for the gold and try everywhere we can: Lion's Gate, ThinkFilm — the bigger indie places and the smaller indie places. Let's just send it everywhere we can." Most of them we never heard back from. I sent out mass amounts of e-mails, and there were a lot of people that seemed interested, and then once we sent them a copy we couldn't even get them on the phone. One day I sent out follow up e-mails to various companies. The first one to respond was Heretic Films, and they just were like, "Thanks for keeping in touch with us. I have it right here, let me give it a look." And within a week we had an e-mail back, "We want to distribute this."

You're a Journalism major at West Virginia University. Why aren't you in film school?
I can't afford it. I applied at Point Park, where I really wanted to go, in Pittsburgh. I went up for my interview, and my portfolio had *Raising the Stakes* and *Faces of Schlock* in there. I made a huge binder full of every press clipping and everything I possibly had. The guy was like, "Oh, yeah, I watched about 10 minutes of this one. I didn't get to this one. I kind of skimmed through this stuff. I don't know if this is really a good idea, because you're going to be making short films. You have to ask yourself if this is what you want to do." And I was like, "These guys don't care about me at all. All they care about is that I'll be going into debt for 100 grand." That's pretty much the way I felt about it. I didn't like their equipment, either. They were talking about switching to HD, and trying to convince me

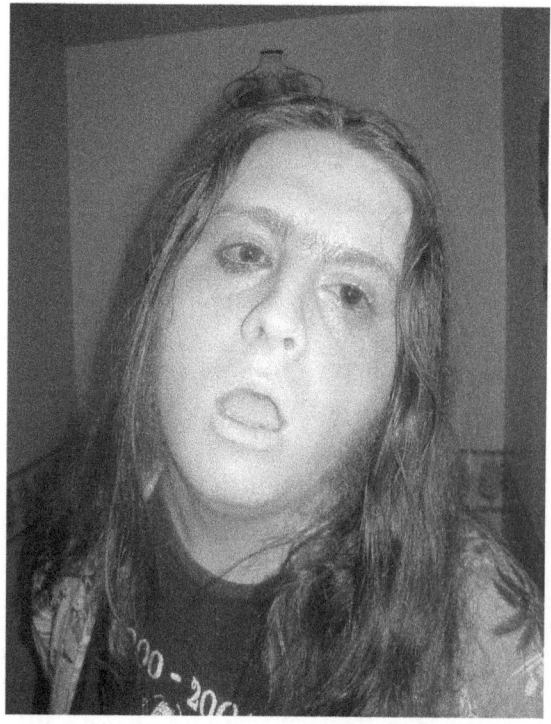

Henrique Couto is ready for his close up in *Die and Let Live* (2008). Courtesy Justin Channell.

that HDV was better than solid state HD, and I disagree with that. Not a fan of the HDV format.

You've completed two features, which most of the people who enroll in that program won't do. You have to laugh at that.

Why go into debt for 100 grand to learn something that I'm already doing? How could I make another movie if I was 100 grand in debt? At West Virginia, I have the PROMISE scholarship, and pretty much just have to pay off whatever student loans I need for living expenses. It works for me; I'll go into journalism for a little bit and keep making movies on my own and see what happens from there.

What's next?

The most likely candidate is a script we're currently developing called *The Mold*, which is going to be a throwback to the 80s grindhouse era, like the Troma stuff; movies that were more gooey and absurd than really bloody and stuff. *Slime City* was one of those...

25

The Martini

Last Words

"Lights... Camera... Action!"

These words typically come to mind when a layperson imagines how a film set is run. In reality, the assistant director will announce, "Picture is up!" which is a call for silence. If anyone on set continues to make noise, the AD will then bark, "Lock it up!" My former DP, John Rosnell, relished any opportunity to deliver his catch phrase, "Nobody moves, nobody gets hurt!"

When all is quiet, the camera operator confirms that film is running through the camera by calling, "Speed!" Then the sound recordist does the same. Either the AD or the DP will say, "Mark it," a commandment to a member of the camera crew to call out the scene and take number and clack the slate board. Finally, the director speaks up: "Action!"

Hopefully, magic occurs.

For a second take, the AD says, "Going again," or "Back to one," meaning "Back to Square One." When people are satisfied with a take, including the sound recordist, the DP and the camera operator use a mag light to inspect the camera's gate, ensuring that no dust particles lurk there, threatening image quality. If satisfied, one of them will declare, "The gate is good," cuing the AD to announce, "The gate is good. We're moving on to a new deal." On a video shoot, the director and the DP will play back the footage, which serves the same purpose. And the crew will prepare the next setup.

"Magic hour" refers to that perfect exterior lighting that occurs at dusk. A "walk and talk" is when two actors burn through an entire scene of dialogue in one shot while walking toward a moving camera.

When a cast or crew member needs to use a bathroom, they inform the AD, "Ten-one-hundred." When an actor has completed his duties for a film, the AD says, "That's a wrap on (actor's name)," which generally leads to a round of applause from the crew and remaining cast. For the last shot of the day, the AD says, "This is the Martini." With any luck, this will be followed by, "That's a wrap!"

I hope you've gained valuable information from this book, and that it enables you to go out and make a horror film — or any film — that reflects your personality and vision. Thank you for your time and interest, and good luck.

That's a wrap.

FADE OUT

Index

Abbott and Costello 186
Academy of Art 65
"The Accomplice" 56
accounting 25, 76
The Addiction 146
Adler, Stella 48
Adobe Premiere 21
After Dark Horrorfest: 8 Film to Die For 221
After School Special 171
Aftermath 239
agoraphobia 201
AIDS 20, 128
Albright, Ariauna 19, 21
The Alien Factor 2, 11
Almereyda, Michael 145, 146
Alphabet City 154
Alternative Cinema 19, 20
Alternative Cinema 29, 33
American Academy of Dramatic Arts 187
American Film Institute (AFI) 65, 72–75
American Film Market (AFM) 205
American Film Partners 213
American Gangster 55
American Theatre of Actors 187
Amtrak 156
Anchor Bay 222, 256
animatronics 133
anthologies 109, 216, 239
Anthony, Len 106
Arachnia 208, 211, 213
Argentina 61
arthroblastosis 103
artwork 81, 83, 116, 130, 236, 239
Ashbury Park 110
Asian Man Records 267
Astoria 135
attaching talent 83, 84
attorneys 25, 27, 64, 76, 78
Aurora 1
Austin Heart of Film 51
auteurs 24, 137
Automatons 146, 151
Avid 215
Aylmer 83, 158

B-Independent.com 265
Backstage 127
Bacterium 206, 214, 215
Bad Biology 164
Bad Worms 103
Balin, Ina 105, 111
Baltimore 247
Baltimore Spring Creek 54
Balun, Chas 233
Band, Charles 17, 21, 22, 23, 257
Barnes, Theo 158
Barrett, Andrew Lee 159, 161
Basement 15
Basket Case 2, 27, 78, 158, 190, 238, 243
Basket Case 2 132, 164, 224
Battle for the Lost Planet 209
Bay Ridge 135
Beck, Alexander 46, 226, 228
Behar, Wayne 157
Being John Malkovich 104
Beloit International Film Festival 245, 246
Best Buy 6, 230, 240, 241, 255
Best Comic Book 245
beta tapes 151, 231, 234
betacams 10, 30, 176
Beverly Hills Corpse 15
Beverly Hills 90210 211
Billy Jack 222
Billy Jack Goes to Washington 222
Biro, Stephen 232–242, 245, 249
Bite Me! 206, 214, 215, 258, 259
Blade Runner 177
The Blair Witch Project 5, 22, 221, 245
Bleecker Street Cinemas 222, 243
Blockbuster 22
Blood Cult 10
Bloodletting 20
Bloody Disgusting 258
blowups 35, 111, 229
Blue Bomb 53
blue screens 161
Boca Ciega 48
Bodeen, DeWitt 109
Boise, Idaho 102

Bolex 143
Bonk, Ron 179
Book of Shadows: Blair Witch 2 22
Bookwalter, J.R. 3, 9–23, 129, 131, 175, 184, 200
Brady, Bob 187
Brain Damage 2, 24, 26, 78, 83, 99, 134–136, 158, 159, 182, 224, 238
The Brain Damage Company 78
Brazil 226
Bretschneider, Steve 201
Brinkley, Bonnie 130, 154
Bronx 135, 224, 243
Brooklyn 117, 122, 135, 154
Brooklyn College 97
Brooks, Conrad 263
Brown, Erin 35, 128, 132, 184, 214, 246, 258
Buckley, Stephen 204
budget penalties 91
Buffalo 63, 95, 197, 242
Buffalo's House of Horrors 184
Bullwinkle 109
Bunce, Kevin 203
Burt's Bikers 103, 107, 108, 111, 113, 120
Butch Cassidy and the Sundance Kid 106
Butthole Surfers 170

cabin in the woods movie 19, 72, 98, 183
California 17, 51, 202, 208, 213
Callahan, Jimmy 120
camera angles 42, 152
Cameron, James 147
Camp Home Video 15, 223, 224, 228, 229
candy glass 161
Cannibal! The Musical 262
Canon Optura 20
Canon XL2 72
Capra, Frank 181
Carma 45, 54
Carpenter, John 204
Carteris, Gabrielle 211
Caruso, David 186, 196
casting 127, 128, 155; ads 127, 132; directors 127
Cat People 109
catalysts 66
caterers 97, 98
CBS 193
CD ROM 39
cell animation 133, 201
Central Park 135
Chaingang 56–58
Chainsaw Sally 37
Channell, Justin 260–269
character sketches 66
Chase, Jenny 172
Cheap Scares! 2, 3
Chepil, Bill 122
Chicago 35
Chicago Underground Film Festival 175

Chickboxer 17
Chiller Theatre Expo 232, 247
Christmas 262
Cincinnati 29
Cinema 5 186
Cinema Home Video 16, 17, 20
Cinema Wasteland 247
Cinemagic 1, 2, 11, 163
cinematography 13, 37, 76
Cinemax 240
Cinevest 208
Citizen Toxie 29
City 193
Clark, Peter 2, 26, 27, 48, 80, 81, 129, 135, 155, 156, 157, 164
Class of Nuke 'Em High 127, 128, 131, 262
Cleveland 11
clichés 46, 47
climax 66
Cohen, Larry 164
Cold War 67
Colorado 161
Combat Shock 262
The Comeback Trail 105, 108, 112
Comic-Con 240, 247, 251
commentary track 39, 205, 234, 239, 253, 259
communications directors 252
completion funds 28
computer generated imagery (CGI) 21, 74, 133, 145, 148, 206, 211, 219
concept art 80, 81, 82, 83
Confederate Zombie Massacre 65, 67
Connecticut 38, 98, 135, 156
Considine, Tim 147
continuity 131, 262
contracts 63, 86, 87, 226, 228, 230
conventions 65, 233, 230, 233, 246, 278, 47, 250
copyrights 86
Corey, Prof. Irwin 105
Corman, Roger 150
costume designers 73, 127, 131
Coulter, Scott 38, 50–52, 100, 127, 132, 134, 155–157
Couto, Henrique 229, 265, 266, 267, 268
cover art 266
Crabbe, Buster 105, 112
craft services 155
Craven, Wes 5, 108, 109, 111, 112
Creature-Corner 249
Creepshow 103
crew 31, 126, 129–133, 142, 154, 184, 216, 270
Cronenberg, David 164
Crosby, Zane 261
Crown, Peggy 201
Cuban missile crisis 52
Cult Figure 48, 103
Culton, Leslie 25
Culture of Fear: The Horror Film 65, 67, 69

Cunningham, Sean 111
The Curse of the Love Canal 2
Curse of the Puppet Master 21
Curse of the Vampire 229
Cyborg 62

dailies 49, 73
Danford, Rick 245
Danforth, Jim 207
Dangerfield, Rodney 103
Dark Fortress 208
Darrow, Tony 187–189
Davis, Andrea 251
Davis, Kurt B. 155
Davis, Paige Kay 229, 250–260
Dawn of the Dead 2, 106–108
The Daytrippers 130
Dead House Music 204
The Dead Next Door 10–12, 15, 16, 131
Deadly Embrace 16
The Deadly Rites 80, 97
Deadly Spawn 2
Deadly Stingers 23
deal summary 91
Death in Venice 104
Death Is a Bitch 30
Death Mobile 99
DeCoteau, David 16, 17, 20
The Deer Hunter 192
deferments 28, 81, 90, 208, 226
The Definitive Document of the Dead 108, 118
De Laurentiis, Dino 139
delivery materials 228, 234, 266
Del Toro, Benicio 147
Del Toro, Guillermo 148, 149
DeMarco, Frank 142
Demo Reels 83
De Palma, Brian 109
De Trizio, Mauro, J. 204
Detroit 10
development 8, 48, 53, 60, 85, 126; agreements 87; funds 92; hell 76–84
Diabolik DVD 233
dialogues 31, 42, 96, 155, 157, 181, 182, 217, 218
Diary of the Dead 106, 108
DiBucci, Michelle 142
Dickinson, Clay T. 130
Dickerson, Ernest 125
Die and Let Live 261, 264–268
digi-beta 234
digital effects 36, 63, 74
digital 8 261
digital video 3, 181, 242
dilution of interests 91
Dinosaur Kid 200
Dior, Rick 143
directing 2, 6, 7, 9, 10, 22–27, 37, 38, 54, 56, 60, 63, 76, 77, 91, 96, 97, 103, 109, 129, 131, 132, 154, 155, 157, 158, 181–185, 194, 230, 259, 260, 270

Director's Workshop for Women 65, 74, 75
Dirty Dancing 226
disclaimers 91
Disney World 262
distribution 5, 6, 8, 9, 15, 16, 25, 28, 75, 85, 94, 102, 104, 112, 123, 145, 151, 204, 205, 213, 221–243, 247, 249, 250–260, 265–268
The Dive 114
Dr. Jekyll and Mr. Hyde 137
Document of the Dead 2, 103, 106–108, 115, 118
Dohler, Don 1, 2, 7, 11, 163
Dollman 62
Donner, Richard 204
D'Onoforio, Vincent 189
downloads 248
drafts 41, 46, 47, 49, 65, 151, 179
Dragon*Con 247
Drainiac 25, 208, 211, 212, 214
Dread Central 249
drivers 131
dubbing 204
DVDs 2, 3, 6, 9, 11, 17, 19, 20, 22, 23, 39, 44, 61, 94, 102, 108, 124, 142, 144, 170, 172, 203, 206, 208, 221, 222, 228–230, 231–242, 245–248, 250–262, 265–267

East Coast 80, 109
Eastwood, Clint 173
Easy Money 186, 197
e-bay 230
E.C. Comics 217
Edgewood 211
editing 9, 10, 12, 13, 20, 21, 23, 31, 33, 35, 36, 44, 104, 122, 128, 132, 181, 199–204, 207, 218, 262
Edwards, James 19
E.I. Cinema 20, 29, 33, 61, 132, 203, 204, 210, 213, 214, 218, 219, 229, 243
86th Street East 224
Electro Video 15
Elm Street sequels 224
Elmer the Parasite 78, 83
"Elmer's Tune" 158
Elwood, Tony 15
e-mail 63, 132, 133, 242, 257
entertainment law 85
Equinox 208
establishing shots 22
An Evening at Dangerfield's 105
The Evil Dead 2, 83
Evil Dead 2 10, 15
expendables 126
expenses 99, 100, 101, 247
Experimental Theatre 48
Exploited Cinema 233
extras 11, 19, 20, 203, 234, 239, 252, 253, 262

Fabrigar, Dale 56
Faces of Schlock 268

fades 1, 44, 47, 48, 67
Failure 243
Fairmont 263
Famous Monsters of Filmland 1, 83
FanExpo Canada 247
Fangoria 1, 10, 15, 51, 175, 180, 226, 243, 248, 258
Fangoria Radio 248, 259
Fangoria Weekend of Horrors 35, 247, 258
Fanta-festival 175
Fantasia 245
FBI 233
FCC 55
Fear Zone 3, 245, 249
Fedele, John 30
fees 60, 64, 96, 97, 226
Ferrara, Abel 145, 192
Fessenden, Larry 73, 133, 137–153, 183, 222
Field, Syd 39, 122, 123
film festivals 7, 44, 65, 68–72, 242, 245, 246, 248, 250, 256
Film Look 17
film schools 13, 38, 39, 42, 66, 124, 138, 163, 206
Film Threat 175, 196
Films in Review 103
Final Cut Pro 21, 199
financing 25, 62, 76, 80, 85, 104, 240
First Amendment 118
5 Minute Horror 48, 55
Florida 48, 65, 232
Ford, Harrison 177
foreign sales 28, 46, 226, 248
The Forever Man 41
Form TX 86
Forum 51, 52
"four walling" 222
France 138, 248
Frankenhooker 132, 164, 186, 190, 191, 192, 195, 232, 235, 237, 238, 239, 240
Freak Productions 265
Friday the 13th 204, 226
Frumkes, Roy 2, 39, 81, 83, 103–125, 135, 187, 188, 194, 196, 197, 198, 245
Frye, Daniel 134, 156
Fuchs, Nancy 83
Fuentes, Augustin 65
Fulci, Lucio 29
Full Moon Pictures 9, 17, 20, 21, 22, 23

gaffers 131
Galaxy of the Dinosaurs 15, 17
Gallo, Phil 161, 199, 200, 201
Garcia, Eddie 116
The Gates of Hell 29
Genesis 239
Germany 6, 67, 236, 239, 250
Ghost 54
Ghoul School 15, 16
Gilbert, Gloria-Anne 251

Gingold, Michael 175, 180
Giovinazzo, Buddy 262
Glass Eye Pix 149
Gleason, Kelly 191, 194
Glickenhaus, Jim 195, 197
Godwin, James 147
Godzilla 125, 226
Gogos, Basil 83
Gold, Jerry 27, 28, 78, 80, 81, 85–95, 226, 228
Goldsmith, Jerry 204
Gone with the Wind 226
Goodfellas 188
Goodwill 73, 74
Gore, Chris 196
Gore-Met Zombie Chef from Hell 228
Gorilla Warfare: Battle of the Apes 208
Gornick, Michael 107
grass roots 255
Gray, David 62, 182
Great Scott Talent Agency 104
Greenway, Peter 143
Grey, Jennifer 189
grindhouse era 269
grips 131
Gruesome 62, 98, 99, 128, 129, 132, 182, 184, 245, 248
Gudino, Rodrigo 7
guerrillas 12, 21
Guinea Pig movies 233, 239, 241
Gunn, James 262

Habit 58, 138–148, 150, 222
The Hacker's Source 249
Halloween 204
Halloween Horror Picture Show 65, 232, 245
Halloweenpalooza 245, 247
Hammer Studios 176
Hansen, Gunnar 222
Harlem 135
Harper, Valerie 193
Harris, Bob 108, 111
Harvard Business School 74
Hawaii 250
HBO 54, 55, 240
HD 268, 269
HDV 269
Healy-Louie, Miriam 139
Hector Dodges 147
Hefner, Hugh 105
Helter Skelter 202
Hemingway 208
Henenlotter, Frank 2, 26, 27, 77, 78, 83, 135, 136, 158, 163, 164, 167, 168, 190, 191, 195, 226, 238, 239, 240
Herbst, Rick 136, 158
Heretic Films 261, 268
Hero's Funeral 54
Hetrick, Glenn 168, 170
Hi 8 Video 24, 200

Hi, Mom 109
high definition 3, 230
The Hills Have Eyes 109
Hiroshima Mon Amour 125
Hirsch, Chuck 109, 114
Hirsch, Judd 104, 112
Hirschman, Ray 156, 157
Hitchcock, Alfred 3, 24
HK Flicks 233
Hollywood 2, 9, 24, 39, 55, 76, 122, 146, 147, 193, 206, 233, 253
Hollywood Chainsaw Hookers 222
The Hollywood Reporter 1
Hollywood Video 22
home video 11, 16, 208, 228
Horror Review 258
Horror Yearbook 249
Horrorfind Weekend 247, 263, 265
Houdini, Harry 103
Howe, Matt 167, 172
Humanoids from Atlantis 17
Huner, Mary 49, 50, 127, 128, 131, 134, 155, 156, 201, 246
Hunting Season 51, 53
Hurwitz, Harry 104, 105, 112

I Was a Teenage Zombie 2, 6, 48, 49, 77, 97, 181, 243
IBM Selectric 179
The Ice Cream Man Hero 195
Ievans, Edgar 27, 77, 78, 135
impact editing 63
The Incredible Mr. Limpett 188
Incredibly Strange Video 263
Independence Day 130
Independent Film Market 140
Indie Spirit Someone to Watch Award 146
Inga 257
insurance 31, 89, 100, 101
International Cinema 125
International Creative Management (ICM) 85
International Famous Agency 85
International Sales 224, 226, 248
Internet 230, 231, 247, 248, 249, 257
Interview with a Vampire 159
investing 25, 27, 28, 76–78, 85, 88–93, 95, 96, 97, 123–125
iPods 241
Iraq 115, 179
Ireland 248
ITV 241
IWC (Idiots with Cameras) Films 267

Jackson, Mick 54
James, Crawford 168, 177
Japan 78, 226, 236, 239
Jennings, James 187
Jeremy, Ron 210
Johnny Gruesome 3, 62, 82, 83, 98, 99, 128, 245, 248

joint venture agreement 27, 28, 81, 89
Jonestown 12
Jonker, Leif 176
Junk 233
Just Desserts 143
Just the 4 of Us 2, 24, 51

Kaufman, Lloyd 262, 263
Kassak, Lydia 116
Kentucky Fried Chicken (KFC) 98
key art 259, 264
Kilgore, Al 109
Killer 15
Kindlon, Dave 158
King Kong 1, 2
King of New York 192
Kingdom of the Vampire 17
Kinky Kong 33
Kinnear, Greg 54
Knotts, Don 188, 263
Kolchak: The Night Stalker 109
Kool-Aid 12
Korea 226
Krause, Tina 171
Kubrick, Stanley 24, 153
Kuciw, Alex 178
El Kuervo 61

Lackey, Mike 113, 187, 194
Lake Erie 217
Lamberson, Greg 8, 26, 43, 127, 183, 253
Land of the Dead 106, 108, 164
Las Vegas 195
The Last Gunfighter 222
Last House on the Left 108, 109, 111, 112
The Last Winter 145, 149, 152
latex make-up effects 50, 74, 133, 134, 148
Laughlin, Tom 222
Lauten, Tom 50, 100, 127, 132, 134, 156
Laverack, Tom 143
Leatherface 57
Leaver, Robbie 152
Leber, Susan 151
Lecter, Hannibal 57
Lee, Eva 155
Lee, Spike 125
Lehman, Reeves 107, 120
Leigh, Janet 3
letter of agreement 27
letterboxed 229
Levi-Hinte, Jeffrey 147, 148
Levine, Jeffrey 54
Levine, Terry 114
Levinson, Barry 54
Lewis, Herschell Gordon 67
Library of Congress 86
Limited Liability Corporation 27, 81, 87, 192
Limited Partnership 27, 78, 81, 87, 92
Limited X 123
Lincoln Center 187

Lindberg, Craig 134, 160, 162
Lion King 1.5 54
Lion's Gate 6, 222, 253, 255, 256, 259, 268
Lively, Josh 261
Lo Cosa 51
locations 19, 21, 31, 76, 97, 111, 126, 134–136
log line 72
logo design 80
Loreti, Nicanor 61, 62
Lorinz, James 121, 186–198, 122
Los Angeles (LA) 15, 20, 29, 58, 59, 67, 75, 105, 193, 196, 197, 206, 243, 250
Los Lobos 77
Lost Highway 121
Lost in Space 163
Louis, Joe 55
Lovecraft: Fear of the Unknown 204
Lowry, Jennifer 158
Lucas, George 145
Lufthansa heist 189
Lumet, Sidney 54, 183
Lustig, Bill 104
Lynch, David 178
Lynch, Julie 46, 53, 128, 131, 159

Maché, Eric 79, 82, 83, 132, 224, 229, 244
Macintosh 21
magazines 11, 20, 24, 122, 163, 242, 248, 249
Mager, Jason 132
Making Slime 229
Makowski, Marc 27, 28, 81, 88, 135, 199, 226
Manfredini, Harry 204
Manhattan 37, 135, 203, 224, 259
Margarita Happy Hour 151
marketing 8, 132, 220, 222, 228, 231, 240, 250–260, 261
Mars 204
Marshall Video 15
Martin 2, 107
The Martini 270
Matis, Lawrence 52
The Matrix 241
Maximum Impact 17
McBain 195
McCabe and Mrs. Miller 104
McCann, Chuck 111
McCarthyism 67
McCrae, Scooter 129, 163–180, 183, 184, 200
McDonald's 99, 212, 238
McDormand, Frances 147
McKenney, James 146, 150, 151
McKeown, Douglas 2
Me and the Mob 193
meal 97–99
Media 100 199
The Meltdown Memoirs 115
Merrick, T.J. 243
methylcellulose 50, 135, 156
Michaels, John 6, 97, 98, 181
micro-budget 2, 5, 9, 24, 25, 39, 42, 44, 61, 64, 71, 76, 83, 84, 94, 96, 99, 100, 126, 129, 163, 181, 206, 221, 230, 261, 266
Middletown 163
Midnight Movie 2, 43, 222, 229, 243, 245
Miller, Donna 201
Miller, Rex 56, 57
Mini-DV 3, 9, 16, 19, 24, 176, 200, 203, 221, 234, 238, 261
mini-majors 256
mini-maxi clause 89, 92
miniatures 134, 211
Mobray, John 117
The Mold 269
Montreal, Canada 245
Moore, Tom 208
Morano, Carl 229
Morgantown 263
Mother's Day 199
Moving Targets 211
The Mugger Mega Bugged 204
Mullen, Patty 195, 237
Mundae, Misty 35, 128, 184, 214, 216, 237, 238, 246, 258
Murder Weapon 16
Muro, Anita 99
Muro, Jim, Sr. 159
Muro, Jimmy 2, 83, 104, 113–122, 135, 182, 187
Muro Collision Yard 136
Museum of Modern Art 104, 106
Museum of Natural History 137
music video 82, 99, 104, 128
Mutant Men Want Pretty Women 210, 212
Mutant War 209, 212
MySpace 12, 57, 63, 237, 241, 242, 245, 247, 248, 257
Mysterious Island 207
Mysterious Planet 207

Nadja 145, 146
Naked Fear 2, 24, 28, 46, 51, 81, 88, 127, 129, 132, 134, 135, 160, 161, 162, 199, 200, 201, 203, 204, 224, 229, 245
National Board of Review of Motion Pictures 103
NBC 193
negatives 108, 111, 112, 228
Net Profits 27, 28, 64, 77, 78, 89, 226
Netflix 230
Never Die Alone 125
New Hampshire 208
New Jersey 15, 122, 135, 161, 208, 224, 232, 247
New Mexico 178
New Orleans 103
New Rochelle 103
New York City (NYC) 2, 29, 43, 58, 83, 103, 104, 105, 108, 123, 125, 136, 137, 139, 142, 147, 175, 186, 193, 195, 196, 197, 209, 222, 224, 243

New York Daily News 224
New York Flash 164
New York Times 118, 188
New York Underground Film Festival 175
New York University (NYU) 48, 104, 105, 106, 118, 138, 156, 163, 186
New York Vampire 43, 53, 61, 229, 243
newsletters 241, 242, 250
newspaper advertising 222, 224
Night of the Living Dead 2, 106, 107, 206; remake 108, 120
Nightbeast 2
A Nightmare on Elm Street 2: Freddy's Revenge 80, 81
9/11 122, 124, 147, 179
1952 54
No Telling, Or the Frankenstein Complex 138, 139, 142, 143, 146, 150, 152
North Carolina 15
Noto, Vic 122
Notre Dame University 65, 69
NYC Horror Film Festival 67, 245
Nyman, Michael 143
Nymphoid Barbarian in Dinosaur Hell 208, 211

O'Connell, Ryan 98, 182
Off Hollywood 106, 107
The Off Season 150
Ogle, Karen 132
Ohio 9, 17, 21, 23, 29, 197, 247
O'Loughery, Dan 184
The Omen 204
on-line distribution 230
one-sheets 236
One Thin Wire 53
Open Water 5, 6, 221, 245
operating agreements 87, 92
optical effects 133
O'Rawe, Tom 15
Osterer, Michael 104
Oullette, Dan 164
The Outer Limits 163
over budget summaries 91
Ozone 3, 14, 17, 19

Panasonic DVX 100-A 267
Panasonic 24p 215
paradigms 39, 66, 122, 152, 169
Park, Mike 267
partnerships 27, 28, 60, 81, 87
PayPal 248
Pedersen, Maria
Pennsylvania 52
Per Sullivan, Erik 142, 149
Personal Demons 3, 41, 61
Pesci, Joe 188
Petrucelly, Brit 26, 156, 157
Pioneer Cinema 37
photography 2, 8, 15, 33, 42, 80, 85, 99, 107, 116, 127, 129, 131, 135, 142, 184, 200, 202, 217, 259; *see also* still photography
Piper, Brett 25, 31, 36, 35, 200, 201, 206–220, 246
Pittsburgh 29, 106, 206, 263, 268
Plan 9 from Outer Space 263
Playboy 188
Play-Mate of the Apes 33
Plutonium Baby 2, 6, 38, 98, 134, 135, 156–158
Point Park College 29, 268
Polonia, Mark 217
Polonia brothers 208, 209, 217
Polymorph 16, 19, 20, 22
POP Cinema 6, 29, 30, 33, 61, 128, 206, 207, 213, 215, 229, 230, 246, 248–260, 268
pornography 5, 177, 178, 228
Potter, Nicole 121, 122
Poultrygeist 224
practical effects 133
premieres 38, 75, 88, 186, 243, 245
press releases 242, 255, 257
Pretty Woman 210
Prison-a-Go-Go 252
Prison of the Psychotic Damned 204
producers 2, 3, 7, 9, 24, 25–27, 38, 56, 58, 60, 61, 62, 65, 75, 77, 85, 90, 93, 96, 97, 98, 115, 139, 148, 149, 210, 226, 230, 178, 259
production 2, 8, 10–12, 24, 27, 28, 29, 56, 61, 63, 73, 74, 85, 100, 102, 106, 115, 126, 129, 130, 131, 154–163, 194
The Projectionist 103–105, 109, 111
PROMISE Scholarship 269
prospectus 10, 77, 90, 91
PSP 241
The Psychic 40, 83
Psycho 172
Psyclops 208, 211–213
publicity 3, 79, 236, 237, 242–249, 252, 259, 263
Puincie 110
Pyun, Albert 62

Queens 135
Quigley, Linnea 15, 222

Rafael, Sukey 107
Raiders of the Living Dead 208, 209, 210
Raimi, Sam 2, 83
Raising the Stakes 261, 262, 265, 267, 268
Rapper X 62, 63, 64
Raso, Mike 15, 29, 30, 31, 33, 35, 36, 62, 203, 213–215, 217–219, 229, 230, 250
Raven, Stark 171, 172, 173
Raven Gets a Life 65, 68, 70, 73
Ray, Fred Olen 222, 228
Ray Bari's Pizza 136
The Redeemer 199
Redford, Robert 140
rehearsals 33

Reichardt, Kelly 140, 150
Rentrak 17
Retro Seduction Cinema 29
Retro Shock-O-Rama Cinema 29
returns 230, 252
reversion of rights 61
rewriting 47, 54, 62
RH Factor 103
Rhodes, David 118
Rhodes family 106
Rice, Ann 159
Richichi, Sal 228
River of Grass 140
RKO National Twin 2
Road Warrior 116
Roberts, Julia 210
Robot Ninja 13, 15, 16
Rochon, Debbie 18, 29, 31, 249
Rock and Rule 240
Rock and Shock 247, 256
rock CD 245
Rogue Cinema 249
Rollin, Jean 178
Romania 21
Rome 176
Romero, George A. 1, 2, 5, 29, 106, 107, 108, 164, 206
La Ronde 122
The Roost 151
Rosemary's Baby 46
Rosenberg, Max 105
Rosnell, John 127, 129, 183
Rosovsky, Ivy 127, 131, 154
Roth, Eli 151
rotoscoping 133
Rubinstein, Richard 106, 107
Rue Morgue 7, 248, 249, 258
Rue Morgue Radio 249
Rue Morgue's Festival of Fear 247
Russo, James 3, 17

Sabin, Robert Craig 24, 45, 46, 47, 48–59, 61, 127, 131, 132, 134, 154–156, 158, 161, 186, 201, 202, 246
The Sad Ballad of Sister Cyborg 178
Saint-Peter, Lucille 158
San Francisco 65, 67
The Sandman 17, 19
Saturday Night Live 216
Saunders, Matthias 129
Savini, Tom 103, 107, 108, 120
Scare Tactics 3
Scareflix 137, 146, 149, 150, 151
Scarsdale 226
School of Visual Arts (SVA) 2, 39, 48, 81, 103, 106, 107, 113, 118, 150, 186, 187, 194, 203
Schweitzer, Al 209
Sciarra, Danny 204
score 77, 100, 143, 199, 204

Scorsese, Martin 138, 188, 189
Scott, Ridley 177
scream queens 128, 131
Screaming Dead 206, 214, 215
Screen Actors Guild (SAG) 84, 123, 124, 127, 130, 192, 201
screenings 49, 102, 118, 177, 237, 243, 245, 250, 260
Screenplay 39, 122, 197
screenplays 9, 24, 25, 27, 29, 30, 31, 38–47, 49, 51, 53, 56, 59–64, 76, 84, 86, 123, 126, 135, 152, 169, 183
The Screenwriter's Handbook 39
screenwriting 6, 9, 17, 18, 24, 26, 27, 38–47, 48, 59–64, 66, 67, 69, 71, 96, 97, 113, 152, 153, 157, 172, 179, 260–262
scripts 2, 10, 19, 24, 25, 30, 38, 39, 41, 42, 44, 46, 47, 49, 52, 53, 57, 62, 64, 65–67, 96, 115, 121, 152, 161, 179, 262
Seduction Cinema 29, 33, 251, 257
The Seduction of Misty Mundae 36
self distribution 222–224
Seminara, George 49
Sevin, Julia 80
Sevin, R.J. 80
Sex Crime of the Century 109
The Shadow Children 178
Shakespeare, William 44, 153
Shapiro-Glickenhaus 190, 191, 195
Shatter Dead 163, 165, 167, 169–179
Shatter Dead: Death and Taxes 179
Shatter Dead II 179
Shaw, David 142
Sheen, Charlie 233
Sherman, Sam 208
The Shining 241
Shinnick, Kevin 31
"The Six Pack" 17
Shock-a-Go-Go 252
Shock-O-Rama 201, 206, 210, 216, 254
Shock-O-Rama Cinema 29, 34, 61, 214, 215, 229, 254
shooting schedules 20, 31, 44, 73, 97, 115, 126, 182, 212, 216
Showtime 53
Shriek Out 104, 105, 112
Shrieker 20
Sikh assassin knife 159
Silent Spring 139
Silver, Jay 147
Simon, Simone 109
Simonelli, Rocco 122, 195, 197
Sirius Satellite 248
16m 2, 10, 17, 24, 83, 107, 108, 112, 114, 129, 154, 155, 181, 216, 222, 228, 229, 243
Sixteen Tongues 163, 166, 168, 169, 170, 171, 172, 173, 174, 176, 177, 178
65/35 split 222
Skin Crawl 29, 30, 31, 34, 35, 36, 37, 217, 218, 259

Skinned Alive 12, 16
Slamdance 69, 148
Slice 56, 57
Slime City 2, 11, 24, 27, 38, 46, 49, 50–52, 56, 61, 77–81, 98–100, 103, 118, 127, 129, 130–132, 134, 135, 144, 154–156, 157, 159, 164, 182, 199, 202–204, 222–224, 228–230, 243, 245, 247–250, 253, 269
Slime City Massacre 249
"Slime Boy" 155
Slime Guys 26, 38, 155
SlimeGuy.com 155, 247, 248
Sloan House 2, 132
Slob 56, 57
The Smithereens 77
Snively, Devi 65–75, 134, 245
Snyder, Dee 248
Snyder, Meredith 141
Snygg, Zach 30, 31
Socrates 72
Soho 48
Sony 19, 176, 215, 262
The Sopranos 201
The Soulless 2, 61, 62
sound editing 20, 154, 203
sound effects 203
Sound Recordist 129
soundtrack 77, 100, 203
South Bronx Hero 156
South Park 262
Spain 226, 248
special effects 38, 49, 50, 62, 72, 100, 103, 131, 133, 134, 135, 145, 147, 148, 155, 156, 182, 215, 216, 219
Speredakas, John 144
Sperling, David 116
Spinosaurus 200
Spivey, Terrence 128, 134, 157
Splatter Beach 217
Star Trek 163
Star Wars 106
Starbucks 55
Starlog 163
Starz 222
Steadicam 2, 114, 182
Steenbecks 187, 199, 207
Sterlace, Greg 24, 243
Sterling, David 17
Stevens, Brinke 18
still photography 107, 131, 132
stills 131, 132, 234, 236, 259
stop motion animation 206, 207, 208, 215, 253
storyboards 12, 13, 84, 116, 134, 194
The Straight Story 178
Strandburg, Ian 74
Strange People in Astoria 186
Straw Dogs 153
Street Trash 2, 24, 81, 83, 103, 104, 108, 113–122, 125, 135, 158, 159, 182, 186–189, 191, 196, 197

Street Trash 3 114
styrofoam 109, 111
Subchapter-S Corporation 89
Sub-Rosa Studios 179
The Substitute 103, 108
Sullivan, Mike 114
Sundance Film Festival 5, 140, 146, 245
Sunshine Hotel 136
Superman 56
Super-8 9, 10, 15, 83, 103, 163, 186
Super 8 Filmmaker 1, 12
"Super Sex" 56
Super-16 111, 201
Survivor 98
Sutt, Paul 170
Swayze, Patrick 226
Sweeney, Tommy 46, 51, 88, 127, 128, 135, 159, 160–162, 201, 202, 227
Sweet Jesus 243
The Sweet Life 122–124, 197
Swirlee 186, 191–195, 197, 198

Taiwan 226
talent 83
Tales That Will Tear Your Heart Out 106, 114, 115, 116, 117
Tamar 128
Tampa 105
Tarantino, Quentin 151, 217
"Tasty" 56
Taxi Driver 186
Taylor, Dayton 142, 148
Teenage Bikini Vampire 65, 68
Tempe Video 15
The Terminator 103
Tet Offensive 107
Texas 208
Texas Chainsaw Massacre 72
Thalia 105
That's Adequate! 105, 112
theatrical exhibitions 2, 5, 93, 221–224, 227, 249
They Bite 210, 211, 213
ThinkFilm 268
third party distributors 252
35mm 2, 10, 21, 22, 24, 83, 107, 111, 159, 222, 229, 243; anamorphic 20, 21
Thomas, Mike 216
Thompson, William 1, 2
The Three Stooges 186
Tieghen, Van, David 138
Times Square 27, 224, 226, 237
Timpone, Tony 258
Todd-AO 143
Todd, Michael 13
Tolochko, Mike 15
Tomaro, Robert 100, 202, 204, 245
Toronto 247
Tourette's Syndrome 103
Town Diary 129

The Toxic Avenger 262
trailers 83, 207, 234
Trapped: Buried Alive 211
treatment 30, 61, 64, 108, 205
Trial of Billy Jack 222
Triola, Victor 186
Trippin' 65, 71, 72, 74
Troma Entertainment 29, 127, 131, 208, 224, 257, 262, 269
The Tulane Hullabaloo 103
Tulane University 103, 104
20th Century Fox 218
24p 30, 72, 215
20/20 233
Two Boots Den of Cin 224
Two Boots Pioneer Cinema 253
Two Evil Eyes 106

Ultra Violent 249
Underwood, Beck 138, 139, 140, 143
Undying Love 2, 8, 24, 28, 43, 46, 50, 53, 81, 126–129, 131, 134, 135, 145, 159, 161, 183, 199, 203, 204, 224, 225, 227, 229, 244, 245
Unearthed Films 6, 232–241
United Artists 104
United Home Video 228
United States 6, 28, 61, 93
Universal Studios 62
urban horror 62

Variety 1, 122, 148, 224
Vermont 213
Vestron 119, 224, 226
VHS 2, 10, 11, 61, 108, 111, 167, 176, 204, 224, 228–232, 247, 249, 253
video distribution 28
Video Mayhem 232
Video on Demand 241
video streaming 248
Village East Cinemas 224, 245
Village Voice 222
Vincent, Jan Michael 16

Wagner, David 19
Waits, Tom 50
Wakefield, Nelson 154, 161, 204
Wall Street 78, 80, 224

Walloga, Edward 26, 28, 81, 135, 155, 157, 161, 224
WalMart 252, 253
Warda, Joe 26, 136, 154, 156
Warner Brothers 191, 241
Washington, D.C. 2, 12
Watt, Mike 29
Webber, Jake 149
Weiss, Michael 252
Welles, Orson 24
Wells, Julian 29, 218, 251
Wendigo 142, 143, 145, 147, 149, 150
West, Ty 133, 150
West New York 2, 154, 201
West Virginia International Film Festival 265
Whacked 54
Whale, James 24
White, Paul 233
White House 12
White Plains 109
Whitten, David 119, 187
The Wild Geese 129
Willerford, Bari 55
Wilshire Boulevard 228
Wingenfeld, Justin 26, 29–37, 217, 218, 229, 259
Winston, Robert James 105
Winston, Stan 103, 108, 194
Witchouse 21, 22
Witchouse II 22
Witchouse 3: Demon Fire 18, 22
Within the Woods 83
Wood, Ed 183
Worcester, MA 247, 256
Wray, Fay 1
Writers Guild of America (WGA) 86
written agreements 26, 27, 86

Ybor City 232
Youngman, Henny 105
YouTube 248

Zarcha, Billy 156, 157
Ziegfeld, Lorenz 118, 119, 186
Zombie Cop 17

www.ingramcontent.com/pod-product-compliance
Ingram Content Group UK Ltd.
Pitfield, Milton Keynes, MK11 3LW, UK
UKHW050540150426
5217IPUK00026B/2012